100 YEARS OF CRYSTAL PALACE FOOTBALL CLUB

100 YEARS OF CRYSTAL PALACE FOOTBALL CLUB

NIGEL SANDS

Frontispiece: The two Palace managers who span the first 100 years at the club – John Robson (left) and Iain Dowie.

Front cover: Crystal Palace celebrate being promoted to the Premier League in 1997. © *Empics*

First published 2005
Reprinted 2006, 2007

STADIA is an imprint of
Tempus Publishing Limited
The Mill, Brimscombe Port,
Stroud, Gloucestershire, GL5 2QG
www.tempus-publishing.com

British Library Cataloguing in Publication Data.
A catalogue record for this book is available from the British Library.

ISBN-10: 0 7524 3608 2
ISBN-13: 978 0 7524 3608 1

Typesetting and origination by Tempus Publishing Limited
Printed and bound in Great Britain

CONTENTS

Crystal Palace FC Roll of Honour	6
Author's Preface	7
Acknowledgements	8
Palace in Précis	9
SEASON BY SEASON ACCOUNTS AND ANALYSES	11

CRYSTAL PALACE ROLL OF HONOUR

FA Premiership
Best Season: Eighteenth place in 2004/05

Football League
Division One: Champions 1993/94
Promoted via play-offs: 1988/89, 1996/97, 2003/04
Second Division: Champions 1978/79, Runners-up 1968/69
Third Division: Runners-up 1963/64
Third Division (South): Champions 1920/21, Runners-up 1928/29, 1930/31, 1938/39
Fourth Division: Runners-up 1960/61

FA Cup
Runners-up 1989/90

Football League Cup
Semi-finalists 1992/93, 1994/95, 2000/01

Full Members Cup
Winners 1990/91

Most-Capped British Player
Eric Young: 19 caps for Wales as a Crystal Palace player

Most League Appearances
Jim Cannon: 571 (1973-1988)

Most League Goals in Club Career
Peter Simpson: 153 (1929-1936)

PREFACE

Once again, I am delighted to offer to Crystal Palace FC and its thousands of supporters a book about our club that I believe everyone who reads will find both comprehensive and stimulating, regardless of their age or the era in which their support was able to be at its most intense.

I little thought, when I attended my first Palace match as a little boy with my father behind the Holmesdale Road goal in September 1946, that, a lifetime on, I would be able to write a book about the Palace like this one! It all leaves me with hugely mixed emotions. I am grateful that I've been able to support the Palace for so long and to contribute to the club as its honorary chaplain and historian, and this is laced with pleasure at the good, even sometimes great, times at the club that I've enjoyed with all the other contemporary fans, as well as sharing the tough, even occasionally grim, ones we have endured here!

So, I invite Palace folk everywhere to accept and enjoy this season-by-season analysis and description of the 100 years of Crystal Palace FC, and I look forward to perhaps the best times of all that I trust still lie ahead, whether I am able to share them or not.

Nigel Sands
Wickham Rectory
May 2005

ACKNOWLEDGEMENTS

All the usual folk who guide me towards the completion of a Palace book need to be acknowledged gratefully once more. This volume in particular, though all of them in general, would not be so informative or attractive without the help of my friends David Keats and Tony Bowden, who research and discover invaluable snippets of Palace information; Neil Everitt, whose photography is unsurpassed anywhere in football; proofreader Colin Duncan; plus of course all the team at Tempus Publishing, who offer their unstinting and unique professionalism to our cause.

Every reader should be grateful to them all: the author is particularly so.

Nigel Sands
Wickham Rectory
May 2005

PALACE IN PRÉCIS: HOW SERIOUS SETBACKS HAVE MARRED PALACE'S PROGRESS

Imagine just how thrilled those first Palace fans from the Edwardian era, who watched, supported and cheered our club in its embryonic days and months in the Second Division of the Southern League, would have been to have known that, 100 years on, the Palace would have matured into an outfit that could meet and beat even the topmost clubs in the nation, provide international players for a range of countries worldwide upon a regular basis and contest major cup finals and semi-finals with at least a measure of distinction. They would have been absolutely overjoyed and delighted!

Equally, although Selhurst Park is today prohibited from housing many more than 26,000 fans, no matter how illustrious the occasion, it would again be the case that our predecessors of 100 years ago would have been ecstatic and amazed to learn that the club of their generation, which seldom drew attendances of more than four figures during its initial five years, would become of such a calibre as to draw sell-out crowds to many of its matches and pack leading stadia for major contests under league or cup auspices.

That said and accepted, it must also be acknowledged that Palace's progress from being tiny minnows into a major club in the English football scene has been anything but smooth! If truth be told, the Glaziers and the latter-day Eagles have certainly appeared at times to be on the brink of, or indeed have suffered, a substantial reduction in prestige. Worse still, as modern-day fans know only too well, Palace have been on the verge of extinction.

Probably the first setback to hit our club occurred in the summer of 1925, at the culmination (one hesitates to call it the 'climax') of Palace's first season at our (then) prestigious new ground Selhurst Park, when defeat by visiting Oldham consigned us to relegation to the Third Division (South) and largely the company of clubs with whom we had contested Southern League and Third Division fixtures. The Palace programme editor of that time expressed the opinion that relegation as a result of that final game of the season would be nothing short of 'a calamity' for our club. With what certainty and truth he wrote for, despite the best efforts of everyone connected with Crystal Palace FC, it was to take almost forty years for our club to regain Second Division status.

Yet within four years of doing so Palace had become members of the top flight and remained within it for the next four seasons – only then to be relegated twice in succession! These demotions had the cumulative potential to consign the club to oblivion. The board of directors was largely untried and the drop from the old First Division to the Third was cataclysmic. Despite hopes – indeed, from some naive quarters, assertions – that an immediate return to the Second Division was ours for the taking, it simply has to be admitted that this seldom looked likely in 1974/75. The following season such a prospect was overshadowed by a marvellous run to the FA Cup semi-finals that ultimately proved to be such a distraction that we finished the term back in fifth place.

Happily, Palace's fortunes were redressed in even more rapid fashion in the late 1970s when two promotions in three seasons restored top-flight football to Selhurst Park but, after a spate of managerial and player defections Palace were sunk without trace at the foot of the 1981 First Division table and there followed a sequence of dreadful seasons in the mid-1980s when further embarrassments were barely staved off and gates fell to an appallingly low level. In a political climate that was stridently anti-football these were extremely difficult days for the directors or followers of football clubs eager to regain former glories.

At the Palace an inspired choice of manager brought Steve Coppell to Selhurst Park and, while Steve inevitably took some time to right matters, once he had secured goalscorers Mark Bright and Ian Wright for the club the Eagles were upward bound once more. After four top-flight seasons, including a first FA Cup final in 1990 and then our most successful term of all in 1990/91 when we finished third in the top flight, Palace fell out of the senior section in controversial circumstances. However, this appeared to have been remedied, first in 1993/94 when Premiership status was restored by claiming the Division One championship and then again in 1996/97 via the play-offs.

However, by 1997/98 the clouds were looming over Crystal Palace FC once more. The club was secured by a super-ambitious new chairman, but was immediately relegated again and then put into administration on 31 March 1999, where it languished for over fifteen months. The chairman, having seriously overreached himself in financial terms, ultimately had to resign and Palace increasingly became a laughing stock in the footballing fraternity as well as a focus for derision in our community.

It was not until 5 July 2000 that Palace came out of such dreadful purgatory and during all that time it appeared to be becoming increasingly likely that either the club would simply fold and cease to exist or that it would be relegated to a level of obscurity beyond the comprehension of most modern-day fans. There was never a worse time to be a supporter of, or be involved with, Crystal Palace FC, although as this little précis has shown there had previously been some awful ones.

At last, wonderfully, the Palace were saved when local Phone Shop tycoon Simon Jordan purchased the club and, after some mixed managerial appointments, brought in Iain Dowie in December 2003. From that point the club's momentum has only been upwards with the climax being the winning of promotion back to the Premiership once more in the play-off final at Cardiff's Millennium Stadium on Saturday 29 May 2004.

1905/06

THE PALACE PIONEERS HAVE A TRIUMPHANT FIRST SEASON

In comparison with many other football clubs, Crystal Palace FC was founded relatively late and our Club's origins lie in the spectacular FA Cup finals and England international matches hosted at the Crystal Palace Exhibition Ground after 1895. The 1901 final drew an amazing crowd of 110,000 to the Palace and it began to be realised that a side playing there regularly could capture sufficient support to be viable.

In 1904 the FA declined to sanction a proposal to this effect from the Crystal Palace company, but twelve months later approved the formation of an independent club that bore the Palace name and played its home matches there. The general manager of the Palace, Mr J.H. Cozens, and his predecessor, Mr Gillman, had both been enthusiastic and the former approached Aston Villa, already a pedigree club in the Football League and twice winners of the FA Cup at the Palace. Chairman of Villa at that time was Mr William McGregor, founding father of the Football League. He fully endorsed the idea and wrote in the *Football Star* in December 1904: 'The high water mark of prosperity in the metropolis has not been reached and I believe a really good team at the Crystal Palace would be a tremendous draw.' McGregor also recommended a young assistant secretary at Villa, Edmund Goodman, for the task of organising both the new Club and its team. It was a brilliant acquisition that remains among the best 'transfers' the Palace club has ever made.

Edmund's own promising football career had been abruptly terminated when he suffered a knee injury that necessitated amputation at the age of just nineteen. For his first two seasons with his new club he was too deeply immersed in the hard secretarial graft of administration to spend sufficient time with the players as manager, but Palace's first manager, Mr John Robson, was appointed under his guidance and he found the Club's superb first chairman, Mr Sydney Bourne.

The manner in which Mr Goodman secured the support and involvement of Mr Bourne as chairman is not only interesting but a clear indication of his shrewdness. Mr Goodman revealed that he scrutinised the books of the Crystal Palace company that dealt with the FA Cup finals and, among the list of those who always took a number of tickets, was Mr Bourne. Mr Goodman contacted him, put the notion of the new club to him, found him fully supportive and, quite soon, had persuaded Mr Bourne to become a director.

Sydney Bourne had been an all-round sportsman and had played football for twenty-two years after leaving school. A Londoner born and bred, he played for a team known as 'The Mosquitoes' in the early 1880s, later for Champion Hill, then Lyndhurst in Hampshire. In his early days he was an eager and aggressive forward, but as time went by he dropped back to half-back, then to full-back and finally to goalkeeper!

Having helped Edmund Goodman in the establishing of the Crystal Palace Club, when the Palace left the Southern League for the Football League in 1920 Mr Bourne was made a life member of the former for the service he had given since 1905. He continued as chairman of Crystal Palace until his death in 1930 and was the last of the original directorate to remain associated with the Club. He was, to the end, an interesting, colourful and most respected personality.

So far then, everything had proceeded most satisfactorily: the new Club was approved by the FA; it had appointed Mr Goodman as its secretary and persuaded Mr John Robson, formerly in charge of Middlesbrough, to come south to manage the playing side. But then an application was made for admission to the Southern League, only to be denied (by one vote, it was later revealed), and thus it became necessary for the Palace to compete in its Second Division, which comprised only thirteen clubs, either reserve teams from sides in the First Division or lesser-known outfits like Grays United and St Leonards United.

The financial implications were considerable, but the seriousness of the situation may be better appreciated by today's reader when it is realised that several clubs had already tried to prove themselves in the Southern League in its earlier years, only to fail and withdraw. St Albans, Shepherds Bush and Maidenhead had all gone to the wall and in the same season that the Palace joined there was another local club, Southern United from Nunhead, who did so – and then resigned the following April.

Whether it was solely because we could not play in the Southern League First Division, or whether we would have done so anyway is unknown, but Mr Goodman also sought and secured admission to the United League. This competition provided matches against the first elevens of the other Southern League clubs. Although it was played largely in midweek, Palace took part in it for two seasons and, in fact, our first competitive game was in the United League, away to New Brompton (later to become Gillingham) on Friday 1 September 1905. We won 3-0 with goals from 'Dickie' Roberts, Ted Birnie and Dick Harker.

The majority of the players assembled in the late summer of 1905 by John Robson were from the North of England or the Midlands. Captain was to be Ted Birnie, himself a Geordie and formerly with Newcastle United, and it was the skipper who uttered the rallying call to his playing colleagues at the commencement of the proceedings: 'We must win nearly every Southern League match and then they will have to have us in the First Division.'

That was, effectively, what Ted Birnie and his boys did – but not before the shock of failing at the first such hurdle! Twenty-four hours after the United League victory at New Brompton, Palace were hosts to Southampton Reserves in the Southern League Second Division but, in spite of romping to a 3-0 lead before half-time, they contrived to lose the game 3-4. Then came a United League defeat at Watford a few days later. However, the tide was turned by a Southern League victory at Swindon (over their reserve side, of course) and thenceforth Palace's first season became a triumphant cavalcade.

Fulham Reserves, champions of the Second Division the previous term, were trounced 5-0, while from 30 September to 18 November ten consecutive victories were recorded, including the

The 1905/06 Crystal Palace team photograph. From left to right, back row: J. Robson (manager), T. Walters (director), A. Daniels (director), J. Thompson, W. Oliver, A. Grant, R. Ross, H. Astley, M. Edwards, A. Cuttlin (director), S. Bourne (chairman), E. Goodman (secretary), A. Birch (trainer). Front row: G. Thompson, R. Hewitson, A. Needham, W. Watkins, E. Birnie, W. Innerd, G. Walker, R. Roberts. On ground: R. Harker, C. Wallace.

Club's first success in the FA Cup on 7 October when we secured a 7-0 victory, which we have never (yet) bettered in that most ancient and distinguished of all competitions, against Clapham.

Another huge victory (7-1) was secured in the preliminary round of the FA Cup when we were paired with Chelsea. In view of the fact that they also had a Football League fixture that afternoon, Chelsea chose to send a reserve side to the Palace for the Cup tie and were humiliated for their folly, while the other outcome was that the FA legislated that any club competing in the cup must in future field its strongest side.

A further cup victory, if a much narrower one, by a single goal over Luton Town took the Palace into the (old) first round proper of the competition after Christmas and here we engaged Blackpool in two 1-1 draws, first at Bloomfield Road, then at the Palace before going down to the powerful Football League side by a single goal in the second replay at Villa Park. However, Palace suffered more than defeat against Blackpool – a badly injured right knee sustained by Horace Astley deprived us of his extremely valuable services at wing half virtually until the end of the season, and that loss could have ruined our progress. But Mr Robson overcame the setback by deploying the local amateur A. Wilson, and Scotsman Alex Grant, in Astley's place, and Palace's Southern League charge continued unchecked.

Featuring regularly for the Palace by the midpoint of the season was Palace's first superstar – George Woodger. He was the only local boy to make a real impact upon our fortunes in this initial season but quickly became a fixture in our side after making his debut in November. George was a prodigy, his poise and delicate ball-playing skills rapidly endearing him to our supporters and earning him the curious nickname of 'Lady'. In 1905/06, George was still acquiring the remarkable talent that was to become so effective and, eventually, earn him an England international cap, but, even so, he became an integral part of our championship-winning side.

As well as several three- and four-goal successes, Palace secured probably their most satisfying result of the entire season when they won 2-0 at Southampton Reserves on

Saturday 10 March. We were denied until late in the game, but goals from Archie Needham and George Thompson ensured the outcome we so desperately wanted – and it was a bonus that it sent us clear of our closest rivals, Leyton, at the top of the table!

By early, April, Leyton were the only other possible contenders for the championship of the division and on the Saturday before Easter Palace travelled over to their Essex headquarters for a match Leyton knew they had to win in order to keep their chances alive. Because of the importance of this game several hundred Palace fans made their journey across town to cheer their favourites – the first record of this happening. The match was won 2-1, with outside right Charlie Wallace and Archie Needham scoring the goals that secured the title.

The next weekend saw the Palace play four matches in five days, beginning on Good Friday when we were engaged at Portsmouth Reserves, who were eager to down the colours of the new champions. Palace had a splendid throng of fans at Fratton Park, the two sides were well matched and a 1-1 result was a fair outcome. Several of the regular members of the side were rested the following afternoon when Wycombe Wanderers came to the Palace, but we won this penultimate Southern League match comfortably enough with a four-goal margin. Then, having met Leyton in a United League match on the Bank Holiday Monday, we played our last fixture in the Southern League on the Tuesday at Fulham and, with a somewhat depleted line-up, held Fulham Reserves to a 2-2 draw in 'a keen match' – the 1906 idiom for a battle royal!

Palace's first championship was eventually secured by a four-point margin and, with a goal-average that was vastly superior to those of all our opponents, was a highly impressive performance by Mr John Robson and his team.

SEASON: 1905/06

GROUND: The Crystal Palace

MANAGER: John Robson

LEAGUE/DIVISION: Southern League Second Division

FINAL POSITION: 1st

BIGGEST VICTORY: 9-1 *v.* Grays United, 4 November 1905

HEAVIEST DEFEAT: 3-4 *v.* Southampton Reserves, 2 September 1905

FA CUP – ROUND ELIMINATED: 1st (old)

LEAGUE CUP – ROUND ELIMINATED: –

FULL MEMBERS CUP – ROUND ELIMINATED: –

LEADING LEAGUE APPEARANCES (MAX: 24): 24 – R. Hewitson, R. Roberts, G. Walker

LEADING LEAGUE GOALSCORERS: 20 – A Needham, 8 – G. Woodger

1906/07

ONLY PALACE'S SECOND SEASON AND WE GAIN OUR GREATEST CUP VICTORY

Palace had a new captain for 1906/07 with Wilfred Innerd taking over the role after Ted Birnie moved to Chelsea, and the club made further progress this term – though not, ironically, in the Southern League. To put it at its best, we struggled there, eventually finishing next to bottom in nineteenth place. However, elsewhere we were quite superb – so read on and gloat!

Palace won the United League title, and remember this competition was not a minor one at all. But best of all we fared quite brilliantly in the FA Cup and it must be doubtful whether any other club has done so well in that most distinguished of knock-out competitions within two years of its foundation. A 4-0 success over Rotherham County in a preliminary round tie staged at Stamford Bridge (because the Crystal Palace was hosting a rugby international) enabled the Palace to enter the old first round draw for the FA Cup where we found ourselves pitted against Newcastle United at their famous St James' Park ground. Frankly, I consider that this victory should still be regarded as Palace's greatest of all – so far of course! – given the relative status of the two outfits. Palace were still in their infancy and possessed a matter of just four months' experience in the senior division of the Southern League, so the contrast could scarcely have been more pronounced. Newcastle were among the foremost clubs in the country at that time. They were the current Football League champions and had been FA Cup finalists the previous season. They were unbeaten at their headquarters for more than a year and fielded several current internationals in their line-up. Regarded by the contemporary pundits as the perfect football team, the Magpies were favourites to win this clash by the biggest margin of the round!

Perhaps Palace's greatest asset in this tie was that a number of our team, like Horace Astley, winger Charlie Wallace and goalkeeper Bob Hewitson hailed from the North-East. Skipper Wilfred Innerd had actually played for Newcastle teams, as had Dick Harker and outside left Dickie Roberts.

The afternoon of Saturday 12 January 1907 was a cold, midwinter one on Tyneside and it was inevitable that Palace would have to endure a lot of Newcastle pressure. This they did successfully, but just as half-time was approaching, the seemingly impossible occurred when Horace Astley eluded the converging full-backs, then raced onto a return pass from George Woodger and thumped a terrific shot past the bemused Scottish international goalkeeper Jimmy Lawrence to give Palace the lead.

Here's how Tyneside viewed the Newcastle-Palace FA Cup tie before our stunning victory!

Nothing Newcastle could offer after the break could retrieve the situation! In fact, incredibly, the margin could even have been greater! George Woodger was twice denied by Lawrence, then lifted another opportunity over the bar – and Palace finished with only ten men after Charlie Ryan had to be carried off ten minutes before the end!

Nevertheless, this success was one of the greatest FA Cup upsets of all time – and neither was our tremendous victory achieved in isolation. Southern League champions Fulham were disposed of by a similar margin in a Crystal Palace replay after a scoreless match at Craven Cottage, and Brentford went the same way in round three after the game at the Palace remained goal-less. This took Palace into the quarter-finals where we were paired with Everton, the cup holders and another club that had already earned a mighty tradition.

A record crowd of some 35,000 turned up at the Palace, in spite of miserable drizzling rain, to witness the confrontation. The Toffees had no fewer than nine internationals in their side but, as at Newcastle, with barely a few minutes to go before half-time, Horace Astley put the Palace ahead. Everton regained their composure during the break and managed an equaliser around the hour so that the last thirty minutes provided compelling entertainment – 'a finer contest than many Cup Finals' according to one seasoned observer.

The replay at Goodison Park could really only go one way after Everton secured an early goal. It was all over when we were three down after half an hour, and it finished 0-4. But by now Crystal Palace had gained a fine reputation as a club that could extend and even beat the greatest sides in the land – and that, after just two seasons, was quite remarkable!

SEASON: 1906/07

GROUND: The Crystal Palace

MANAGER: John Robson

LEAGUE/DIVISION: Southern League First Division

FINAL POSITION: 19th

BIGGEST VICTORY: 5-1 *v.* QPR, 5 January 1907

HEAVIEST DEFEAT: 0-6 *v.* Portsmouth, 6 April 1907

FA CUP – ROUND ELIMINATED: 4th (old)

LEAGUE CUP – ROUND ELIMINATED: –

FULL MEMBERS CUP – ROUND ELIMINATED: –

LEADING LEAGUE APPEARANCES (MAX: 38): 37 – W. Innerd, 36 – R. Hewitson, C. Wallace, R. Roberts

LEADING LEAGUE GOALSCORERS: 10 – H. Astley, 8 – C. Wallace

1907/08

A GLORIOUSLY SUCCESSFUL SOUTHERN LEAGUE SEASON

If season 1906/07 had seen Crystal Palace excel in the FA Cup, its successor would witness a hugely impressive showing in the more mundane, more important (and, some would argue, much more demanding) Southern League competition, in which we were engaged for the second time in the First Division.

That would not be to suggest that the Palace took the FA Cup lightly. No club that has tasted FA Cup glory ever takes it lightly and, certainly, the Palace did not! But three consecutive away draws eventually took their toll: we won 4-2 at Coventry in the first round in January, then beat Southern League Plymouth 3-2 at their Home Park headquarters, but bowed out at Grimsby in deplorable conditions later in February, where the Mariners scored the only goal of the game.

The Palace club was now managed by Edmund Goodman who made a clutch of early summer signings, of which that of Welsh international winger Bill Davies from Stoke City was the most significant. Bill had craft, pace and guile and gained Palace's first full international honour during this 1907/08 season, when he was capped for the Principality against Scotland on Saturday 7 March.

Mr Goodman also attempted to find a goalkeeper to replace Bob Hewitson, who had left us for Oldham, but it was not until three months into the season that he was able to secure a top-class custodian, who was to grace the Palace scene until the First World War and become a huge favourite with our supporters: he was the tall, good-looking, studious Joshua (usually nicknamed 'Joe') Johnson, and he played so many games for the club in those years (295 in total) that he still remains among our leading all-time appearance-makers.

Another great Palace personality in the early years of our club was Harry Collyer. Sporting his distinctive 'Pentonville' haircut, he drew huge praise from the pundits for his safe and stylish role at right-back. So much did Harry impress that he was given a trial for England in 1909/10 and he appeared in several representative fixtures for the Southern League.

Palace did not begin 1907/08 at all well, winning only once in our first five fixtures, and that was at Southampton, though it was a thrilling and praiseworthy victory. We were in arrears from only the third minute and fell further behind soon afterwards. We could have been in for a humiliation, and then what would have been the prospects for 1907/08? Bill

The 1907/08 Palace team photograph has Mr Goodman on the far right, sporting a fashionable boater hat!

Davies began the comeback before half-time, George Woodger equalised and left-back Matthew Edwards struck the winner from the penalty spot. Nonetheless, it was not until mid-October in our fourth home game, that most Palace fans witnessed a victory, though when it came it was certainly impressive, 4-1 over Swindon Town, and included a 'proper' hat-trick from George Woodger – that is to say three goals – our first three in fact – all scored in succession.

Palace's form remained erratic throughout the autumn, but it certainly improved after 'keeper Johnson's arrival and then became as good as anyone's in the division for the last third of the season, and that was despite losing Dickie Roberts' services in the Plymouth cup tie. Johnson's debut was quite unforgettable: it was at Bristol Rovers on a waterlogged pitch after the local river had broken its banks and, with a somewhat injury-depleted side, 'Joe' was magnificent. He kept his team in the game despite intense Rovers pressure, saved a penalty, and the Palace only capitulated to a late strike to lose by the odd goal in three.

Eventually, the Palace finished fourth. George Woodger accumulated an impressive 13 goals, popular Dickie Roberts weighed in with 8 from the wing before his injury and a new signing, Jimmy Bauchop from Norwich, hit six in the last eight games. Jimmy was a tough character: he was a proven goalscorer wherever he played, he never stopped long at any of his clubs (and he played for at least nine!). He also possessed something of a short temper and became Palace's first player to be dismissed when he was sent off in September 1908 in a London Cup match against local rivals Croydon Common.

SEASON: 1907/08

GROUND: The Crystal Palace

MANAGER: Edmund Goodman

LEAGUE/DIVISION: Southern League First Division

FINAL POSITION: 4th

BIGGEST VICTORY: 4-1 *v.* Swindon Town, 12 October 1907

HEAVIEST DEFEAT: 0-4 *v.* Plymouth Argyle, 14 September 1907, 0-4 *v.* Luton Town, 26 October 1907

FA CUP – ROUND ELIMINATED: 3rd (old)

LEAGUE CUP – ROUND ELIMINATED: –

FULL MEMBERS CUP – ROUND ELIMINATED: –

LEADING LEAGUE APPEARANCES (MAX: 38): 37 – H. Swann, 35 – G. Woodger

LEADING LEAGUE GOALSCORERS: 13 – G. Woodger, 8 – R. Roberts

1908/09

A STUNNING FA CUP WIN ENLIVENS A POOR LEAGUE SEASON

Palace's Southern League season of 1908/09 was a poor one and was made even more disappointing when compared with its immediate predecessor. It was almost a mirror image of the hugely successful 1907/08 term, with our best results coming early in the campaign followed by an awful second half in which we went thirteen games without a victory after beating Watford 3-1 at our headquarters on Saturday 19 December, and won just twice in the eighteen League fixtures in the early months of 1909.

Palace were joined for this season by sparkling little outside right George Garratt, formerly of Plymouth, Aston Villa and West Bromwich Albion. He was a tricky customer on either flank, tough, strong and unselfish, and so reliable that he seldom missed a match through injury. George played 185 League and Cup games for Palace over five seasons, gained several minor representative honours and became a great favourite with our supporters. Another useful arrival for 1908/09 was full-back Ted Collins, who joined us from Carlisle and deputised for or partnered Harry Collyer most effectively, while wing half John Brearley, who had joined us from Spurs in the summer of 1907, had an excellent season, missing just one game.

The Palace club undertook an interesting summer tour of 'the continent' in late May 1908. In reality, and understandably, we limited our travels and played six matches in Slovakia. We won all of them but manager Edmund Goodman was not impressed by the local referees and opined upon the party's return to English shores that they were 'the great blot on continental football'!

Palace began 1908/09 in fine style: we won six of our first ten matches and suffered only one defeat, so that by the time amateur striker Charlie McGibbon and George Woodger had accounted for visiting Luton on Saturday 10 October before a crowd of some 10,000, Palace were at the top of the Southern League table for the first time in their existence. Centre forward McGibbon was a stunningly successful acquisition, secured from New Brompton by manager Goodman in the first couple of weeks of the season. He became the first Palace striker to net a hat-trick on his debut for the club when Palace beat Brighton 4-0 at our headquarters on 19 September, Jimmy Bauchop netting our other goal (in fact our third). But Charlie left us for Southampton after the end of this season and was not heard of again after early January.

Archie Needham, who netted one of the finest Palace goals of all time.

Although our League season deteriorated out of all recognition (we ultimately finished sixteenth) we were still among the Southern League's leading clubs when we met the giants of Wolverhampton Wanderers in the first round of the FA Cup in mid-January and sprang a surprise by holding the cup-holders 2-2 at their imposing Molineux ground. That said, the prospect of us repeating that feat, let alone of improving upon it in the replay was considered remote. And that sensible viewpoint was confirmed when the visitors netted in the first minute – or was it?

Palace were able to make the speedy response that was required upon the heavy, liberally sanded turf when another Palace amateur, Billy Lawrence, took a pass from John Brearley, rounded the full-back and shot firmly past the goalkeeper. Early in the second half Ted Collins was hurt but somewhere around the middle of the half Palace took the lead through our irrepressible right winger George Garratt. Wolves levelled with eight minutes of ordinary time remaining.

Extra time, in the fading light and on the now badly cut-up pitch, produced such drama that no Palace fan who saw it could ever forget it. Jimmy Bauchop took full advantage of another superb pass from John Brearley, but it was in the dying moments of the match that Archie Needham scored one of the finest goals in all Palace's history. He received the ball in the centre circle inside the Palace half and ran at the Wolves defence, striding through tackles as well as the strength-sapping mud, before lashing it into the net and falling exhausted in the Wolves penalty area. There he accepted the acclaim of the fans and the congratulations of his colleagues. No wonder that Palace supporters who saw it were still talking about it six or seven decades later!

SEASON: 1908/09

GROUND: The Crystal Palace

MANAGER: Edmund Goodman

LEAGUE/DIVISION: Southern League First Division

FINAL POSITION: 16th

BIGGEST VICTORY: 5-1 *v.* Leyton, 5 September 1908

HEAVIEST DEFEAT: 1-5 *v.* Watford, 24 April 1909

FA CUP – ROUND ELIMINATED: 2nd (old)

LEAGUE CUP – ROUND ELIMINATED: –

FULL MEMBERS CUP – ROUND ELIMINATED: –

LEADING LEAGUE APPEARANCES (MAX: 40): 39 – J. Brearley, 38 – J. Johnson

LEADING LEAGUE GOALSCORERS: 16 – J. Bauchop, 14 – C. McGibbon

1909/10

A RESPECTABLE SEASON UNDER GEORGE WOODGER

George Woodger became Palace's third captain when Wilfred Innerd returned to his native North-East in the summer of 1909 and a series of impressive early results soon put our club among the leading contenders for the Southern League title of 1909/10. Chief among these was the 6-0 rout of Southend in September in which J.W. Williams scored five of our goals. Palace in fact had a new striking partnership for 1909/10 in Williams and George Payne. Williams could play in any forward position and had joined us from Birmingham City. He soon proved highly popular with the Palace fans, who christened him 'Ginger' on account of his auburn hair, but some of the local press gave him the sobriquet 'The Palace Terrier' which most aptly describes his neat, eager and busy style, his snappy tackle and zest for goals. So well did he fare with us that he gained Welsh international honours and 1909/10 was his first and best season for us, although he played regularly for four-and-a-half years.

George Payne came to us from Tottenham in 1909/10. He was an astonishing marksman with 25 Southern League goals from just 34 outings – 21 of them before Christmas, including hat-tricks in consecutive games in October and four against New Brompton in November!

Although the Palace became the only side to beat champions-to-be Brighton, at their Goldstone Road ground that season (2-1, with goals from Payne and Williams, one in each half), we were nothing like such a strong side in the second half of the term, and slipped eventually to finish seventh – respectable enough and a considerable improvement on 1908/09 certainly, but disappointing nonetheless in view of the splendid showing and high hopes raised earlier in the campaign.

A feature of the 1909/10 season was the three new defenders in our side, all of whom would go on to become invaluable members of later, more successful Palace teams, and a new half-back who was to become an inspirational captain.

The first of the defenders was already known before his arrival at Palace because he had starred with Croydon Common, who had won the Southern League Second Division championship in 1908/09. Bob Spottiswood was a wing half, fierce and determined. He missed just one Southern League game for us in 1909/10, gained Southern League honours, went on to make 189 appearances for our club before the First World War and helped to form one of our best ever half-back lines with two other new men, Jimmy Hughes and Harry Hanger.

Big Jimmy Hughes was a powerful bulwark of a centre half and it is no coincidence that our best seasons in the Southern League were achieved while he was marshalling our defence. Dominant in the air, strong in the tackle and able to deliver a stream of stylish, sweeping passes to either wing, it was no surprise that he too was chosen to play for the Southern League. Only the First World War prevented him from amassing a huge total of appearances for us – as it was, with four seasons lost to the hostilities, Jimmy played 209 first-class games for us with remarkable consistency.

Harry Hanger came to the Palace for this 1909/10 season from Bradford City and this cultured wing half became a splendid club captain after George Woodger's departure in October 1910. He was popular with his colleagues as well as with the fans and his inspirational captaincy helped the club to within an ace of the Southern League championship in 1914.

Last of the new players of note in 1909/10 was left-back Joe Bulcock, who made an immediate impact, and was chosen to represent the Southern League against the Football League at Stamford Bridge in April before going to South Africa with an FA touring side. Like the others, Joe was to provide sterling service to the Palace and helped to form some of our best defences in the early years.

George Woodger, Palace's captain for 1909/10.

SEASON: 1909/10

GROUND: The Crystal Palace

MANAGER: Edmund Goodman

LEAGUE/DIVISION: Southern League First Division

FINAL POSITION: 7th

BIGGEST VICTORY: 6-0 *v.* Southend United, 25 September 1909

HEAVIEST DEFEAT: 0-3 *v.* Watford, 22 January 1910, 0-3 *v.* Southend United, 23 February 1910

FA CUP – ROUND ELIMINATED: 1st (old)

LEAGUE CUP – ROUND ELIMINATED: –

FULL MEMBERS CUP – ROUND ELIMINATED: –

LEADING LEAGUE APPEARANCES (MAX: 42): 42 – J. Williams, 41 – J. Johnson, R. Spottiswood

LEADING LEAGUE GOALSCORERS: 25 – G. Payne, 20 – J. Williams

1910/11

PALACE'S STRONGEST SQUAD YET REACH FOURTH PLACE

It was obvious to everyone who followed pre-First World War football, virtually from the start of the 1910/11 season, that George Woodger would not long remain a Palace player. He was so clearly of a class above most of his contemporaries in the Southern League; he yearned for full England recognition but he, and everyone else, knew that the only way he could gain it would be to play for a major Football League club. Thus, while Crystal Palace and our fans were sorry to see our captain leave us, it was certainly no surprise at all when he moved to First Division Oldham on 30 September 1910 for a fee variously described at between £450 and £800 – a substantial enough sum for those days — and he did eventually fulfil his ambition to play for England.

Woodger's replacement at centre forward, Charlie Woodhouse, was another astute signing for the club by Edmund Goodman. He netted on his debut on 1 October when we beat Leyton 5-4 at the Crystal Palace in a splendid game. He was a strong rumbustious leader of our attack, played in every remaining Southern League fixture of 1910/11 and finished as our top scorer by a distance, with 15 strikes from his 33 appearances. He had come to us from Halesowen.

Another newcomer at this stage who was to become a Palace regular up to the First World War was inside forward Charlie Hewitt, a bustling bundle of energy with considerable experience. Once George Woodger had left us, it was Charlie who became the great supplier for the wing wizardry of George Garratt, but he was also a most useful goalscorer, hitting 39 Southern League goals for us. One of them was on his Palace debut when we tanned Plymouth 6-1 at the Crystal Palace on Saturday 15 October. Plymouth had been something of a bogey team for us: this was a second consecutive victory over the Pilgrims at the Palace but the Westcountrymen had previously and repeatedly beaten us there. On this occasion Palace were able to repay several old scores: George Garratt and Ginger Williams netted close together midway through the first half and the latter made the outcome certain soon after the break. Charlie Woodhouse, Hewitt himself and Woodhouse again, in that order, simply added to Argyle woes on the day, though fairness demands an acknowledgement that we lost the Home Park return 1-5 four months later.

The victory over Plymouth was the beginning of a superb Palace sequence of seven Southern League wins in nine outings interspersed, and then followed, with two draws, and the Palace only

Right: Charlie Hewitt joined the Palace for 1910/11.

tasted defeat for the first time in two-and-a-half months at Brighton on Boxing Day after Jimmy Hughes had to go off early with a badly wrenched knee.

Much of the above implies that it was probably Palace's strongest Southern League squad to date that was available to manager Edmund Goodman for 1910/11, and certainly the team did do well. We secured four 'doubles', yet nobody beat us twice, although there was the odd statistic whereby we failed to even score in any of the four matches against the relegated clubs, Southend and Portsmouth. A creditable late run of two home wins, over West Ham United and Exeter City, plus two away draws at Queens Park Rangers and Luton Town, meant that come the last game of the season Palace could have finished as runners-up to champions Swindon, but a heavy defeat at Northampton consigned us to fourth place, with the Cobblers themselves finishing second.

Our single FA Cup match in 1910/11 deserves a mention: former adversaries Everton came to the Crystal Palace again in the first round in mid-January. This time their calibre was much superior and they returned to Merseyside with a 4-0 victory. It would be rather different the next time the clubs were paired in the competition but that was to be a decade or more in the future.

SEASON:1910/11

GROUND: The Crystal Palace

MANAGER: Edmund Goodman

LEAGUE/DIVISION: Southern League First Division

FINAL POSITION: 4th

BIGGEST VICTORY: 6-1 *v.* Plymouth Argyle, 15 October 1910

HEAVIEST DEFEAT: 0-5 *v.* Northampton Town 18 April 1911

FA CUP – ROUND ELIMINATED: 1st (old)

LEAGUE CUP – ROUND ELIMINATED: –

FULL MEMBERS CUP – ROUND ELIMINATED: –

LEADING LEAGUE APPEARANCES (MAX: 38): 37 – H. Collyer, 36 – J. Johnson

LEADING LEAGUE GOALSCORERS: 15 – C. Woodhouse, 8 – C. Hewitt, J. Williams

1911/12

A SUDDEN DEATH AT THE PALACE BRINGS TED SMITH'S ARRIVAL

Crystal Palace began 1911/12 with an excellent sequence of results, which meant that, initially at least, we carried the look of possible, even potential, champions of the Southern League. The reason for such optimism lay in a series of scores that involved us in just one defeat in the first eleven matches and included several important successes. West Ham were beaten at the Crystal Palace on the opening day of the season, Saturday 2 September, with a goal from Ginger Williams just before half-time, Coventry were dismissed 3-0 in October and Norwich routed 6-0 later that month when our forward line ran riot in the second half with five goals in a twenty-minute spell, in which they were described as 'beyond praise' by one seasoned scribe.

Leading goalscorer at this time was rampant centre forward Charlie Woodhouse, who notched six goals in four games in mid and late October and early November, but Charlie died suddenly and his death inevitably proved a heavy blow to the club. Incidentally, Charlie is buried in Elmers End cemetery, adjacent to Birkbeck station, but his grave would benefit from attention if any modern-day Palace fans could spare him an hour or two.

Versatile forward Dick Harker had rejoined us for this season and filled in up front in Woodhouse's absence. Dick probably had his best game of the term when Ted Smith arrived from Hull City and made his Palace debut alongside him at West Ham at the end of December 1911: both men secured hat-tricks and Palace won 6-1 at Upton Park, easily our best result there. Ted hit another three the following Saturday too in a 4-1 beating of Bristol Rovers. He simply went on from there. He topped our list of goalscorers for each of the four remaining pre-war seasons, and again in 1919/20 and during that period his record was the equal of any in the game.

Ted hailed from Birmingham and was burly and strong, weighing in at 12 stone 7 pounds and standing some 5 feet 9.5 inches tall. As a header of the ball, he was phenomenal and it was amazing how many of his goals came from his head. But he also possessed an extremely powerful shot, and remember that in those days the leather ball collected any moisture on the pitch and could finish up weighing several pounds! Altogether, Ted notched 124 senior goals for the Palace and there is no question that if the First World War had not reduced the impact

Ted Smith, who hit hat-tricks in his opening pair of Palace games.

of his career it would be he and not Peter Simpson who would have been our leading goalscorer of all time.

Palace finished 1911/12 brightly enough with three victories and only one defeat in the last six games, but our prospects of fulfilling the early season hopes were banished between mid-January and early March, when we played seven Southern League matches (four at home) and failed to win even one of them. Ted Smith was usually on target, but our problem was that there was little support from elsewhere now, and the opposition were all too well aware of our limitations.

Modern readers will blanche (and modern footballers quail!) at the fact that the Palace played four League games in an eight-day period over Christmas 1911, including three matches in four days, and then, over Easter 1912, turned out four times in five days!

In fact it was in the Easter Saturday game against Watford at the Palace, played in blazing sunshine throughout, and the second match of the latter sequence, where Palace at last began to assert themselves again. The Hornets were well beaten with second-half goals from Ted Smith and Charlie Hewitt scarcely doing us justice. Then Millwall were beaten 3-0 on Easter Monday with a vintage Palace performance. After a defeat at Brighton on the Tuesday, Palace drew with New Brompton and at Exeter, then beat Brentford in the final game to finish seventh.

It was the Bees' second defeat of the season at the Crystal Palace, because we had beaten them 4-0 in a first round FA Cup replay in mid-January after a scoreless draw at Griffin Park. The prize was a home tie against Sunderland from the First Division of the Football League. The Wearsiders held us 0-0 on a bone-hard, icy Palace pitch, then crept through in extra time of the replay with a goal contrived by the great Charlie Buchan.

SEASON: 1911/12

GROUND: The Crystal Palace

MANAGER: Edmund Goodman

LEAGUE/DIVISION: Southern League First Division

FINAL POSITION: 7th

BIGGEST VICTORY: 6-0 *v.* Norwich City, 28 October 1911

HEAVIEST DEFEAT: 1-4 *v.* Brighton & Hove Albion, 9 April 1912

FA CUP – ROUND ELIMINATED: 2nd (old)

LEAGUE CUP – ROUND ELIMINATED: –

FULL MEMBERS CUP – ROUND ELIMINATED: –

LEADING LEAGUE APPEARANCES (MAX: 38): 35 – H. Collyer, 34 – J. Johnson

LEADING LEAGUE GOALSCORERS: 19 – E. Smith, 15 – J. Williams

1912/13

ANOTHER SOUND SOUTHERN LEAGUE SEASON

Without a shadow of doubt, Palace's best summer signing during the 1912 close season was that of left-back Horace Colclough from Crewe Alexandra. Horace played just nine times for us this term, in both the full-back positions, but in 1913/14 he took over at left-back and was quite superb, going on to gain a full England international cap – the first in Palace's history.

But manager Edmund Goodman was aware of the quality of his squad and realised that there was little he could do to improve it for the season ahead, although a useful arrival who could fill a variety of forward or midfield roles was Ernie York, who made 28 appearances in four different positions, and we were occasionally favoured with the distinguished England and England amateur international half-back, Revd Kenneth Hunt, who had played against us for Wolves in the great FA Cup tie back in 1909 and been lavish in his praise of his team's conquerors afterwards.

Harry Collyer and Joe Johnson received thoroughly deserved benefit games (though in those days these matches were selected from the formal fixture list). During this season the Palace won the London Challenge Cup for the first time, beating West Ham in the replayed final at Tottenham by a goal to nil with Ginger Williams netting the vital strike. No fewer than five Palace players were called to represent the Southern League in the inter-league contests.

There was also no doubting the Southern League highlight of the season. It came in mid-November with an 8-0 thrashing of Southampton at the Crystal Palace, although only a modest (estimated) crowd of some 8,000 actually watched it. Saints had been one of the leading Southern League clubs in the competition's earlier days but at this time they were at a somewhat low ebb and this defeat at a fog-shrouded Palace still remains their (equal) heaviest ever. Palace went to the top of the Southern League table as an outcome of this huge victory in which we led after only five minutes through Ginger Williams, were five up at half-time and crashed in three more in the last quarter of an hour when Saints were complaining about the light and requesting an abandonment! Ginger Williams hit a hat-trick; Charlie Hewitt went one better!

But Palace were not quite consistent enough over the whole season to win the Southern League championship: our old foes, Plymouth, did that, though we took three of the four points from our matches against them, 0-0 at Home Park the week before the rout of Southampton and 1-0 at the Palace thanks to a blasted Ted Smith penalty three minutes from time in mid-March, when both clubs had an important player absent for a Southern League representative fixture being played at Millwall.

Palace's FA Cup run in 1912/13 was more interesting than usual because it brought us our first competitive meeting against the club most closely associated with our 1905 foundation; mighty, distinguished Aston Villa. To reach that (old) third round tie we had beaten two Football League sides, Glossop and Bury, both 2-0 and both at the Crystal Palace. The latter, on Saturday 1 February, drew one of the best crowds of the season to the Palace, despite constant and heavy rain, and those 14,000 hardy souls were well rewarded by an excellent display from our favourites against a club that retained all its former top-flight lustre despite being relegated the previous summer. Ted Smith headed us in front from a flighted Harry Hanger free-kick a little after a quarter of an hour, then Bill Davies scored a wonderful goal to ensure victory with twenty minutes to go, beating three defenders with his consummate dribbling skills and then the goalkeeper for a spectacular individual strike.

At Villa Park, in front of the biggest crowd to watch a Palace game before the First World War – some 44,500 – we were opposed by our star winger from 1905-07, Charlie Wallace. Charlie and his colleagues were altogether too much for us: they won 5-0 and went on to win the FA Cup at the Crystal Palace in the spring, beating Sunderland before a record Palace crowd of over 120,000 fans!

The Revd Kenneth Hunt – the only parson to play for Crystal Palace FC.

SEASON: 1912/13

GROUND: The Crystal Palace

MANAGER: Edmund Goodman

LEAGUE/DIVISION: Southern League First Division

FINAL POSITION: 5th

BIGGEST VICTORY: 8-0 *v.* Southampton, 16 November 1912

HEAVIEST DEFEAT: 0-2 *v.* Reading, 23 November 1912, 0-2 *v.* QPR, 21 December 1912, 0-2 *v.* Portsmouth, 4 January 1913

FA CUP – ROUND ELIMINATED: 3rd (old)

LEAGUE CUP – ROUND ELIMINATED: –

FULL MEMBERS CUP – ROUND ELIMINATED: –

LEADING LEAGUE APPEARANCES (MAX: 38): 37 – J. Johnson, 34 – H. Collyer, W. Davies

LEADING LEAGUE GOALSCORERS: 25 – E. Smith, 11 – C. Hewitt

1913/14

PALACE MISS THE SOUTHERN TITLE ON GOAL AVERAGE ALONE

The summer of 1913 spelt the end of a Palace era because manager Edmund Goodman permitted sparkling winger George Garratt to leave us for Millwall. George had played 185 League and Cup games for the Palace since 1908 and was hugely popular with our fans, as well as a clever and dangerous raider, but Mr Goodman could afford to let him leave without a qualm because two young wingers were coming swiftly to the fore – John Whibley and Ben Bateman, who won three amateur international caps during this 1913/14 season. Their most substantial contribution to the Palace cause would come largely after the First World War, but they were both valuable members of the 1913/14 Palace side, which would come unbearably close to winning the Southern League championship.

As previously indicated, it was in this season that Horace Colclough seized his opportunity brilliantly, made the left-back position his own and gained Palace's first full England international honour when he represented his country against Wales at Cardiff (a 2-0 win for England) on 16 March 1914 as well as becoming yet another Palace player to earn Southern League representative honours.

Palace's cup exploits this term were varied: our FA Cup run was certainly rather less interesting than in 1912/13. We met two of our Southern League contemporaries and home advantage proved decisive. Palace beat Norwich 2-1 in the (old) first round on Saturday 10 January with an early goal from Charlie Hewitt and another from Ted Smith after Norwich had equalised, but our hero of the afternoon was actually goalkeeper Joe Johnson, because he saved a late Norwich penalty! We lost in round two, at Upton Park, going down to two goals conceded in front of 18,000 London football fans. However, Palace retained the London Challenge Cup, beating Tottenham (who included Jimmy Bauchop) 2-1, the winner coming from Bill Davies, and thus became the first club to win that trophy twice in succession.

Nevertheless, it was the Southern League title that the club and its followers wanted to win, and we came so close to doing so. By early 1914 it was clear that the race was between ourselves and Swindon Town. The two matches between us had been completed by the first Saturday in February: both sides won at the other's headquarters and it was evident that there was little to choose between them. Palace lost at home to a single goal in October but inside

P.T. Keene, who netted twice in Palace's 3-1 win over champions Swindon Town.

left John Bright (who replaced Ginger Williams from early December and the latter was transferred to Millwall in February) and Ben Bateman earned our first ever win at the County Ground and took us ahead of Town on goal average at the top of the table. Now the race was really on!

Palace actually played the final eight games without defeat, but we only managed to win three of them. Matters were always close and the leadership of the table changed hands (or should we say 'feet'?!) several times. The decisive afternoon was the Saturday before Easter when Palace secured a fine 3-1 victory over visiting Coventry, only to learn with dismay that Swindon had trounced Portsmouth 5-0 and had thereby managed to slip ahead of us on goal average. Neither club could put in a championship-winning run – Palace drew all three Easter weekend matches and beat Norwich in our last home game. Thus, the last Saturday of the season was reached with Swindon ahead of us, but only on goal average and everything hinged upon the results of the clubs' final matches of the season. We were at Gillingham, Swindon at Cardiff.

Truth told, we did not play at all well at Gillingham and fell behind in the first half. Ted Smith put us level when he ran from inside his own half, but we could not get a winner – and then learned that Swindon had fought out a 0-0 draw in south Wales. The club and its supporters were bitterly disappointed to be denied by such a slender margin, but true sportsmanship was revealed in that a telegram was immediately despatched from our headquarters to Swindon bearing our congratulations to them on winning the title despite our best efforts.

SEASON: 1913/14

GROUND: The Crystal Palace

MANAGER: Edmund Goodman

LEAGUE/DIVISION: Southern League First Division

FINAL POSITION: 2nd

BIGGEST VICTORY: 5-1 *v.* Reading, 15 November 1913

HEAVIEST DEFEAT: 0-3 *v.* QPR, 22 November 1913

FA CUP – ROUND ELIMINATED: 2nd

LEAGUE CUP – ROUND ELIMINATED: –

FULL MEMBERS CUP – ROUND ELIMINATED: –

LEADING LEAGUE APPEARANCES (MAX: 38): 38 – E. Smith, 34 – J. Johnson, H. Hanger, H. Colclough

LEADING LEAGUE GOALSCORERS: 26 – E. Smith, 8 – J. Bright

1914/15

PALACE FORCED TO LEAVE THEIR HOME

By the time the 1914/15 football season opened on Saturday 5 September our country was already at war with Germany and, while every club at every level of the game was inevitably affected by members of the playing and administrative staffs being called up or volunteering to join the Army, the Palace would ultimately suffer more by these hostilities than most other clubs.

Our early Southern League progress this term was decidedly sluggish. It is interesting in the modern game how a 'near-miss' on promotion or a major cup success in one season can detrimentally affect a club at the start of the next. It is not a new phenomenon, and certainly appears to have happened to Crystal Palace in 1914. Having been so narrowly denied the 1913/14 Southern League title, our club was hit by a severe loss of form. We failed to win a match in 1914/15 until our eighth outing, at Southampton on 17 October, and failed to win at home until 7 November when Ted Smith netted the only goal of the game against Portsmouth with a typically powerful strike some fifteen minutes before the end. Palace had been at the bottom of the table for several weeks by that time, but at least this victory lifted us away from there!

Probably Palace's best League performance in the first half of the season was when we faced the champions Swindon at the Crystal Palace a fortnight after the victory over Portsmouth. Ben Bateman was on leave from Army service and was the key to our splendid 3-1 success. Ted Smith netted after only ten minutes, only for Swindon to show their character with a speedy equaliser. Palace forged ahead again two minutes after the break through P.T. Keene, our outside left deputising for Bill Davies, and the same player settled the outcome, converting a typically brilliant penetrative run by man of the match Ben Bateman.

This deserved if unexpected success worked wonders for our players' confidence. Even without Ben Bateman we won 4-1 at Plymouth the following week, when Ted Smith claimed a hat-trick, then again two weeks later at West Ham, who were previously undefeated. Bill Middleton and Ted Smith scored for us in the opening eight minutes and the Hammers' sole reply came very late indeed.

Although Palace's playing form had improved enormously in the early winter months of 1914/15 there was no doubt that our attendances had fallen away badly this season. The war in

Europe was affecting the lives of a growing number of folk, including football fans, and the 'pull' of a football match inevitably lessened week by week.

Thus the FA Cup brought pleasure as well as relief to the Palace club officials when we were drawn to meet Football League side Birmingham City at their St Andrews enclosure. Sure enough, there was a much bigger crowd (estimated at 18,000) for the game in Birmingham than we would have anticipated at the Crystal Palace, while the Palace team did really well, holding the Blues to a 2-2 draw. All the goals came one after the other just after the hour: Birmingham scored from a penalty, Bill Davies then Bill Middleton netted for us and Birmingham replied immediately.

Then the Palace directors made a decision that remains unique at our club. It was agreed to waive the right to stage the replay at our ground and to accept Birmingham's offer to host the contest again. The decision was condemned at the time, but our financial predicament precluded any other course. Palace did well again and took Birmingham to extra time, but the Blues scored three goals in the added half hour.

The following month the Admiralty requisitioned the Crystal Palace and closed it to the public, making it impossible for us to continue to play there. Several Southern League clubs offered their grounds to enable us to complete our home fixtures, but the directors decided to move across to the Herne Hill running track, where the distinguished amateurs West Norwood had their base.

Palace lost three of our first four games at Herne Hill, but then, in April and typically perversely, produced our best spell of the entire season, comprising four straight wins, three of them on our borrowed ground! We finished the season fifteenth out of twenty participating clubs, but by then virtually everyone's interest lay in a far greater contest being fought out in Europe.

Ben Bateman.

SEASON: 1914/15

GROUND: The Crystal Palace to February 1915, Herne Hill from March 1915

MANAGER: Edmund Goodman

LEAGUE/DIVISION: Southern League First Division

FINAL POSITION: 15th

BIGGEST VICTORY: 4-1 *v.* Plymouth Argyle, 28 November 1914, 4-1 *v.* Reading, 6 February 1915

HEAVIEST DEFEAT: 0-5 *v.* Cardiff City, 30 January 1915

FA CUP – ROUND ELIMINATED: 1st (old)

LEAGUE CUP – ROUND ELIMINATED: –

FULL MEMBERS CUP – ROUND ELIMINATED: –

LEADING LEAGUE APPEARANCES (MAX: 38): 38 – H. Colclough, 36 – R. Spottiswood

LEADING LEAGUE GOALSCORERS: 20 – E. Smith, 5 – W. Middleton

1915-1919

THE FIRST WORLD WAR BRINGS TROUBLED TIMES TO CRYSTAL PALACE FC

Football during the First World War hostilities was frowned upon to say the least by the British authorities, and as a result coverage of the sport is tantalisingly brief in the newspapers of the period. Some clubs actually suspended operations entirely for the duration of the war but the Palace administration does not appear to have even considered such a step. Much more practically, the formation of the London Combination for the 1915/16 season, with the provision of matches against the top Football League sides in the metropolis, was a positive reaction and was unquestionably welcomed by ourselves and the other Southern League clubs located in the capital.

Palace's problem, for the first three wartime seasons certainly, was the location of our temporary home stadium, allied to the absence of most of our pre-war players. Herne Hill was never a happy base for us (although it was an early, perhaps even the earliest, instance of a senior football club having to play on another club's ground) and such experiences have seldom proved popular or successful. Nevertheless, Herne Hill was a football ground and, as previously pointed out, the home of an eminent southern amateur club, but the twin effects of playing on someone else's ground combined with the absence of most of our players, who were engaged in distant war work or in the Services and were replaced by 'guests', must have been to produce an almost surreal atmosphere to most of our matches there. The team was called 'Crystal Palace' to be sure, but that was all it had about it to mark it out as 'ours'. Frequently in that period there were teams playing in our colours and under our name that did not contain a single pre-war Palace player! And on a borrowed ground at that!

It was inevitable that there would be more than the occasional farcical result and also that the balance of such would be against us at Herne Hill, although, taken overall, the Palace performed creditably enough for a Southern League side in the London Combination. But the mood of everyone connected with our Club can be imagined when news of the deaths of skipper Harry Hanger and former favourites 'Ginger' Williams and Joe Bulcock was received.

In summary, the 1915/16 London Combination season comprised two competitions, the principal one of which took place between August and late January and involved twelve clubs. Palace finished ninth, with two big defeats by Chelsea certainly hampering our prospects. After

Left: Joe Bulcock – a Palace star at left-back who was killed in the First World War.

Opposite: This Ordnance Survey map clearly shows the location of The Nest, directly opposite Selhurst railway station.

a friendly held on the last Saturday of January against Croydon Common on their ground, The Nest at Selhurst, (won 2-0), devoted to raising money for the War Comforts Fund, a supplementary competition was held from February to early May with home and away fixtures against seven opponents. Palace beat Reading 10-1 at West Norwood in one of these (though the Biscuitmen only had ten men for most of the match) and we avenged both the earlier Chelsea defeats, so thus managed to finish in the top half of the table in this smaller competition.

For 1916/17 the London Combination devised a single more impressive League contest. With fourteen clubs, including Luton and Southampton, and forty fixtures apiece, it obviously required an element of double-pairing. A unique and extraordinary Palace debut occurred in our first game under this auspice, against Brentford when a young air mechanic named W. Johnson, who had previously played for West Norwood and was a late selection for 'our' team, hit all four Palace goals in our 4-0 defeat of the Bees. The lad only played one other match for us, at Luton three weeks later, and netted in our 1-3 defeat.

In games against the bigger London clubs Palace usually suffered, but we did a double of sorts over Arsenal, whom we beat twice at West Norwood, though perhaps our most interesting results were a sequence of 2-2 draws at Christmas time: at Portsmouth on 23 December, against Southampton at home on Christmas morning and at The Dell on Boxing Day, and we finished a creditable eighth in the final table.

Season 1917/18 saw a similar competition run by the London Combination. It was reduced in the number of clubs taking part to ten, but each one played all the others four times. We

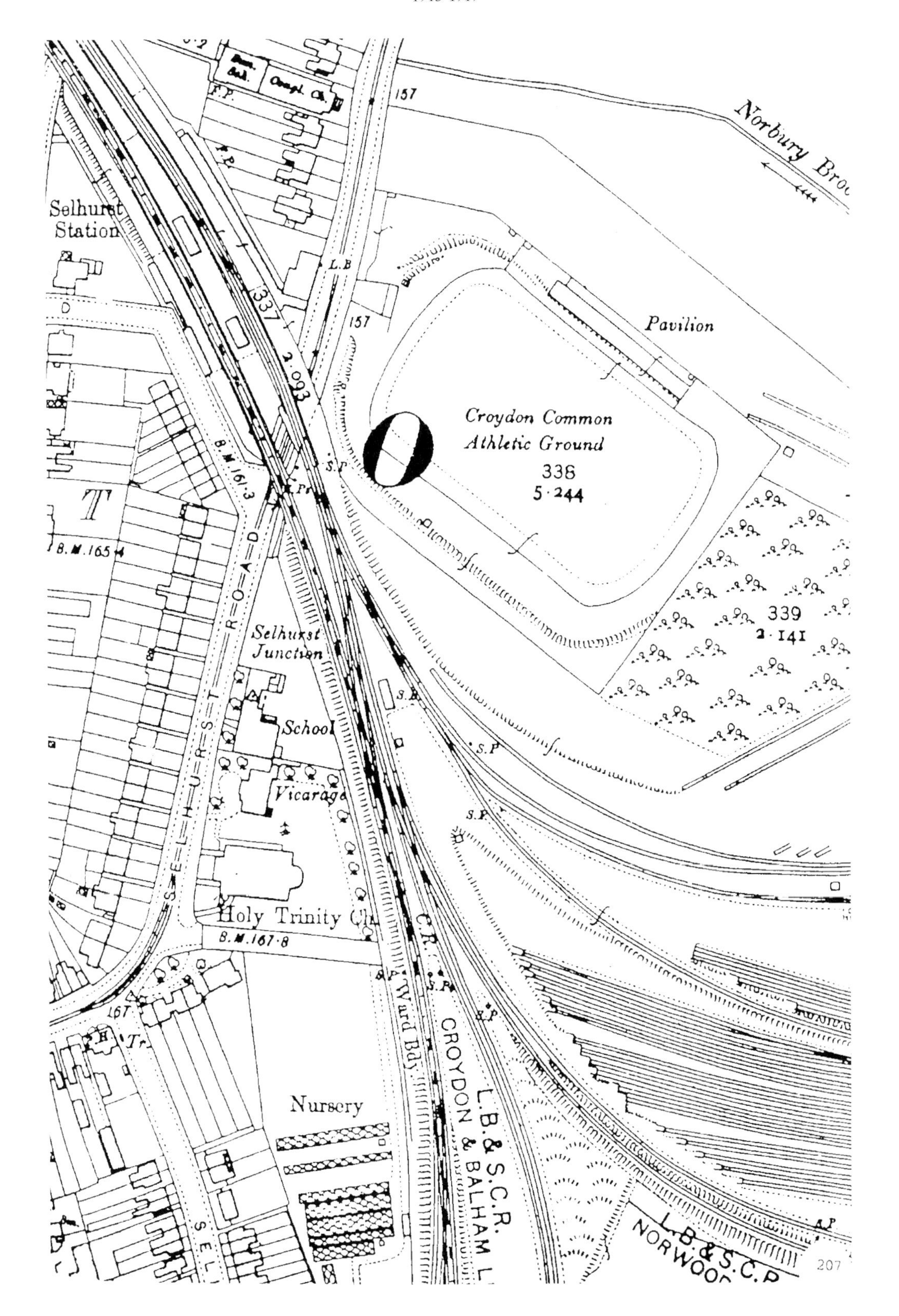
Norbury Brook
Selhurst Station
Pavilion
Croydon Common Athletic Ground
338
5·244
337
2·093
339
2·141
Selhurst Junction
School
Vicarage
Holy Trinity Ch
S E L H U R S T R O A D
Nursery
Ward Bdy
CROYDON & BALHAM L
L.B. & S.C.R.
L.B. & S.C.R.
NORWOOD
B.M.161·3
B.M.165·4
B.M.167·8
157
167
207

suffered an early season 1-7 defeat at Fulham and a 0-8 one at Tottenham in mid-February, but the worst one of all was 0-11 at West Ham in the final game of the competition on the Saturday after Easter. It was Palace's misfortune that the championship rested on the outcomes of the Irons' game against us and Chelsea's at Clapton Orient – and despite West Ham's mammoth total, Chelsea took the title by winning 6-1 in East London. Palace finished seventh.

Palace then rounded off their season by playing both Queens Park Rangers and Clapton Orient twice more (that is, for the fifth and sixth times!) in War Fund matches, winning all but the first one at Park Royal.

However, the best news for Crystal Palace FC during the war years was that the Club found a new home – and it did so during the summer of 1918. It was named 'The Nest' and for six years it did the Palace proud!

The Nest, on the site of the present-day Selhurst railway sidings, was built around the turn of the century upon land that had originally belonged to the Church Commissioners. It became the home of Croydon Common in 1908 and, because Croydon's colours were red and white they were accordingly nicknamed 'the Robins' and their ground inevitably was dubbed 'The Nest'. Common ceased to function at the end of 1915/16 and the ground remained untenanted for two years until Crystal Palace took out a lease from The London, Brighton & South Coast Railway Company, dated 27 June 1918 and played the last of the First World War seasons there. An interesting feature of Palace's time at The Nest originated in the earlier ownership of the land, for it was stipulated that no matches were permitted to be held at The Nest on Good Friday or Christmas Day and, although Southern and Football League fixtures appear always to have taken this into account, the restriction either lapsed or was relaxed in our favour in 1923 and 1924.

At the time that Crystal Palace moved to The Nest it was described as 'a small ground with a two-hundred-seater stand on one side and mounds of earth to stand upon at the other side, with a ditch at the back touching the railway line'. There was no terracing or barriers and only one means of entry or egress, opposite Selhurst Station, but additional turnstiles were erected in the summer of 1919. Iron railings around the playing pitch were installed during the 1920/21 season and 'considerable alterations' were made to the ground after Palace won promotion at the end of that term. Nevertheless, several Second Division clubs complained about the accommodation and facilities at The Nest and these cannot have been enhanced by a fire in the grandstand during a London Challenge Cup tie against Charlton (2-1) on Monday 31 October 1921.

In contrast to Herne Hill, The Nest was a happy home for Crystal Palace FC, and, as we shall see, proved to be a most successful one. But to begin with, the move to Selhurst had the hugely positive effect of extending the supporting base of the Club, because many – perhaps most – of the followers of Croydon Common transferred their allegiance to their new local team, my own grandfather among them. Admittedly this was made somewhat easier for Common fans by the poignant fact that during 1918/19 half a dozen or so games were played for the Palace by Croydon's strong and highly capable former full-back Jack Little, who had appeared regularly for the Robins' 1914 Southern League Second Division championship side, while in addition in 1919/20 Palace included former Common star Cyril Smith, a clever if diminutive inside or centre forward, in several early Southern League games upon the resumption of full competitive football.

The additional support immediately assisted Palace's financial position via the turnstiles and with Selhurst so readily accessible from Croydon itself and, further out, the towns of northern

Surrey, Palace's catchment area became a huge one. This fact was reflected over several subsequent decades at both The Nest and at Selhurst Park where, even when Palace teams were rather poor ones, our attendance figures were well ahead of clubs with much better sides.

We shall subsequently see how the years that the Palace spent at The Nest were highly successful ones and that during the time we were there we made tremendous progress, with the tight, humble little enclosure an ideal place from which to launch giant-killing feats against prestigious clubs... all to be revealed in subsequent pages!

Meanwhile, Palace were settling into their new base during the last of the wartime seasons, 1918/19. We played our first home fixture at our new address on Saturday 31 August with a charity match in aid of Croydon Hospitals against Millwall. The Mayor of Croydon, Alderman Howard Houlder welcomed the sides and kicked off. Millwall scored first but Palace won 4-1 with outside left J. Baker netting twice for us.

As in the previous term, the London Combination comprised ten clubs, with four fixtures against the others. Palace began with five victories and won seven of our first nine outings but, inevitably, were unable to sustain such a pace and finished in seventh place again. With the hostilities now ended, interest and attendances rose: Chelsea in February and Brentford in March both pulled attendances in excess of 10,000; Tottenham on 5 April over 12,000.

Then the London Combination home match against Arsenal on Good Friday had to be played at neighbouring Millwall (presumably because of the restriction noted above) and drew another 'very large crowd'. Palace lost to Chelsea in the semi-final of the London Victory Cup the following day and concluded their first season at The Nest with three exuberant friendlies. Now, like everyone else, we awaited a return to proper League action after the summer.

SEASON: 1915/16

GROUND: Herne Hill

MANAGER: Edmund Goodman

LEAGUE/DIVISION: London Combination, Principal and Supplementary competitions

FINAL POSITION: 9th and 6th

SEASON'S BIGGEST VICTORY: 10-1 *v.* Reading, 4 March 1916

SEASON'S HEAVIEST DEFEAT: 1-7 *v.* Watford, 6 November 1915

FA CUP – ROUND ELIMINATED: –

LEAGUE CUP – ROUND ELIMINATED: –

FULL MEMBERS CUP – ROUND ELIMINATED: –

LEADING LEAGUE APPEARANCES: –

LEADING LEAGUE GOALSCORERS: –

SEASON:1916/17

GROUND: Herne Hill

MANAGER: Edmund Goodman

LEAGUE/DIVISION: London Combination

FINAL POSITION: 8th

BIGGEST VICTORY:4-0 *v.* Brentford, 2 September 1916, 4-0 *v.* QPR, 27 January 1917

HEAVIEST DEFEAT: 1-8 *v.* West Ham United, 11 November 1916

FA CUP – ROUND ELIMINATED: –

LEAGUE CUP – ROUND ELIMINATED: –

FULL MEMBERS CUP – ROUND ELIMINATED: –

LEADING LEAGUE APPEARANCES: –

LEADING LEAGUE GOALSCORERS: –

SEASON: 1917/18

GROUND: Herne Hill

MANAGER: Edmund Goodman

LEAGUE/DIVISION: London Combination

FINAL POSITION: 7th

BIGGEST VICTORY: 4-0 *v.* Brentford, 29 September 1917, 4-0 *v.* West Ham United, 26 December 1917

HEAVIEST DEFEAT: 0-11 *v.* West Ham United, 6 April 1918

FA CUP – ROUND ELIMINATED: –

LEAGUE CUP – ROUND ELIMINATED: –

FULL MEMBERS CUP – ROUND ELIMINATED: –

LEADING LEAGUE APPEARANCES: –

LEADING LEAGUE GOALSCORERS: –

SEASON: 1918/19

GROUND: The Nest, Selhurst

MANAGER: Edmund Goodman

LEAGUE/DIVISION: London Combination

FINAL POSITION: 7th

BIGGEST VICTORY: 6-1 *v.* Clapton Orient, 2 November 1918

HEAVIEST DEFEAT: 1-6 *v.* Brentford, 25 January 1919

FA CUP – ROUND ELIMINATED: –

LEAGUE CUP – ROUND ELIMINATED: –

FULL MEMBERS CUP – ROUND ELIMINATED: –

LEADING LEAGUE APPEARANCES: –

LEADING LEAGUE GOALSCORERS: –

A postcard showing a match in progress at the Croydon Common ground.

1919/20

CLOSE FINISH IN PALACE'S LAST SOUTHERN LEAGUE SEASON

Naturally it was back to Southern League duty for Crystal Palace FC in August 1919 and inevitably we started with a line-up bearing little resemblance to the ones of the immediate pre-war days although the captain was again the prolific goalscorer Ted Smith. Partly due to Ted's 19 goals from 31 appearances Palace fared well in the renewed Southern League championship, but Ted's efforts were now augmented by dapper little Scottish Junior international inside or centre forward John Conner, who totted up 18 League goals. As a result the Palace finished third in May 1920, just two points behind champions Portsmouth and runners-up Watford and taking the final decision right to the last match.

But perhaps the feature of the immediate post-war Palace side that was most remembered by the contemporary fans and that is most deserving of notice all these years later, was the defensive triumvirate of Jack Alderson in goal, Jack Little at right-back and Ernie Rhodes on the left. Mention has already been made of Jack Little's origins and transfer from defunct Croydon Common, but Ernie had been at the Palace rather longer, having joined the Club in the summer of 1913. However, it was only now that he made his major contribution. He was strong physically in the mould of traditional 1920s full-backs, but he was always cool under pressure, thoughtful about his game and had a keen eye for the volleyed clearance, so that it was entirely fitting when the Football League honoured him with a place in one of its representative sides in the autumn of 1921.

Finding a worthy post-war successor to Joe Johnson, Palace's superb goalkeeper between 1907 and 1915, was obviously going to be an enormously difficult task, but Palace's manager, still the great Edmund Goodman, now entering his fifteenth season with our Club, actually discovered an even better one! Jack Alderson hailed from Crook, in County Durham, but was stationed at Woolwich in the latter stages of the First World War, and it was while he was there that he guested for the Palace during the late winter and spring of 1919, and signed professional forms for us immediately after leaving the Forces. Tall, lean and almost cadaverous in appearance, Jack was a goalkeeper of the highest class. He went on to play 205 first-class games for us and is one of only two Palace goalkeepers to have gained a full England cap while at the Club. His value became enormous to us after we had joined the Football League. He developed into a phenomenal penalty-saver, formed part of what was statistically Palace's best defence for over half a century, and if subsequently the highest point of his career was the international cap he earned for England

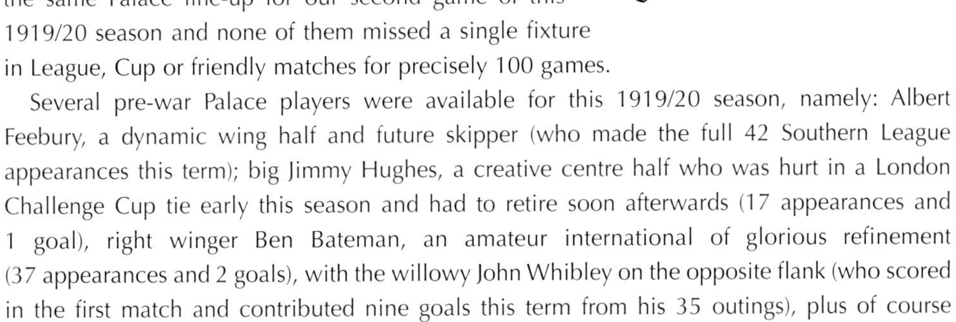

Right: Jack Alderson – a goalkeeper of the highest class.

against France in Paris (a 4-1 win for England) on 10 May 1923, in another sense it came soon after the end of the First World War. A youthful soldier, struck dumb from shell shock in the trenches, was behind Jack's goal watching a Palace game, when one particularly brilliant piece of goalkeeping so enthralled him that his speech was instantly restored.

Palace fans who saw these three men play together used to tell of an understanding between them that bordered on the uncanny: they were first together in the same Palace line-up for our second game of this 1919/20 season and none of them missed a single fixture in League, Cup or friendly matches for precisely 100 games.

Several pre-war Palace players were available for this 1919/20 season, namely: Albert Feebury, a dynamic wing half and future skipper (who made the full 42 Southern League appearances this term); big Jimmy Hughes, a creative centre half who was hurt in a London Challenge Cup tie early this season and had to retire soon afterwards (17 appearances and 1 goal), right winger Ben Bateman, an amateur international of glorious refinement (37 appearances and 2 goals), with the willowy John Whibley on the opposite flank (who scored in the first match and contributed nine goals this term from his 35 outings), plus of course skipper and centre forward Ted Smith as mentioned above.

SEASON: 1919/20

GROUND: The Nest, Selhurst

MANAGER: Edmund Goodman

LEAGUE/DIVISION: Southern League First Division

FINAL POSITION: 3rd

BIGGEST VICTORY: 4-0 *v.* Brighton & Hove Albion, 26 December 1919

HEAVIEST DEFEAT: 1-5 *v.* Southampton, 13 March 1920

FA CUP – ROUND ELIMINATED: 1st (old)

LEAGUE CUP – ROUND ELIMINATED: –

FULL MEMBERS CUP – ROUND ELIMINATED: –

LEADING LEAGUE APPEARANCES (MAX: 42): 42 – J. Alderson, J. Little, A. Feebury

LEADING LEAGUE GOALSCORERS: 19 – E. Smith, 18 – J. Conner

1920/21

PALACE ARE CHAMPIONS ON FOOTBALL LEAGUE DEBUT

After just one post-war season, the Southern League's First Division was taken en bloc into the Football League to become its new Third Division, and with that decision began the most successful period in the first sixty years of Crystal Palace FC, for, under Mr Goodman, the Glaziers became the first champions of the new section as well as gaining a prestigious victory in the FA Cup. Mr Goodman chose to add just three men to his playing squad and, in the light of the previous season's most capable showing, plus these arrivals, any rational pundit would have agreed that Palace had as sound a chance as any of their opponents.

Most important of the new acquisitions was Irish wing half Roy McCracken, who joined us from Belfast Distillery and was a neat, polished and clever schemer, but he was to suffer a badly broken leg midway through this season. In October, however, Roy was selected for Northern Ireland and thus became the first international from the new Third Division. He became a thoroughly consistent performer in our colours and was certainly seen at his best in the more refined atmosphere of the Second Division in later seasons.

Tall and dependable in defence and a current international, Welsh centre half J.T. Jones came to the Palace from Stoke City, but could only find a niche in our side in place of the stricken McCracken. Lancashire-born Tom Storey arrived from Middlesbrough to play on the right wing or at inside right in two spells this term and scored on his debut at Plymouth early in September.

Yet the most romantic figure in our side was the popular, good-looking Phil Bates at centre half. Phil had suffered a nasty injury to his right arm while on active service in the First World War and it had become quite useless, hanging limp and withered at his side. The injury didn't prove a handicap in this 1920/21 season and he was a splendid, probing, attacking pivot in those days before the idea of the 'stopper' centre half had been conceived.

If Palace's entry into the Football League was to prove an immediately triumphant one there was no indication of such a likelihood on the opening day of the season, 28 August, when Palace were down in south Wales at Pennydarren Park, the home of Merthyr Town, where we lost by the odd goal in three. There followed the midweek home game, against Plymouth, the first Football League match to be hosted at The Nest, which remained scoreless, but Palace then made their intentions and abilities clear for all to see with a run of six consecutive victories, including doubles over Norwich and Brentford, for the fixture list in those days had the clubs' home and away games in successive weeks.

Already, during these early autumn months, that great little goal-poacher John Conner was scoring important goals to ensure that we were among the front runners at that stage, while all the forwards were proving that they were capable of putting their names on the scoresheets. Conner and Whibley disposed of Merthyr in the Selhurst return; Storey's header at Plymouth continued the run in midweek and was followed by a late Whibley winner at Norwich. When the Canaries flew into our Nest (their ground at that time was called by the same name) John Conner settled a game of missed chances seventeen minutes from the end and thereby sent Palace to the top of the table. A brace from Ted Smith set us firmly on the way to victory at Brentford and we hit the Bees for a second four-goal beating when they came to our headquarters on 2 October, although this time we had to come from behind to win because Brentford netted early on.

Our impetus faded a little in October, when we lost the away games at Bristol Rovers and Reading, although the home games against those opponents were won comfortably enough and our crowds at The Nest rose steadily to ground records of 16,000, then 18,000, pushing the accommodation towards its limit.

However, come early November, with the Palace well to the fore in the race for the title, disaster struck. A midweek match against Southend at The Nest saw the Palace in some difficulties. Skipper Ted Smith had to spend some time off the field after an injury and Southend played a pretty physical game with their right-back twice cautioned by the referee – a rare event in those days and at least equal to a sending off today. In the end Palace were unable to get back on terms and we lost 2-3, but the frustration was just too much for some of our supporters, who swarmed onto the pitch and surrounded the visitors' worst offender in an ugly mood. Retribution from the FA soon followed – not only had we lost the match but The Nest was to be closed for two weeks, including Palace's next home match against Exeter at the end of November.

Palace were forced to play this game at Southampton although the Palace won it well, 2-1. Tom Storey gave us just the start we wanted with a goal in the fifth minute and Ted Smith notched a header after a quarter of an hour. Exeter rallied, replied before half-time and a thrilling second half ensued in mud and falling rain, with our 'keeper Jack Alderson in sparkling form and Palace holding onto their lead. There was a touch of intended humour when the band played *Home Sweet Home* upon our return to The Nest in mid-December, but we lost the match against Swansea 0-1 and lost our Northern Ireland international with a broken leg, so that the last few weeks of 1920 were far from easy and there was still no hint of what was to follow.

A marvellous Boxing Day victory over Brighton drew a crowd of 22,000: an Albert Feebury penalty nullified Brighton's fortieth-minute opener but the match was won by captain Ted Smith. His first goal was straightforward, knocking home an effort from John Conner that had rebounded off the crossbar, but his second was delightful. Ted played a one-two with John Conner, raced onto the return and hit a spectacular rising shot into the netting. Ted only played once more this season, being sidelined by illness and the need for an operation, but the value of his leadership and experience had kept us in contention for honours.

Palace then knocked Manchester City out of the FA Cup by winning 2-0 at The Nest and a hard-won double over Millwall in mid-January sent us back to the top of the Third Division table, but the title was won because of a magnificent run-in to the end of the season. After losing at Grimsby on the first Saturday in February the Palace beat the Mariners in the midweek return

Palace's summer 1920 photo of the men who would go on to become the first Third Division champions.

to begin an undefeated sequence of sixteen games, including eight consecutive victories before Easter, which took us to the brink of success. The vital pair of fixtures proved to be the ones against Southampton, our closest rivals for the championship. On Easter Monday Palace were back at The Dell and fell behind in the seventy-fifth minute in front of a 21,000 crowd. Jack Alderson kept us alive with some brave saves before Phil Bates equalised with the last kick of the game, his lob deceiving the Southampton defence as it looped into the net. At The Nest the following afternoon Southampton again went ahead, in the first half this time, but formidable pressure in the second period brought its reward, the equaliser being lashed home with a few minutes remaining by our tough little inside left Alf Wood.

Three more drawn matches followed, but a 5-1 demolition of Northampton on a heavy, slippery pitch in the last home game made promotion all but certain. Then a point from the return at the Cobblers' headquarters left no doubt. In both matches against Northampton John Conner had scored twice, and the clever little centre forward hit 9 goals in Palace's last 5 games to emphasise his ability to score at crucial times and record a fabulous 29 League goals this season. That ensured that the Palace were champions of the Third Division and had thereby secured a place among some of the great names in the game in the Second Division.

However, there was one other little matter outstanding, in which another victory would bring the already successful season to an emotional, passionate and totally satisfactory conclusion.

As luck would have it, the final match of our Third Division programme was at Southend of all places! The fracas at The Nest in November nearly had the direst consequences for us. Never was a final match contested so keenly! Certainly not one where nothing but honour was at stake! And you can imagine the satisfaction that was felt down Selhurst way when it was learned that John Conner had blasted a goal in each half to avenge that other little business!

Which all left one last game of the season – a cup final, no less! Palace had reached the London Challenge Cup final by beating Fulham and Charlton back in the winter. This final was actually Palace's second of four consecutive appearances in the final in the immediate post-war years: it was staged at Tottenham and our opponents were Clapton Orient from the Second Division – so, considerable prestige rested on the outcome. Again, John Conner won the match, ten minutes into the second half, to secure the trophy. This explains why pictures of Palace's championship-winning side also show the London Cup on parade, and demonstrates that Crystal Palace would be fully capable of holding their own the following season in the higher sphere against more senior opposition.

SEASON:1920/21

GROUND: The Nest, Selhurst

MANAGER: Edmund Goodman

LEAGUE/DIVISION: Football League Third Division

FINAL POSITION: 1st

BIGGEST VICTORY: 5-1 *v.* Northampton Town, 23 April 1921

HEAVIEST DEFEAT: 0-3 *v.* QPR, 18 December 1920

FA CUP – ROUND ELIMINATED: 2nd (old)

LEAGUE CUP – ROUND ELIMINATED: –

FULL MEMBERS CUP – ROUND ELIMINATED: –

LEADING LEAGUE APPEARANCES (MAX: 42): 42 – J. Little, E. Rhodes, J. Conner

LEADING LEAGUE GOALSCORERS: 29 – J. Conner, 9 – E. Smith

1921/22

PALACE'S FIRST SEASON IN THE SECOND DIVISION PRODUCES TWO FABULOUS VICTORIES

Manager Edmund Goodman made several signings in the summer of 1921, though these were more to deepen the pool of talent available than to change the formation. Most significant of the new arrivals were goalkeeper George Irwin, who proved an able if occasional deputy for Jack Alderson, and subsequently would manage Crystal Palace himself, and a pint-sized inside or centre forward called Albert Harry – of whom much more will be heard!

There were some much-needed ground improvements at The Nest and the season opened with the most prestigious fixture of the whole term. Our highly attractive visitors were Nottingham Forest, and they pulled in an estimated 20,000 crowd, many of them eager to see at first hand the famous England goalkeeper Sam Hardy, who was making his Forest debut. But the occasion was to be Palace's from beginning to end, and would provide the first of two fabulous victories gained by our club this term. J.T. Jones, Palace's Welsh international centre half, gave us the lead after twenty-five minutes with a powerful header that left Hardy grasping nothing but air and, even though Forest equalised, we had restored our lead through John Conner before the break with another headed effort. Then in the second half we ran riot: Ted Smith put us in full command following a clever move initiated by Roy McCracken in his comeback game after the dreadful injury he had suffered the previous winter, then John Whibley dribbled through from the halfway line, outpacing the Forest defence, drawing Hardy, and lashing the ball past him for a glorious goal.

Forest soon recovered from this setback; not only did they beat us in the return match a week later but they comfortably won the Second Division championship. For our favourites it was a marvellous victory, but it did not preface any lasting success among the more illustrious company of the Second Division: although Palace did reach the final of the London Challenge Cup, we lost to Arsenal by a single goal.

Our other wonderful success of 1921/22 came about because Palace were drawn to meet Everton at Goodison Park in the old first round of the FA Cup in early January 1922. We not only won, but we did so in such tumultuous fashion that this victory almost equals that of the early Palace heroes at the same stage of the 1906/07 FA Cup at Newcastle. We won this one 6-0! Just eighteen months out of the Southern League and here we were, sinking a top-flight side without trace at their own distinguished headquarters! The impact of that result upon the world of domestic football cannot be understood today: the contemporary press extolled the Palace as a 'wonder-team', which is roughly the modern-day equivalent of screaming headlines and excessive media hype.

So, the question must be 'how did we do it?' Unquestionably it was one of those days when everything went right for one side, but it is clear that the Palace were seldom on the defensive and actually had the ball in the net twice more, with another effort that hit the bar. Jack Alderson calmly peeled and ate an orange at one stage of the proceedings!

John Whibley started the rout, heading in Ben Bateman's fourth minute corner. Croydon-born Bert Menlove doubled the lead midway through the first half with a deflected shot and, although Everton rallied somewhat they proved quite unable to break through our ranks, so that it was left to the Palace to score four more times in the last quarter of the game. John Conner converted a Whibley centre, Menlove headed home another cross, Alf Wood made it five and, after Everton had missed a penalty, John Conner completed matters five minutes from time.

With hindsight the other most significant event of 1921/22 was the goalscoring debut of Albert Harry, who notched a brace from his original position of centre forward when Bury were our visitors at The Nest in late March. One of them was a header too! From that moment the Palace crowd had a new favourite to cheer – and they did so for the next twelve years!

J.T. Jones, who scored Palace's first ever Second Division goal.

SEASON: 1921/22

GROUND: The Nest, Selhurst

MANAGER: Edmund Goodman

LEAGUE/DIVISION: Football League Second Division

FINAL POSITION: 14th

BIGGEST VICTORY: 4-1 *v.* Nottingham Forest, 27 August 1921, 4-1 *v.* Bury, 25 March 1922

HEAVIEST DEFEAT: 1-5 *v.* Stoke City, 3 December 1921

FA CUP – ROUND ELIMINATED: 2nd (old)

LEAGUE CUP – ROUND ELIMINATED: –

FULL MEMBERS CUP – ROUND ELIMINATED: –

LEADING LEAGUE APPEARANCES (MAX: 42): 40 – E. Rhodes, 37 – B. Bateman

LEADING LEAGUE GOALSCORERS: 8 – J. Conner, 7 – B. Menlove

1922/23

LITTLE ENOUGH TO ENTHUSE ABOUT... UNTIL EASTER MONDAY

The summer of 1922 saw news beginning to circulate in South Norwood and other neighbouring suburbs of London about the land that Crystal Palace FC were about to purchase for their new ground, although no name for it had yet been decided upon.

Meanwhile, Mr Goodman negotiated what probably remains the most complex transfer deal in the entire history of our club. No fewer than six players were involved in an exchange with Second Division rivals Coventry City: J.T. Jones, along with inside forwards Tom Storey and Alf Wood, moved to the Midlands, while in return the Palace welcomed centre half Bert Millard, full-back Charlie Cross and, later in the summer, inside left Billy Morgan. The transfer can be clearly seen to have been one that favoured the Palace and Mr Goodman proved once again just what an astute leader of our club he was. The last two players mentioned were typically inspired additions: Cross took over from 'Dusty' Rhodes at left-back early in the season and made a fine partner for Jack Little, going on to play 221 League games in our colours, while Morgan made a more explosive contribution. He became a useful goalscorer in the ensuing two seasons, while fully justifying the £500 fee we had paid out to acquire him in one match alone – the next season's review will reveal all the glorious detail!

However, in all honesty successes were few and far between for the Palace during the 1922/23 season. Top scorer was George Whitworth, a brave, strong raider who had guested for the Palace during the First World War seasons and joined us in March 1922 when we needed a quality striker to replace Bert Menlove, who had moved on to Sheffield United. George hit 17 League goals from his 36 outings, but the big centre forward had little support from elsewhere. The few highlights of the season came towards its finish.

After a 4-1 defeat at Leeds the previous weekend, everyone at or connected with Crystal Palace must have viewed the Easter programme of matches with dismay, because our Good Friday and Easter Monday opponents were the champions-elect Notts County, while their closest rivals for the title, FA Cup finalists West Ham, were at The Nest on Easter Saturday. Fans' fears proved to be well-founded. County won, albeit narrowly, at The Nest and then West Ham administered a 5-1 hiding. That experience was humbling, and the team must have appeared like lambs for the slaughter as the match against the exuberant Magpies at Meadow Lane approached.

A cartoon of an early Palace *v.* Corinthians friendly encounter, played at our former headquarters on Saturday 3 February 1923.

Palace hung on in the first half and were pleased enough to reach the dressing room at the break with the scoresheet still blank and dignity at least somewhat restored, although County had hit our crossbar during the proceedings. But then, early in the second half, Palace slammed in three goals in an amazing eight-minute spell and went on from there to record a marvellous, if hugely unexpected, victory.

During that blitz upon the County goal, the Palace forwards produced a gala performance. They showed pace and initiative as they overran a bemused home defence. Neither they nor their fans could believe what was happening to them as lowly Palace ran riot. Billy Morgan cracked the first with a low drive, leading scorer George Whitworth blasted the second following a faulty clearance, then dapper little Bill Hand calmly lobbed the goalkeeper for the third. It was an incredible performance! Our tiny outside left completed the rout towards the end when he converted Ben Bateman's perfect cross, but the fact that this 5ft 6in character did so with a header speaks volumes about the calibre and extent of the Palace success!

It is no exaggeration to say that Palace's Second Division status hung upon this result. Before the game we were in a perilous position in the table, but this success triggered a new confidence that ensured points from a praiseworthy draw at West Ham the following Saturday, another at home to South Shields and a big win over bottom club Wolves in the last home game.

SEASON: 1922/23

GROUND: The Nest, Selhurst

MANAGER: Edmund Goodman

LEAGUE/DIVISION: Football League Second Division

FINAL POSITION: 16th

BIGGEST VICTORY: 5-0 *v.* Wolverhampton Wanderers, 28 April 1923

HEAVIEST DEFEAT: 0-6 *v.* Derby County, 25 December 1922

FA CUP – ROUND ELIMINATED: 1st (old)

LEAGUE CUP – ROUND ELIMINATED: –

FULL MEMBERS CUP – ROUND ELIMINATED: –

LEADING LEAGUE APPEARANCES (MAX: 42): 40 – J. Alderson, R. McCracken, 39 – J. Little

LEADING LEAGUE GOALSCORERS: 17 – G. Whitworth, 7 – W. Morgan

1923/24

ANOTHER FABULOUS CUP VICTORY HIGHLIGHTS OUR LAST SEASON AT THE NEST

Palace made a summer 1923 signing that generated a lot of interest: we secured Chelsea centre forward Tom Hoddinott. Tom was a Welsh international, tall, slim and possessing pace and elegance. With 13 goals this season, he and George Whitworth (who netted 16) made a good striking pair but, regrettably, this was to be the only season in which Tom showed his true ability on our behalf.

Palace finished one place better in the Second Division (fifteenth) in 1923/24 than in the previous term, but the season was a much more evenly balanced one for us than its immediate predecessor. It only took the Palace three matches this time to gain our first victory but our top League performances were certainly during the month or so before Christmas.

Tom Hoddinott's best game for the Palace occurred when title challengers Stoke City came to The Nest on 24 November. Tom put on a great display – he hit a first-half hat-trick to destroy the Potters, led his line with vision and verve in a fog-shrouded game and helped Palace to a morale-boosting victory. Our next win came three weeks later against The Wednesday. This time George Whitworth scored our three goals in a convincing victory. True, we lost 0-6 at Hillsborough a week later, but captain Albert Feebury was badly injured and was never able to play again. Undoubtedly it was Whitworth's hat-trick in the first match (allied to a goal he would score against the Owls in 1924/25) that so impressed the Wednesday officials that they eventually signed him towards the end of the following season.

Able to step immediately into the strong, driving wing half role that had been held since pre-war days by Albert Feebury but had now been vacated by him was young Bobby Greener, who had joined us from the North-East a couple of years before. Bob was to have a fabulous Palace career over the next decade as a player with 317 first-team appearances and then, subsequently, as club trainer and a member of the ground staff, eventually totalling thirty-four years' service.

However, the Palace reserved their finest performance of 1923/24 for an FA Cup tie. Tottenham, from the higher reaches of the First Division, were our illustrious visitors for an old first round encounter on Saturday 12 January 1924. The heavy pitch soon cut up and a typical cup match ensued, with plenty of excitement and drama for the fans. It soon became clear that either a piece of sheer brilliance from the sophisticated north Londoners or some opportunist finishing by the Palace would settle the outcome.

Right: Palace skipper Billy Morgan, whose two goals defeated Spurs in an FA Cup tie.

The breakthrough came just after half an hour. Roy McCracken won the ball and slipped a pass to Albert Harry, who had a marvellous match. The little winger was away. He beat Spurs' skipper, England international wing half Arthur Grimsdell, tore past the left-back and cut in on goal before delivering a cross that was never more than a couple of feet off the ground. Several players went for it, but it was Palace's Billy Morgan, diving low among the flying boots and studs, who got to it and glided a perfect header past the Spurs goalkeeper for an inspirational goal. Ten minutes after the break it was all over, Billy Morgan netting from close range after shots from Tom Hoddinott and Bill Hand had been blocked. Morgan was to do little more for the Palace in his career with us, but he had done enough in the ninety minutes against Tottenham to earn a permanent niche in any Palace chronicle.

There was huge excitement at the Palace and, in the wake of such a superb victory. hopes were high of a run into the latter stages of the FA Cup competition. First Division Notts County were eventually overcome 2-1 in a titanic struggle in the second round, after three goal-less draws and in the third replay of our club's longest-ever cup-tie. But disappointment was to follow because our old rivals from the Third Division, Swindon Town, came to The Nest for the third round and beat us with a great display inspired by Harold Fleming.

Palace won four and drew two of the last (League) matches at The Nest, with the finale a 3-1 success over Barnsley, a fitting and appropriate farewell to the ground that had served the club so well.

SEASON: 1923/24

GROUND: The Nest, Selhurst

MANAGER: Edmund Goodman

LEAGUE/DIVISION: Football League Second Division

FINAL POSITION: 15th

BIGGEST VICTORY: 5-1 *v.* Stoke City, 24 November 1923

HEAVIEST DEFEAT: 0-6 *v.* Sheffield Wednesday, 22 December 1923

FA CUP – ROUND ELIMINATED: 3rd (old)

LEAGUE CUP – ROUND ELIMINATED: –

FULL MEMBERS CUP – ROUND ELIMINATED: –

LEADING LEAGUE APPEARANCES (MAX: 42): 41 – J. Alderson, 39 – C. Cross, W. Morgan

LEADING LEAGUE GOALSCORERS: 16 – G. Whitworth, 13 – T. Hoddinott

1924/25

PALACE'S FIRST SEASON AT SELHURST PARK ENDS IN CALAMITY

Selhurst Park was formerly a brickfield, with two chimney stacks on the site of the present-day playing pitch. It had cost the Palace £2,750 to purchase back in 1922. The stadium – if it could originally have been called such – was designed by Archibald Leitch, probably the leading authority on football grounds at that time, and built by Messrs Humphreys of Knightsbridge to a contract valued at something over £30,000. Unfortunately, however, an industrial dispute delayed work on the main stand so much that some of the seats and other fittings were incomplete when the ground was formally opened prior to Palace's first match of 1924/25 against The Wednesday on 30 August 1924.

The ceremonial opening took place a few minutes before the teams ran out onto the pitch. Sir Louis Newton, Lord Mayor of London, undertook that responsibility and was accompanied by Mr Sydney Bourne and Mr F.J. Nettlefold, Palace's chairman, and president respectively. The latter, it has quite recently been discovered, provided £24,000 towards the cost of building the ground and then, some ten years later, absolved the Club of that entire, huge debt. Other Palace directors accompanied them. The ceremony itself consisted of the cutting of claret and blue ribbons across the entry to the original players' tunnel, followed by a brief speech from the Lord Mayor.

Although the Second Division of 1924/25 contained several other great clubs, it is difficult to imagine more select opposition for the opening game at Selhurst Park. The Wednesday line-up was packed with pedigree players, including present or future internationals. However, another international who might have been expected to appear was conspicuous by his absence. Jack Alderson had refused to re-sign for the Palace, because the Club would not allow him the benefit match to which he believed he was entitled. It was a great pity that such a fine performer should leave us in such acrimonious circumstances.

Alderson's replacement was Billy Harper, formerly of Manchester City and Sunderland, no mean goalkeeper, but comparison with Alderson was not really possible until Billy Callender had taken over and grown to maturity a season or so later.

The match against The Wednesday attracted a crowd of some 25,000 to our new headquarters. This was more than double the number to have seen the same fixture at The Nest in the previous two seasons, but most were in for a disappointing afternoon, because a goal conceded just four minutes after the start was sufficient to defeat us. It was scored by

Wednesday's inside right Joe Marsden, their close-season signing from Sunderland. To be honest, it appears that Wednesday controlled the game from that moment and were clearly in a class above our favourites, although the Palace did have opportunities to get on terms, only to spurn them all, and we hastened our own downfall by being much too elaborate in front of goal.

To their credit, the Palace quickly shrugged aside the disappointment of defeat against The Wednesday and soon strung together a series of creditable results. Only two days later they went to Coventry and secured an impressive 4-1 victory while our next home game, against Hull City (1-0), saw us record our first success at our new ground. By early October we were in the top third of the table and by 1 November we were fifth after despatching Derby County 2-0.

But the high spot of the season was undoubtedly the return fixture against The Wednesday, in Sheffield, two days after Christmas, which was played in deplorable conditions of pouring rain, driving wind and on a quagmire of a pitch!

Palace produced a performance of real character and professionalism and, during the first half, were forced to weather (no pun intended!) enormous Wednesday pressure when the home side had the wind and the rain behind them. But, in what was only Palace's second attack, we scored! Half-time was imminent: Bill Hand was the instigator; George Whitworth the executioner. Palace's tough little inside left broke clear down his flank before swinging over a cross for Whitworth to demonstrate real talent. He took possession, advanced, then, as the 'keeper came out and the defenders began to close in, despatched a crisp low shot that skidded along the sodden turf and entered the net just inside the foot of the post.

The second half was less one-sided and in this period the honours again largely went to our defence, who showed tenacity and resilience in dealing with the home attackers, but by the end The Wednesday realised that they had lost the day.

The Palace side had benefited throughout those autumn and early winter months from the inclusion at centre half of ex-guardsman Jimmy Hamilton. Jimmy was a dominating figure at the heart of our defence and had a lot to do with our progress in the first half of 1924/25. He was to have a grand career with the Palace, totalling nearly 200 appearances, and it can clearly be argued that the nasty eye injury he sustained when Blackpool were our visitors at the end of February, which rendered him unavailable for virtually the rest of the season, was a major reason for the disaster story that follows.

Palace's greatest weakness over the second half of 1924/25 lay in our forwards' inability to score sufficient goals. George Whitworth was absent from mid-February for five matches – in which Palace lost three times and gained a 0-0 draw! Also, George's decisive goal at Hillsborough had confirmed his prowess to the Wednesday administration and perhaps his concentration on Palace matters was somewhat distracted upon his return: certainly he left us for Sheffield before the end of the season. Thus, without George at his best for us, we were unquestionably lacking up front and, even with him, we only once scored more than one League goal in a game after mid-December! No wonder our Second Division position crumbled alarmingly! His last goal in our colours enabled us to record our only victory in the last fourteen games, though it was both extremely welcome and a gloriously struck valedictory, coming late in the home match against Chelsea on 1 April. It complemented an excellent defensive performance throughout a testing London derby and came from a perfect cross by Albert Harry.

That win apart, our results showed a seriously worrying deterioration throughout the second half of the season and we inevitably slipped down the table. The decline proved impossible to

Jim Mercer's celebrated cartoon of the opening match at Selhurst Park against The Wednesday on 30 August 1924.

arrest and, by the time the season drew to its climax, we were in grave danger after Good Friday and Easter Saturday defeats at Selhurst Park by Stoke and Barnsley, both 0-1. Palace bravely extracted a point at Stoke (1-1) in the Easter Monday return, but then crumbled badly at Wolves (1-3) in our last away game on Saturday 18 April.

The Palace programme finished with two home matches and it seemed that a couple of points from these games would be sufficient to keep us in the Second Division. On 25 April 1925 Fulham came to Selhurst Park and our hopes soared when Cecil Blakemore gave us a twentieth-minute lead. However, before half-time Fulham were level and then they forged ahead. With little time remaining, the Palace surged forward in a final onslaught on the Cottagers' goal and, when Albert Harry crossed the ball, it appeared to be handled by a Fulham defender. The referee pointed to the penalty spot, but was immediately engulfed by the visiting team. They persuaded him to consult a linesman (less well positioned than he himself had been) and, having done so, he reversed his decision, signalled a goal-kick, and thereby denied the Palace's hopes of salvaging a precious point.

That weak decision by the official, allied to the fact that two of the other strugglers, Oldham and Barnsley, both won, meant that the scene was set for a climactic finale, for Palace's last match was at home to Oldham – and we had to win it to survive.

The atmosphere for Palace's opening match at Selhurst Park had been festive: for this dramatic show-down against Oldham on 2 May it was laden with tension, even before the teams appeared in front of a crowd variously estimated at between 15,000 and 20,000. Palace made four changes from the side beaten by Fulham, but the most significant one was the inclusion of young Billy Callender in goal for his first senior appearance of the season.

For seventy-five minutes the battle raged without a goal and, it must be admitted, the demands of the occasion appeared to be too much for our men. We were tight enough in defence, but over-anxious in front of goal, and neither side troubled the goalkeepers.

With a quarter of an hour or fractionally less remaining, there came the fateful blow. Oldham's outside right had always been their most dangerous player and now he managed to get over a cross despite the attentions of Charlie Cross and Joe Nixon. Oldham's centre forward was ideally positioned and he turned the ball fiercely goalwards, though accounts vary as to whether it was a header or a shot. Callender rose in a valiant attempt to try to tip it away – he managed to get a touch, but not enough to divert it sufficiently. The death thrust had been administered and Selhurst Park was as quiet as any tomb as Palace's first season there ended in such bitter disappointment.

Palace's programme editor of the day wrote that he believed that 'it would be a calamity' if we were to be relegated, and who would argue that he had exaggerated? It took the Palace a full thirty-nine years to restore Second Division football to Selhurst Park.

SEASON: 1924/25

GROUND: Selhurst Park

MANAGER: Edmund Goodman

LEAGUE/DIVISION: Football League Second Division

FINAL POSITION: 21st

BIGGEST VICTORY: 4-1 *v.* Coventry City 1 September 1924, 4-1 *v.* Bradford City, 15 November 1924

HEAVIEST DEFEAT: 0-5 *v.* Hull City, 17 January 1925

FA CUP – ROUND ELIMINATED: 2nd (old)

LEAGUE CUP – ROUND ELIMINATED: –

FULL MEMBERS CUP – ROUND ELIMINATED: –

LEADING LEAGUE APPEARANCES (MAX: 42): 41 – W. Harper, A. Harry, 37 – R. Greener

LEADING LEAGUE GOALSCORERS: 13 – G. Whitworth, 11 – C. Blakemore

1925/26

PERCY CHERRETT SIGNS UP AND PALACE ARE TRANSFORMED

If Palace's first season. at Selhurst Park had ended in such disappointment the only way to describe the beginning of the next one is 'horrific'! With 1925/26 just three weeks old, relegated Palace had lost all five of their fixtures back among their old Third Division contemporaries with an adverse goal aggregate of 5-16, so we appeared to be in real trouble. Certainly we lacked confidence and a reliable goalscorer but manager-secretary Edmund Goodman had weathered previous crises and knew exactly the man he wanted.

His name was Percy Cherrett. He was a strong, bustling centre forward with a proven goalscoring record and he was languishing in the Plymouth Argyle reserve team. He made his Palace debut at Brighton on 19 September (2-3), but the following Wednesday Percy made his first appearance at Selhurst Park. Our fans warmed to him immediately as the big man scored a couple of goals and tore Bristol City's defence to ribbons while Palace ran out 5-2 winners. The next Saturday we romped to a 4-0 victory over Watford, three of the goals coming from Percy Cherrett headers, and in the end he finished that season with 26 strikes from his 35 League outings, having formed an exciting goalscoring partnership with Cecil Blakemore. The pair thrived on the splendid service provided by wingers Albert Harry and the newly signed flame-haired outside left George Clarke.

Two particular matches at Selhurst Park in which Percy starred were of lasting interest to Palace fans. On Saturday 28 November 1925 Palace and Plymouth figured in an amazing 5-5 draw on a snow-covered pitch to record the highest-scoring draw ever played on our ground in a first-class game, while one of the great occasions at our headquarters took place on Saturday 30 January 1926 when the Palace beat Chelsea 2-1 in a fourth round FA Cup tie and set up an attendance record of 41,000, which was to last for nearly forty years! I am sure that readers can make an educated guess as to who it was that put the Palace on the road to that superb result with a magnificent performance while also scoring a quality first goal!

Cherrett was in fact the last major signing made for the Palace by Mr Edmund Goodman, for that worthy gentleman retired from the post of manager at our club in December 1925. Of course he continued as secretary, but he was succeeded as manager by Mr Alex Maley, who joined from Hibernian in Edinburgh and began a policy of recruiting men from north of the border. Probably Mr Maley's most successful signing was that of Scottish international full-back

Bobby Orr from Greenock Morton, who joined us for 1926/27 and went on to make 70 League appearances for us over two seasons.

An event of importance in the 1925/26 season at Selhurst Park remains unique in the Club annals. The occasion was the only full England international match ever to be staged there. Fittingly, on St David's Day, 1 March 1926, England met Wales before a splendid Monday afternoon crowd of over 23,000. To the delight of the large contingent from the Principality the visitors won 3-1 and were much the better side on the day.

Palace's second season at Selhurst Park coincided with the offside law being altered. The earlier rule, which required three men to be between the receiving player and the opponents' goal-line was amended so that now only two men were required. The immediate effect of the alteration was a great increase in the number of goals scored because it naturally took defences some time to adjust. Unfortunately, while the Palace were able to score goals as freely as most clubs – certainly after Percy Cherrett's arrival – we also found it impossible to stem the tide at the other end. This was never better demonstrated than in the amazing fifth round FA Cup tie in which we took part at Manchester City as the reward for having beaten Chelsea. City ran out winners by 11 goals to 4!

Percy Cherrett.

SEASON: 1925/26

GROUND: Selhurst Park

MANAGER: Edmund Goodman to 24 November 1925, then Alec Maley

LEAGUE/DIVISION: Football League Third Division (South)

FINAL POSITION: 13th

BIGGEST VICTORY: 4-0 *v.* Watford, 26 September 1925

HEAVIEST DEFEAT: 1-6 *v.* Bournemouth, 1 May 1926

FA CUP – ROUND ELIMINATED: 5th

LEAGUE CUP – ROUND ELIMINATED: –

FULL MEMBERS CUP – ROUND ELIMINATED: –

LEADING LEAGUE APPEARANCES (MAX: 42): 41 – C. Cross, R. Greener, 40 – A. Harry

LEADING LEAGUE GOALSCORERS: 26 – P. Cherrett, 19 – C. Blakemore

1926/27

PALACE IMPROVE TO REACH SIXTH PLACE

The Palace team of 1926/27 was certainly more consistent than its predecessors of recent seasons and for the first time in five years we won the opening game of the term, with a goal each from Percy Cherrett (a header) and Cecil Blakemore (an overhead bicycle-kick, in the last minute) proving too much for Queens Park Rangers at Selhurst Park, although the visitors had netted within thirty seconds of the first whistle!

Even if we lost only once in the first eight games, that still left us two points and five places adrift of the leaders at the end of September – the old Third Division (South) was certainly a hard taskmaster! Palace eventually finished in sixth place, but that was nowhere really because we were no fewer than seventeen points behind the champions, Bristol City. Season 1926/27 was aptly summed up in that the number of goals we scored – 84 of them – was only exceeded by four clubs, whereas just five defences conceded more goals than our own.

Unsurprisingly Percy Cherrett was again our top goalscorer with 32 strikes from his 40 appearances. He was supported by Cecil Blakemore with 16 while George Clarke hit 13 more from the left wing, including a hat-trick in a 5-3 victory over visiting Southend in mid-November. The highest-scoring match of the term was our 7-4 victory over Bristol Rovers in March: we beat Norwich 7-1 but lost 1-7 at Plymouth! Intriguingly, our first round FA Cup matches against Norwich offered just one goal from 180 minutes' play – and the Canaries netted that after a quarter of an hour in the replay at Carrow Road after the initial match had provided only Palace's second (of two) scoreless games of the season!

Palace's two Third Division (South) games against the champions elect provided fabulous entertainment. We beat Bristol City 4-2 with a depleted side at our headquarters in an early season contest that grew tempestuous at times, with Cecil Blakemore netting a hat-trick. The return at Ashton Gate at the end of January was a nine-goal thriller: City led 5-1 at the break but Palace responded in the second half to make it 5-4 without being able to net an equaliser.

Coming to the fore at the Palace this season were two men who were to feature for many years and play major roles in the Selhurst Park story between the wars – Billy Turner and George Clarke.

Billy had joined the Palace as a tough little inside forward. He was a fixture in our sides for some eleven seasons and accumulated so many appearances that he remains within the top ten

Billy Turner.

places in our all-time charts to this day! He rarely scored many goals himself, but everyone who saw him play agreed that he helped to make hundreds of them: there was also no doubt that right winger Albert Harry played much better with Billy there beside him and that our forwards could become devastating if Billy was directing our attack.

Billy became known to Palace fans as 'Rubber': certainly his resilience and adaptability were an unusual feature in the pre-war game. Later in his career Billy played in the wing half positions and then, towards the end, even as a full-back! He won the hearts of Palace fans with his wholehearted commitment to the Club and Palace manager Jack Tresadern once said of Billy, 'He's 100 per cent wherever you play him!'

It has always been the considered view of Palace fans of that period and of Palace historians since then, that had George Clarke arrived even a month before the end of the 1924/25 season, then Palace would never have been relegated from the Second Division. Certainly he immediately became a permanent feature in our sides after his arrival in the summer of 1925 and remained so for seven seasons.

There is little doubt that George, a magnificent winger with craft, artistry and a lethal shot, was the best outside left our Club has ever had. Not only was his loyalty to the Palace quite undisputed but his goalscoring record from the flank (99 League goals for us in his career and a fabulous 22 in the single season of 1927/28) puts him in a realm above all previous and subsequent players in that position. He was, quite simply, a prince among Palace wingers.

SEASON: 1926/27

GROUND: Selhurst Park

MANAGER: Alec Maley

LEAGUE/DIVISION: Football League Third Division (South)

FINAL POSITION: 6th

BIGGEST VICTORY: 7-1 *v.* Norwich City, 30 October 1926

HEAVIEST DEFEAT: 1-7 *v.* Plymouth Argyle, 12 February 1927

FA CUP – ROUND ELIMINATED: 1st

LEAGUE CUP – ROUND ELIMINATED: –

FULL MEMBERS CUP – ROUND ELIMINATED: –

LEADING LEAGUE APPEARANCES (MAX: 42): 42 – W. Callender, G. Clarke, 40 – P. Cherrett

LEADING LEAGUE GOALSCORERS: 32 – P. Cherrett, 16 – C. Blakemore

1927/28

NEW BOSS FRED MAVIN LEADS PALACE TO FIFTH-PLACE FINISH

Palace's start to the 1927/28 season in the Third Division (South) was a poor one. Even if a run of misfortune in the matter of injuries was partly to blame, there was still no excuse for a pair of 1-6 reverses, at Southend in mid-September and at Luton a month later, so when the Palace were knocked out of the London Challenge Cup by our old amateur rivals, Leyton, on 12 October, there was nothing for it but for manager Maley to resign.

Under Mr Goodman's temporary charge there was no immediate improvement, at least not until we dispensed a 5-0 hiding to visiting Charlton, who had previously been undefeated, on the afternoon of bonfire night, then followed up with a creditable point from a 3-3 thriller at Swindon and another home win, 2-0 this time, over Newport County.

Thus, when Mr Fred Mavin, formerly the manager of Exeter City, took up his responsibilities at Selhurst Park in late November, the worst of the tide had been turned but the new boss inspired the Palace team to a much better all-round performance in the remainder of the season. We were able to finish 1927/28 in fifth place, though still a long, long way behind the champions, our New Cross neighbours Millwall.

The season was a huge success for George Clarke, who registered 22 League goals from his 40 appearances out on the left wing – a record not only unsurpassed at our Club but never even threatened by any Palace winger in the years since then.

Season 1927/28 also saw the arrival of centre or inside forward Harry Havelock at the beginning of November. Strong and well built, Harry was a useful goalscorer for the Palace, but he was most unlucky with injuries upon his arrival. Having scored twice upon his debut against Charlton, he had to miss the next League game at Swindon. Then, two weeks later, he sustained such a nasty leg injury in the FA Cup tie at Dartford (3-1) that he did not reappear for us for ten months. That said, Harry's 39 League goals for the Palace from 67 games tell of a striker of some ability and a valuable acquisition.

Palace's best spell of the entire season came late on in the term, during the spring of 1928 when, between 10 March and Easter Saturday, 7 April, we won six consecutive League matches. Admittedly, none of the opponents were from the leading bracket of sides in our division, but certainly of interest was the 3-2 midweek defeat of Torquay, who were in their first season as members of the Football League and, accordingly, were making their first appearance at

Billy Callender – another brilliant Palace goalkeeper.

Selhurst Park. This had actually been delayed from its original Boxing Day date because of a postponement necessitated after a foot of snow had fallen overnight.

During this successful spell Palace had also beaten Swindon (1-0), who would eventually finish proceedings one place below us, to avenge a second round FA Cup defeat in a replay here back in December. Albert Harry scored the decisive goal early in the second half of the League match, but the feature of the contest was the quite brilliant goalkeeping of both custodians, Billy Callender and Ted Nash (the latter would spend the 1932/33 season with the Palace in the twilight of his long and distinguished career) on a pitch that was wet and soft after a deluge of rain earlier in the day.

Perhaps the result that gave the Club and its fans most satisfaction was secured in the only away game in the six-match sequence when Palace routed Charlton 4-0 at The Valley to complete an aggregate 'double' of 9-0!

A critical appraisal of 1927 must acknowledge that, again, it was the Palace's defensive weakness that cost us any chance of contesting the single promotion place from the division, for we conceded more goals than all but one of the other clubs in the top half of the table, although, thankfully, there were no more heavy or embarrassing defeats like the ones we had incurred early in the season. Nevertheless, third-placed Plymouth won 2-0 at Selhurst Park in the last match of the season – their goalkeeper converted a penalty for the second! — and even the lowly sides knew that we were always vulnerable. Bristol Rovers (who finished nineteenth) brought our six-match winning run to an end on Easter Monday and Gillingham (sixteenth) beat us 3-1 in the next game.

SEASON: 1927/28

GROUND: Selhurst Park

MANAGER: Alec Maley to 12 October 1927, then Fred Mavin from 21 November 1927

LEAGUE/DIVISION: Football League Third Division (South)

FINAL POSITION: 5th

BIGGEST VICTORY: 6-1 *v.* Bournemouth, 4 February 1928

HEAVIEST DEFEAT: 1-6 *v.* Southend United, 10 September 1927, 1-6 *v.* Luton Town, 8 October 1927

FA CUP – ROUND ELIMINATED: 2nd

LEAGUE CUP – ROUND ELIMINATED: –

FULL MEMBERS CUP – ROUND ELIMINATED: –

LEADING LEAGUE APPEARANCES (MAX: 42): 40 – J. Hamilton, G. Clarke, 34 – C. Cross

LEADING LEAGUE GOALSCORERS: 22 – G. Clarke, 14 – I. Hopkins

1928/29

PALACE MISS PROMOTION BY A WHISKER

Palace manager Fred Mavin spent a productive summer in the transfer market on behalf of his new club during the 1928 close season. From his former club Exeter City, Mr Mavin secured the man he wanted to skipper his restructured Palace side, full-back Stan Charlton, and alongside him was Tom Crilly who arrived from Derby County. The partnership between Crilly and Charlton became an attractive feature of Palace line-ups and it was certainly significant that during the period they were together at Selhurst Park we were able to mount two serious assaults on the Third Division (South) championship.

Up front Mr Mavin secured Lewis Griffiths from Torquay United and inside left Hubert Butler from Chorley and the new-look Palace team soon showed that it would more than hold its own. Defensive frailties were revealed in the autumn but then a tall, slim, elegant but totally dominating centre half joined us. Jimmy Wilde made his debut in a testing first round FA Cup tie against the regional champions of the Southern League, Kettering Town. Their centre forward had made quite a name for himself – he was Peter Simpson! But Jimmy gave a flawless display, marking out the pivot's position as his own, and Palace progressed with a 2-0 win.

In the League, we then embarked upon a seventeen-match unbeaten run (never yet improved upon within a single season) and, from mid-table, began to have the look of possible champions, moving to within a point of the top of the division after Easter. But the competition was fierce. With a month of the season remaining at least six clubs had serious aspirations, the Palace now clearly among them. None of them was able to sustain the run of good results that would have settled the issue and, come the last week, a 2-1 win down at Exeter and a 3-0 success over Gillingham at Selhurst Park put us level with Charlton at the head of the table, with everything resting upon the outcome of the matches on Saturday 4 May 1929. However, Charlton had a considerably better goal average so that, while they were away up at Walsall, it was necessary for us to gain a point over them from our home match against Brighton.

A crowd of over 22,000 flocked to Selhurst Park for the climax, but Brighton provided such tough opposition that we were only able to edge in front via a seventieth-minute penalty, converted by skipper Stan Charlton. The tension was almost tangible, because of course in those days there was no means whereby the crowd could know what was evolving elsewhere and whether our narrow lead, which became a victory, had proved sufficient to take us back to the Second Division if Charlton, as it began to be rumoured, had dropped a point in the Black Country. But then their commendable 2-0 win was announced to our fans and it was realised

Left: Stan Charlton led Palace to within a whisker of promotion in 1928/29.

that, near to success as the Palace had come, all had been in vain and we were still rooted in the Third Division.

An interesting aspect of the closing stages of this 1928/29 season at the Palace was the signing, and then the inclusion in our League side, of several men from the Kettering Town team that had come to Selhurst Park to meet the Palace in the first round FA Cup tie. Goalkeeper Jim Imrie and inside forward Andy Dunsire joined us in March and played several games, but winger or centre forward George Charlesworth made a bigger impact. However, the most significant signing from Kettering, delayed until June 1929, was that of the man who still remains our Club's most prolific striker, the great Peter Simpson himself. Like Ian Wright over half a century later, Peter came to us from a non-league set-up, quickly established himself as an exciting goalscorer who could turn and win matches, became an enormous favourite with the fans at Selhurst Park and went on to establish Club records, almost, it seemed, at will.

SEASON: 1928/29

GROUND: Selhurst Park

MANAGER: Fred Mavin

LEAGUE/DIVISION: Football League Third Division (South)

FINAL POSITION: 2nd

BIGGEST VICTORY: 6-1 *v.* Swindon Town, 2 February 1929

HEAVIEST DEFEAT: 1-8 *v.* Northampton Town, 27 October 1928

FA CUP – ROUND ELIMINATED: 5th

LEAGUE CUP – ROUND ELIMINATED: –

FULL MEMBERS CUP – ROUND ELIMINATED: –

LEADING LEAGUE APPEARANCES (MAX: 42): 41 – W. Callender, S. Charlton, A. Harry

LEADING LEAGUE GOALSCORERS: 20 – H. Havelock, 18 – L. Griffiths

1929/30

THE ADVENT OF PETER SIMPSON

Despite finishing as runners-up in the Third Division (South) the previous summer, Palace's 1929/30 season did not start at all well, for we only managed to draw and then lose our opening two home games. Manager Fred Mavin decided to opt for the untried talents of Peter Simpson in an attempt to augment our goalscoring capacity and the Scotsman from Leith made his League debut for us on Saturday 14 September when Norwich City were our visitors.

The occasion crystallised Peter's ability to score goals and emphasised just what a brilliant marksman he was, for it remains unique in Palace annals as the only time that a Palace player has netted a hat-trick in his first Football (or even Premier) League appearance! Despite early Palace pressure, Norwich took the lead on that warm, sunlit afternoon with just ten minutes gone. Palace's response was furious and intense, so much so that our equaliser was both long overdue and thoroughly deserved when Peter netted with a hard, low volley from an Albert Harry cross. Norwich endured what a local correspondent described as a 'severe bombardment' after this, but they managed to hold out to reach the break still on terms.

Six minutes after the interval Palace gained the lead and this time Peter was indebted to his other winger, George Clarke, who finished a dazzling run with a tempting, drifting cross that Peter met with a diving header for a spectacular, close-range strike. Palace were now determined to put the outcome beyond Norwich and were successful in doing so when Peter's header from a right-wing centre was mishandled by the goalkeeper and flew high into the net.

Norwich reduced their arrears near the end, but Palace now had mettle and resolution and defended with poise and control to ensure that we gained the full reward for our efforts that afternoon.

Thus, Peter's impact at the Palace was an immediate one, and he went on to create a new Club record of 36 League goals this term, making himself something of a target for the bigger clubs. Shortly we shall see that in 1930/31 his form was quite phenomenal, as he hit 46 goals in the Third Division (South), still the Club record for an individual striker in a single season. He would go on to top our goalscoring charts for each of his first five seasons with us, eventually totalling 165 first-class goals in our colours, so that, even thirty years after he had retired, Peter remained a popular local figure at his newsagent and tobacconists shop at West Croydon.

PALACE CENTRE HAS A FIELD DAY.

SIMPSON BANGS IN SIX.

SCINTILLATING SIMPSON.

SIMPSON'S SIX.

PALACE CENTRE'S REMARKABLE SCORING FEAT.

CRYSTAL PALACE AND EXETER CITY.

Six Successive Goals for Simpson.

Left and opposite: Peter Simpson netted a club-record 36 League goals in his debut season, and hit six against Exeter on 4 October 1930.

Really his efforts for Crystal Palace were quite exceptional, and his name will always rank among the immortals at our Club.

Yet, it has to be admitted, even with the benefit of the talents of Peter Simpson, the Palace were not able to climb out of the Third Division (South) in 1929/30. The reasons were twofold. Firstly, when Peter himself was not scoring goals for us, hardly anyone else was able to do so either! Harry Havelock was second-top League scorer with just 12 strikes, then came Billy Turner with 5! The second problem was that, once again, we were leaking far too many goals at the back, 74 of them in total, and there is no way any club can hope for success with that sort of burden. Those defensive frailties were embarrassingly exposed in the FA Cup, where the Palace were drawn to meet top-flight Leeds United at Elland Road and lost 1-8! Admittedly, there were mitigating circumstances because right-back Tom Weatherby was crocked early on and spent most of the game as a passenger on the right wing.

Making one of his early appearances for the Palace in that disaster at Leeds was former England amateur international outside left Laurie Fishlock. Laurie was no mean footballer, but he was a magnificent cricketer. He quickly became Surrey's left-handed opening batsman and played at The Oval for more than twenty years.

Peter Simpson.

SEASON: 1929/30

GROUND: Selhurst Park

MANAGER: Fred Mavin

LEAGUE/DIVISION: Football League Third Division (South)

FINAL POSITION: 9th

BIGGEST VICTORY: 6-1 *v.* Merthyr Town, 14 December 1929

HEAVIEST DEFEAT: 1-6 *v.* Exeter City, 12 October 1929, 1-6 *v.* Plymouth Argyle, 21 December 1929

FA CUP – ROUND ELIMINATED: 3rd

LEAGUE CUP – ROUND ELIMINATED: –

FULL MEMBERS CUP – ROUND ELIMINATED: –

LEADING LEAGUE APPEARANCES (MAX: 42): 40 – A. Harry, 38 – T. Wetherby

LEADING LEAGUE GOALSCORERS: 36 – P. Simpson, 12 – H. Havelock

1930/31

PALACE ARE THIRD DIVISION (SOUTH) RUNNERS-UP AGAIN

Crystal Palace were always near the top of the Third Division (South) table in 1930/31, but modern-day readers should bear in mind that only the winners were promoted from the regional Third Divisions and that therefore 'near' would not be good enough in the final analysis. Not surprisingly, our forte was up front, where we were usually in fabulous form. Peter Simpson was virtually unstoppable: he hit five hat-tricks and a four as well as six in succession in a 7-2 defeat of Exeter. George Clarke totted up 21 from the wing and Hubert Butler contributed 14 at inside left. Altogether we scored 107 League goals, easily the best in the division at the time and only once bettered at our Club – in 1960/61 with the aid of a longer programme of matches.

There was no question that the forward line of 1930/31 was Palace's best in the first forty years of our Football League career and for sheer effectiveness ranks among the finest we have ever had. Albert Harry at outside right was fast and direct, while inside him was either powerful Harry Havelock or the evergreen Billy Turner. Peter Simpson and Hubert Butler developed a fine understanding together, with George Clarke absolutely devastating out on the left flank.

Unfortunately for the Palace, in the Third Division (South) that season there was also the team with the best defence in the entire Football League, Notts County, and it was soon apparent that, no matter how many goals all the other teams might score, County were going to concede so few that no-one would be able to prevent them from winning the title race. The Palace-County games were interesting as the best goalscorers met the best defence: a 2-2 draw ensued up at Meadow Lane in early December while matters also finished even (1-1) at the Palace in April.

Typical of events in 1930/31 were Palace's two extraordinary Christmas clashes against local rivals Brentford. The Bees had two former Palace men in their line-up at Griffin Park on Christmas morning, one of them being our old favourite Cecil Blakemore, and they ran us absolutely ragged. It was 1-5 by half-time and 2-8 at the end. The following afternoon at Selhurst Park saw a different state of affairs! George Clarke and Peter Simpson had us two up in ninety seconds! A Jimmy Wilde free-kick made it 3-0 just after half an hour and although Jack Lane (who was soon to be playing for the Palace) reduced Brentford's deficit before half-time, Albert Harry and George Clarke extended our advantage after the break to leave the Yuletide honours even and everyone somewhat breathless after the festivities.

Peter Simpson – 46 strikes this season.

Palace chairman Sydney Bourne, who died on 19 September 1930.

Other important events during the 1930/31 season were the death of chairman Sydney Bourne in September and a change of manager in October. Mr Bourne had served the Club supremely well from its inception and, until nearly the end of his life, was to be seen at Selhurst Park on match days with his inevitable cigar and Palace rosette. At the match against Newport County the day after his passing the teams wore black armbands and the flag was flown at half-mast while the Palace dispensed a resounding 7-1 victory to provide just the sort of farewell the Chairman would have wished.

Almost exactly a month later, after Palace's 5-2 defeat of Fulham, manager Fred Mavin resigned because of the ill health of his wife. This was regarded as a severe loss to the Club but, within forty-eight hours, the directors were able to announce the appointment of Mr Jack Tresadern, formerly an international wing half with West Ham and Burnley and the manager of Northampton Town, as our new manager.

Older fans were excited at the prospect of our fourth round FA Cup tie against Everton at Selhurst Park, but the Toffees precisely reversed Palace's 6-0 victory of 1922. Dixie Dean got four of them, although Palace were depleted by an early injury to Billy Turner and the absence of Billy Callender and Bob Greener, who had sustained injuries in the protracted third round tussle against Reading.

SEASON: 1930/31

GROUND: Selhurst Park

MANAGER: Fred Mavin to 18 October 1930, then Jack Tresadern

LEAGUE/DIVISION: Football League Third Division (South)

FINAL POSITION: 2nd

BIGGEST VICTORY: 7-1 *v.* Newport County, 20 September 1930

HEAVIEST DEFEAT: 2-8 *v.* Brentford, 25 December 1930

FA CUP – ROUND ELIMINATED: 4th

LEAGUE CUP – ROUND ELIMINATED: –

FULL MEMBERS CUP – ROUND ELIMINATED: –

LEADING LEAGUE APPEARANCES (MAX: 42): 42 – P. Simpson, 41 – A. Harry

LEADING LEAGUE GOALSCORERS: 46 – P. Simpson, 21 – G. Clarke

1931/32

PALACE UNBEATEN AT HOME ALL SEASON

This 1931/32 season was Jack Tresadern's first full one in charge of Crystal Palace and, while the fourth-placed finishing position to which he inspired the Club in the Third Division (South) was, in one sense, satisfactory enough, in another it was disappointing after being runners-up in two of the previous three terms. Certainly Jack could not be faulted at Selhurst Park where Palace deserved the highest commendation for remaining undefeated throughout the entire season. This should have provided the platform from which we could launch a serious bid for a return to the Second Division; but Palace were in much less convincing form away from home.

The opening fixtures revealed the dichotomy. Palace romped to a magnificent 7-1 win in our first game, at home to Torquay, when Peter Simpson scored four times – the first goal after just seven minutes – and little more than forty-eight hours later we won again at Clapton Orient with Peter notching all three Palace goals. But on the following Saturday we were comprehensively beaten 1-6 at Bristol Rovers.

Another bad away defeat was the one at Coventry in early February when the Sky Blues ruthlessly exposed our defensive frailties in comprehensive fashion to the extent of 0-8. Goalkeeper Ronnie Dunn saved a penalty too! Ronnie had joined us in the spring of 1931 to become the understudy to Billy Callender, having previously starred in a pair of British Army representative fixtures that were staged at Selhurst Park. But events would conspire to force him to become Palace's first-choice 'keeper much more quickly than he or the Club would have chosen. At the time of the Coventry fiasco Ronnie was in the second of two spells he had in our first-team during 1931/32 when he accumulated 14 senior appearances, and he went on to play 167 Third Division (South) games for us, plus 8 FA Cup ties during which time Palace only once finished outside the top six in our division. But because we never finished top, or even seriously threatened to do so, Ronnie, along with several of his Palace contemporaries, was only really appreciated by our fans and not on the bigger stages that his talents deserved. Palace supporters of the 1930s recalled Ronnie with no little esteem: for most of his career with us he was producing form that was little short of Alderson or Callender – and that is some company to be in.

Also on his way to becoming a Palace regular at this stage was full-back Oswald Parry, who had joined us from Wimbledon in 1931. Tall and strong, the big blond Welshman made the left-back position his own during 1932/33 and eventually went on to play precisely 150 first-team matches for us before he moved to Ipswich Town in the summer of 1936.

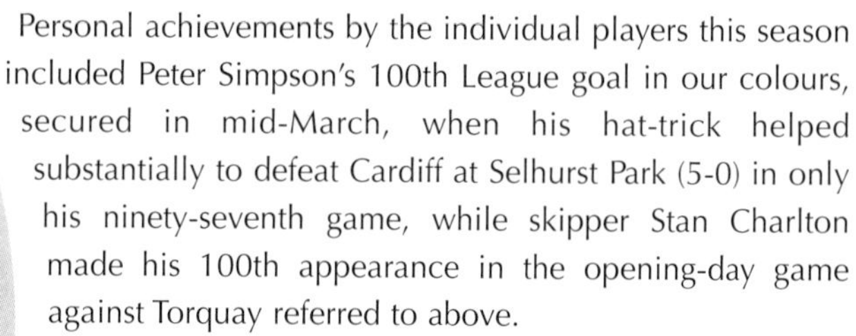

Left: Goalkeeper Ronnie Dunn.

Personal achievements by the individual players this season included Peter Simpson's 100th League goal in our colours, secured in mid-March, when his hat-trick helped substantially to defeat Cardiff at Selhurst Park (5-0) in only his ninety-seventh game, while skipper Stan Charlton made his 100th appearance in the opening-day game against Torquay referred to above.

An unfortunate omen occurred in mid-December when Palace were knocked out of the FA Cup by a non-league club for the first time. A narrow 1-0 victory over Reading had pitted us against Bath City in round two on their glutinous Twerton Park pitch. Peter Simpson had put Palace ahead after a quarter of an hour with a trademark header and Palace seemed to have the tie won as the second period progressed. But, with only thirteen minutes remaining, the referee awarded Bath a contentious penalty. The kick was driven wide, but was ordered to be retaken on the grounds of encroachment and this time Billy Callender was beaten. Thus encouraged, Bath came at the Palace like men possessed and netted the winner five minutes later from close range. The defeat itself was hard enough to take at the time: regrettably it turned out to be the precursor of all too many such defeats that would follow in the years ahead.

SEASON: 1931/32

GROUND: Selhurst Park

MANAGER: Jack Tresadern

LEAGUE/DIVISION: Football League Third Division (South)

FINAL POSITION: 4th

BIGGEST VICTORY: 7-0 *v.* Torquay, 29 August 1931

HEAVIEST DEFEAT: 0-8 *v.* Coventry City, 6 February 1932

FA CUP – ROUND ELIMINATED: 2nd

LEAGUE CUP – ROUND ELIMINATED: –

FULL MEMBERS CUP – ROUND ELIMINATED: –

LEADING LEAGUE APPEARANCES (MAX: 42): 42 – A. Harry, 38 – W. Turner, G. Clarke

LEADING LEAGUE GOALSCORERS: 23 – P. Simpson, 19 – G. Clarke

1932/33

TRAGEDY STRIKES AT SELHURST PARK

The word 'tragedy' is an over-used one in football but tragedy in its fullest and most proper meaning erupted at Selhurst Park in the summer of 1932. It concerned Palace's brilliant young goalkeeper, Billy Callender.

Billy had been our regular custodian since 1926 and was thought by some of his contemporaries to have sufficient skill and character to follow his illustrious predecessor, Jack Alderson, into the full England international side. He had joined the Club in October 1923 as a nineteen-year-old from his local club in Northumberland and saved a penalty in his first match for us, against West Ham's reserve side. By the end of 1931/32 Billy had played 225 senior matches for the Palace, enjoyed a benefit match (in which he acted as linesman!) and become one of the most popular men ever to play for us.

Billy was engaged to be married, but his beloved fiancée was stricken with polio and her health deteriorated steadily. Two weeks into the 1932 close season she died and Billy took it very hard indeed – so much so that on Tuesday 26 July he was found dead in one of the dressing rooms at Selhurst Park, having hanged himself.

Those who knew Billy Callender were still speaking of him with affection and regard sixty years later, to provide us with a measure of the standing and ability of a man who, but for one of life's tragedies, might have reached the highest honours in the game.

Fortunately for Crystal Palace, Billy's deputy, Ronnie Dunn, had the character and ability to replace him in the Palace side and in the affections of our fans. Ronnie missed just one game in this 1932/33 season and that was due to a dose of 'flu! He remained our first-choice 'keeper for four seasons.

Season 1932/33 saw Palace finish fifth in the Third Division (South), but probably its most dramatic and noteworthy event on the playing pitch was the incredible 6-6 draw between the Palace and Portsmouth reserve sides at Selhurst Park on the season's opening day!

Peter Simpson remained our top goalscorer – he notched 14 League goals for us this term – but was only able to appear in less than half our matches after sustaining a groin injury at Newport in mid-December and his absence obviously cost us dear. Peter's deputy was young Frank Manders, who had signed for us on his seventeenth birthday in June 1931. He soon became a prolific scorer for our reserve side and was to graduate to the senior eleven as an ideal partner to Peter, but at this stage Frank was merely Peter's temporary stand-in.

Palace's potential to take the title of the Third Division (South) in 1932/33 was demonstrated in the defeat of the champions to be, Brentford, when the Bees came to Selhurst Park in early

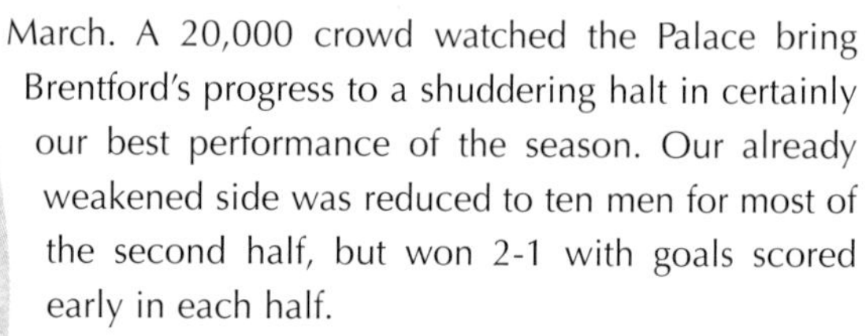

Left: Frank Manders.

March. A 20,000 crowd watched the Palace bring Brentford's progress to a shuddering halt in certainly our best performance of the season. Our already weakened side was reduced to ten men for most of the second half, but won 2-1 with goals scored early in each half.

The most significant event at the end of 1932/33 was the retirement of secretary Edmund Goodman, thus severing the last link with the Club's formation almost thirty years before. Mr Goodman's comments were typically gracious: 'I have had very happy days with the Club and wish it every success for the future,' he said. 'No-one will be more delighted than I when the Club regains a place in the Second Division and then I shall look forward to seeing them in the First.' It is a matter of regret that Mr Goodman did not live long enough to witness either event, but then neither did thousands of loyal Palace people of that inter-war period, so long did the Club languish in the lower reaches of the Football League.

SEASON: 1932/33

GROUND: Selhurst Park

MANAGER: Jack Tresadern

LEAGUE/DIVISION: Football League Third Division (South)

FINAL POSITION: 5th

BIGGEST VICTORY: 5-0 *v.* Brighton & Hove Albion, 31 August 1932

HEAVIEST DEFEAT: 2-6 *v.* Coventry City, 18 March 1933

FA CUP – ROUND ELIMINATED: 1st

LEAGUE CUP – ROUND ELIMINATED: –

FULL MEMBERS CUP – ROUND ELIMINATED: –

LEADING LEAGUE APPEARANCES (MAX: 42): 41 – R. Dunne, 39 – A. Harry

LEADING LEAGUE GOALSCORERS: 14 – P. Simpson, 13 – C. Roberts

1933/34

PALACE ADRIFT IN MID-TABLE

During the summer months of 1933 Palace manager Jack Tresadern took over the additional responsibilities of Club secretary and then, on the eve of 1933/34 and perhaps mistakenly, announced that 'this season is going to be Palace's year'. Palace did indeed begin the new term as if this was going to be the case, but the initial three straight wins proved to be one of many false dawns at Selhurst Park in the inter-war era. The Crystal Palace side proved simply to be a quite ordinary one in the League's regional Third Division and finished in twelfth place. Perhaps the best indication of our true abilities in 1933/34 for modern day readers would lie in the fact that Palace finished the season twenty points adrift of the champions Norwich City, who had demonstrated all too clearly the gulf between the clubs by winning the pair of Christmas matches and preventing us from scoring in either.

A relative success was achieved by reaching the fourth round of the FA Cup, where we were paired with mighty Arsenal, then at the peak of their inter-war greatness, at Highbury, only to receive a 0-7 chastening for our impudence in front of a crowd of 56,000 – until the 1990 FA Cup finals the biggest crowd ever to watch a Palace game.

However, the story of 1933/34 revolved around the club's three strikers —Peter Simpson, Ronnie Rooke and Albert Dawes. Ace scorer Peter Simpson was by now a marked man and the constant heavy attention he received from some of the Third Division defenders had reduced his pace a little and made him injury-prone. While he contributed 20 goals for Palace from his 25 League appearances (including his last major haul for us, all four goals in our 4-0 victory at Aldershot in November) to remain easily our top goalscorer, this was to be the last season in which the great man would claim that distinction.

However, in the Palace reserve side there was just the fellow to take over Peter's mantle – or so it seemed. Ronnie Rooke, big, powerful and strong, had been lashing goals for our second string at a stupendous rate for a year or so but, regrettably, whenever he was introduced to the first team, he failed to reproduce such form. Altogether, Ronnie hit 160 goals for our reserves in three-and-a-half seasons, and he was to benefit greatly from a transfer to Fulham in 1936, before going onto gain a wartime international honour and top the League goalscoring list with Arsenal in 1948, but, prior to the Second World War at least, he could not do it for us. This 1933/34 season saw his debut as a twenty-year-old and a contribution of 2 goals from 6 outings. When he reappears later in this book, when he became our manager in 1949, he would again cause frustration and disappointment.

Left: A youthful Ronnie Rooke.

A striker of superior calibre was Albert Dawes, who was scoring goals regularly for Northampton Town, the club where Jack Tresadern had previously been in charge. In a brave (if vain) attempt to resurrect Palace's flagging challenge for the top place in the division, Mr Tresadern obtained the services of the cultured and powerful inside left in January 1934. Albert responded with a thoroughly commendable 16 goals from his 22 League outings with us in the remainder of 1933/34 but even this was not sufficient to rescue another lacklustre season. Albert's tally included a seven-goal haul from the three Easter matches, with a hat-trick against visiting Aldershot on the Saturday the highlight, and he rounded off his season with another three-goal feat to help dismiss Queens Park Rangers when the west London side came to Selhurst Park for our last home game of the term. Accordingly, such buoyancy as existed among Palace supporters at the conclusion of this season could accurately be attributed almost solely to the explosive exploits of the Club's new striker.

SEASON: 1933/34

GROUND: Selhurst Park

MANAGER: Jack Tresadern

LEAGUE/DIVISION: Football League Third Division (South)

FINAL POSITION: 12th

BIGGEST VICTORY: 5-0 *v.* Gillingham, 2 April 1934

HEAVIEST DEFEAT: 1-5 *v.* Coventry City, 6 January 1934

FA CUP – ROUND ELIMINATED: 4th

LEAGUE CUP – ROUND ELIMINATED: –

FULL MEMBERS CUP – ROUND ELIMINATED: –

LEADING LEAGUE APPEARANCES (MAX: 42): 39 – O. Parry, 38 – R. Dunne, J. Wilde, W. Turner

LEADING LEAGUE GOALSCORERS: 20 – P. Simpson, 16 – A. Dawes

1934/35

NEW PALACE OUTSIDE LEFT BOB BIGG HAS AN EXCITING DEBUT SEASON

In retrospect the 1934/35 season appears to have been rather a mundane one, but it is a mistake to view any football season critically in such a way and, at the time, 1934/35 had its major excitements and uplifts, allied to a similar number of disappointments.

Understandably, the typical Palace line-up for this season was by now considerably altered from the earlier years of that decade. Ronnie Dunn was playing at the peak of hs form in goal with Ted Owens and Oswald Parry in front of him. Ted had joined us in the summer of 1934 in a rare Palace deal with Preston North End and remained with the club until after the Second World War. He was as tough as teak, had a magnificent season for us in 1934/35, missing only a single match because of an injury incurred down at Torquay (1-7) on Christmas Day and certainly ranks as one of manager Jack Tresadern's best signings.

Jimmy Wilde was still our pivot and made all 42 League appearances, while sturdy, strong Nick Collins made his bow this term in the left half berth he was to retain for over ten years. Billy Turner was still at the Palace and replaced injured Alf Haynes at right half before Christmas, but there was a new face at outside right following Albert Harry's departure, with Scotsman Jimmy Carson joining us from Bradford. Frank Manders was our regular inside right and hit 14 Third Division (South) goals for us from his 36 appearances, the same number as the great man himself, Peter Simpson, who played in 28 games in what was to be his last season in the Palace colours. Top scorer was Albert Dawes with 19 goals from 31 matches, including five against Cardiff City on 1 September to add to his exploits for us at the end of the previous season.

But at outside left was another newcomer in Bob Bigg, who was to have an impressive debut season and would eventually prove to be our best left winger since George Clarke and for a very long time to come. Bob was brought up in Thornton Heath and became immensely popular at Selhurst Park. He started off in perfect fashion by scoring the club's first goal of the season on his debut at Aldershot with a header on the half-hour. Curiously the Shots' equaliser came from another header, also from *their* outside left, but Palace led again through Albert Dawes and created far more chances than their hosts but paid the penalty for profligate finishing, for Aldershot were able to equalise in the very last minute of the game for a 2-2 draw.

Bob's talent was not just evident on his debut against one of the weaker sides in our section. He performed consistently well throughout the season and his 16 League goals from the flank in his first League season was a marvellous haul even in those days. He came to Third Division

Bob Bigg netted on his Palace debut.

(South) maturity in mid-April with a hat-trick in a 6-0 rout of injury-hampered Newport County then, six days later, notched Palace's last two against another injury-affected side, Swindon (7-0), on Good Friday.

In today's game, where substitutions for all sorts of reasons are accepted as the norm, it must be difficult for modern readers to understand that, regardless of their severity, injuries caused the loss of a player (sometimes more than one) to their side and that a team could simply do nothing other than accept that situation, get on with the match as best it could, with the injured player sometimes returning to the field and providing 'nuisance value' out on one of the wings. That was what had happened to the Palace at Torquay on Christmas morning: we had Ted Owens and Nick Collins off the field hurt and Alf Haynes limping! As previously stated, the Gulls took full advantage in the pouring rain.

The Third Division (South) side of the season was Charlton Athletic. Palace drew 2-2 at The Valley in October but by the time of the return in mid-February it was understood by everyone that we simply had to win to have the least chance of challenging for the title, for Charlton had a six-point lead over us at that stage. A season's-best crowd of 25,250 came to witness the outcome but most of them were disappointed. Peter Simpson had Palace back on terms just before the break but Charlton snatched a winner with seven minutes left after a defensive error following a Palace throw-in, and ultimately we finished the season in fifth place.

SEASON: 1934/35

GROUND: Selhurst Park

MANAGER: Jack Tresadern

LEAGUE/DIVISION: Football League Third Division (South)

FINAL POSITION: 5th

BIGGEST VICTORY: 7-0 *v.* Swindon Town, 19 April 1935

HEAVIEST DEFEAT: 1-7 *v.* Torquay United, 25 December 1934

FA CUP – ROUND ELIMINATED: 1st

LEAGUE CUP – ROUND ELIMINATED: –

FULL MEMBERS CUP – ROUND ELIMINATED: –

LEADING LEAGUE APPEARANCES (MAX: 42): 42 – J. Wilde, 41 – E. Owens

LEADING LEAGUE GOALSCORERS: 19 – A. Dawes, 16 – R. Bigg

1935/36

TOM BROMILOW'S 'GOLDEN OPPORTUNITY'

There were major upheavals at Selhurst Park in the summer of 1935. First, Peter Simpson left us for West Ham at a substantial fee. Palace fans were naturally sorry to see Peter go, but it had become inevitable that he would leave us for a better-placed club at some stage and everyone wished the sharpshooter well. Secondly, there was a managerial change, and most Palace folk were surprised when Jack Tresadern moved across London to take charge at Tottenham. Palace had not seriously challenged for promotion under his stewardship and, with the quality of some of the players he had available in his five-year tenure, that is a serious indictment.

The new boss was Tom Bromilow, who had won League championship medals with Liverpool in the early 1920s and played 5 times at wing half for England. He had previously been manager at Burnley but seemed more than pleased to come to Selhurst Park. 'This is my golden opportunity,' he said upon arrival, and in fact Tom was to prove the best inter-war manager at our club, second only to Edmund Goodman.

'Golden opportunity' it may have been, but Mr Bromilow was unable to grasp it immediately, either for himself or for our club! Thus, although the Palace finished in a tolerable sixth place, our 1935/36 season will only be remembered for some interesting new signings, the infamous Pools War and the death of two chairmen.

Palace beat Cardiff City in the first match of the season with Bob Bigg claiming a rare winger's hat-trick, but in mid-October Second Division Norwich City sparked a flurry of transfer activity at Selhurst Park when they came in with a generous offer for Frank Manders. It would have been folly to have declined, so Mr Bromilow permitted the deal, then invested the proceeds shrewdly in Bob Birtley, a right-sided utility player from Coventry, and Jack Blackman, a vigorous, bustling centre forward from Queens Park Rangers. Both were first-rate signings and made useful contributions in this season and right up to the Second World War. Both netted on their Palace League debuts (a 5-0 rout of Millwall on 2 November) while Jack Blackman became a valued member of our training staff in the early post-war years. His 52 League goals from 99 outings is impressive by any standard and, as we shall see, during the Second World War seasons he was to prove invaluable.

Scoring goals was not a problem for Palace during 1935: we hit 96 of them in the Third Division (South) with Albert Dawes notching 38 and Jack Blackman 19, but by conceding 74 we forfeited any hopes we might have harboured of climbing out of that section. Additionally, we were embarrassed by a non-league club in the FA Cup when Margate dismissed us (1-3) in the second round.

Partly in reaction to that ignominious defeat, Mr Bromilow made his best signing for our club when he secured Fred Dawes from Northampton Town in February 1936. Fred was the brother of Albert and a composed full-back. He would go on to become one of our most faithful and reliable players and easily our longest-serving captain right up to the days of Jim Cannon. Fred played 222 League games for the Palace plus another 15 FA Cup ties and was the only Palace man to make 100 appearances on each side of the Second World War.

There had been growing acrimony between the Football League and the Pools giants over the use by the latter of the League's fixtures and matters boiled over in the early weeks of 1936. In an attempt to thwart the Pools companies from using the fixtures the League suspended the published programme of matches for 29 February at short notice and substituted other pairings, so that the Palace were hosts to table-toppers Coventry (3-1) instead of Torquay. By the time the Gulls fulfilled their fixture at Selhurst Park (1-0) on 14 March the opposition to the Pools companies had largely evaporated because gates everywhere had been detrimentally affected and the League retreated from the issue.

Early in October 1935, Palace's highly regarded chairman, Louis Bellatti, died suddenly at his home. Mr Bellatti was only Palace's second chairman in thirty years, but within six weeks it became necessary to appoint the fourth because poor Mr R.S. Flew, his successor, also died without the least warning.

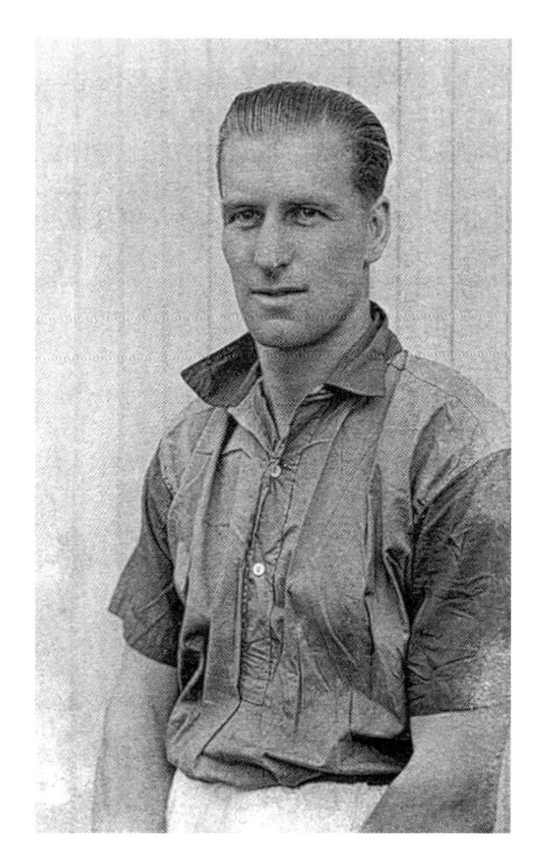

Fred Dawes joined the Palace in February 1936.

SEASON: 1935/36

GROUND: Selhurst Park

MANAGER: Tom Bromilow

LEAGUE/DIVISION: Football League Third Division (South)

FINAL POSITION: 6th

BIGGEST VICTORY: 6-0 *v.* Newport County, 18 December 1935

HEAVIEST DEFEAT: 1-8 *v.* Coventry City, 9 November 1935

FA CUP – ROUND ELIMINATED: 2nd

LEAGUE CUP – ROUND ELIMINATED: –

FULL MEMBERS CUP – ROUND ELIMINATED: –

LEADING LEAGUE APPEARANCES (MAX: 42): 41 – J. Wilde, R. Bigg, A. Dawes, s27 – J. Blackman

LEADING LEAGUE GOALSCORERS: 38 – A. Dawes, 19 – J. Blackman

1936/37

TURBULENT TIMES AT CRYSTAL PALACE FC

There was astonishment throughout London's footballing circles at the end of June 1936 when Palace manager Tom Bromilow tendered his resignation after just twelve months in charge at Selhurst Park. It was evident to everyone that all was far from well here and Mr Bromilow was succeeded by one of the directors, Mr R.S. Moyes, whose stay was to prove both turbulent and brief.

Mr Moyes performed one excellent piece of business on behalf of the Palace when he obtained Scottish international centre half George Walker from Notts County. Tall and well-built, Walker made 41 appearances for us in his first season and took over the club captaincy from Fred Dawes, because he was recognised as a charismatic figure, a model professional and a great leader. For two-and-a-half seasons George missed just three matches and his absence in the second half of 1938/39 could be argued to have cost us the long-sought promotion.

An intriguing signing made by Mr Moyes was that of centre forward Jack Palethorpe from Aston Villa in October. Jack was an extraordinary fellow – he had gained the tag 'Lucky' because wherever he went his club won something! He lived up to his nickname with the Palace – briefly. He hit a brace on his debut to help defeat Newport County and netted in our defeat at Southend a week later. In the end his magic failed to work for us: his meagre return of 8 goals from 29 appearances betrays a man who found the rugged nature of the Third Division (South) not greatly to his liking.

Mr Moyes' problems had actually begun before the season started, for Albert Dawes fractured his jaw in a trial match and was unable to play in the opening games, then he aggravated it upon his return and was sidelined again. Fortunately Jack Blackman, Bob Bigg and Bob Birtley were all in good form, but while we were not struggling we were equally nowhere near the top of the table and went out of the FA Cup at the first hurdle in a replay at Southend. Mr Moyes attempted to restructure matters – he sold Ronnie Rooke to Fulham and signed goalkeeper Vincent Blore from West Ham, but then, in early December, little after five months since his appointment, Mr Moyes himself resigned! A week or so later, so did the chairman! Amid all this, Albert Dawes was permitted to leave for Luton Town just before Christmas and then it was announced that Tom Bromilow would re-assume responsibility at Selhurst Park from 1 January!

Such happenings naturally devastated players and supporters alike. Our League position, never healthy, suffered further and morale was far from improved when Albert Dawes returned to Selhurst Park early in January with his new teammates and helped the Hatters administer a severe beating. Inevitably, Albert scored one of the visitors' goals but their man of the match

Left: Former director Mr R.S. Moyes became Palace's manager at the start of the 1936/37 season.

was the legendary Joe Payne, who ensured our defeat with two second-half strikes, with Palace going down to a 0-4 defeat to the champions elect.

That Tom Bromilow's task was a difficult one no-one at the Palace in midwinter 1936/37 would deny, but to his great credit he righted the ship straight away. We were helped by a run of four home games in the next five fixtures, but Swindon (2-0) and Bristol Rovers (3-0) were beaten; we earned draws at Cardiff (1-1) and against Gillingham (1-1); then restored some self-respect with an 8-0 rout of Exeter City. We finished the season in our poorest position since joining the Football League, that of fourteenth, but discerning fans of the period realised that it could all have proved so very, very much worse.

SEASON: 1936/37

GROUND: Selhurst Park

MANAGER: R. S. Moyes to December 1936, then Tom Bromilow from January 1937

LEAGUE/DIVISION: Football League Third Division (South)

FINAL POSITION: 14th

BIGGEST VICTORY: 8-0 *v.* Exeter City, 6 February 1937

HEAVIEST DEFEAT: 0-4 *v.* Luton Town, 9 January 1937, 0-4 *v.* Swindon Town, 17 April 1937

FA CUP – ROUND ELIMINATED: 1st

LEAGUE CUP – ROUND ELIMINATED: –

FULL MEMBERS CUP – ROUND ELIMINATED: –

LEADING LEAGUE APPEARANCES (MAX: 42): 42 – F. Dawes, E. Owens, 41 – G. Walker

LEADING LEAGUE GOALSCORERS: 12 – J. Blackman, 11 – R. Bigg

1937/38

PLEASING PALACE PROGRESS AND OUR FIRST CUP-TIE AGAINST LIVERPOOL

Although the anger kindled by the departure of Albert Dawes was still smouldering when Palace fans considered the prospects for the forthcoming 1937/38 season, there was no doubt that there were, at last, some genuine grounds for hoping that our club could make another sustained impact upon the race for the single promotion place from the Third Division (South).

Right at the end of the previous season manager Tom Bromilow had purchased one of the best wing halves ever to play for the Palace, Leslie Lievesley, from Torquay. Les was a powerful, dynamic fellow at all but six feet and over twelve stone, and his acquisition was unquestionably a key reason for our enhanced showing in the 1937/38 season. Les put in 53 consecutive appearances after joining us and, with George Walker and Nick Collins, helped to form an outstanding half-back line that is still spoken of with awe at Selhurst Park today.

Also from the West Country arrived a splendid goalkeeper, Arthur Chesters, from Exeter City, while a clever winger, Harvey Pritchard, came from Coventry to fill the gap caused by Bob Bigg's badly broken leg the previous spring. Another useful winger was Jackie Horton, who had previously played for Charlton but arrived from Chelsea.

Taken overall, the 1937/38 season represented a much better showing than the previous recent ones and, but for some really bad luck with injuries, we might even have pushed the top two clubs for the promotion spot. Typical of our misfortune was the story of our two full-backs. Fred Dawes suffered a complicated knee injury in mid-December that kept him out for the rest of the season, while Ted Owens missed the middle three months after being carried from the field in the FA Cup tie at Accrington (1-0). One outcome of this was that, when Palace tackled Liverpool in our first appearance in the third round for four years, we had to do so with two reserves in those crucial positions – and one of them, Sam Booth, had only been able to resume training himself a day or two before the match! But how well our makeshift defence played! Liverpool seldom threatened, while our best chance, a low drive from winger Johnny Horton late in the proceedings, was unwittingly deflected to safety off the centre half after it had beaten the goalkeeper.

That took matters to an Anfield replay where, after Liverpool had missed a penalty, Palace took the lead through Ernie Waldron. Liverpool replied ten minutes later with a goal that every Palace player and our little knot of fans were convinced had been handled into the net, and

Left: Winger Jackie Horton.

then in extra time Nick Collins conceded an unfortunate own goal and Joe Fagan converted another, late, Liverpool penalty.

Drafted in from Reading, though not eligible for the Liverpool cup tie, to help cover the key absences at full-back, was Fred Gregory, a dependable enough defender but also an exciting occasional centre forward, from where he netted 5 times in 2 games early in 1938/39. Fred did not miss a single match after joining us in 1937/38 and lashed home a couple of penalties to aid the goalscoring cause.

But for Palace fans the best news of the entire season was received in mid-February, when it was announced that 'Our Albert' was coming home to Selhurst Park. Thus, by early April, Palace's considerably reorganised team had forged its way from mid-table to sixth place and three points adrift of the leaders – but that was to prove the peak of Palace's efforts for the term and we closed the season in seventh place.

For a change the plaudits could go to the Palace defence, which conceded fewer goals than at any time since the 1921 promotion. Up front we lacked a consistent goalscorer, although Jack Blackman bustled his way to 16 strikes from his 29 games to show that, if he were given a decent service, he could produce what was wanted.

SEASON: 1937/38

GROUND: Selhurst Park

MANAGER: Tom Bromilow

LEAGUE/DIVISION: Football League Third Division (South)

FINAL POSITION: 7th

BIGGEST VICTORY: 4-0 *v.* QPR, 5 March 1938, 4-0 *v.* Mansfield Town, 2 April 1938

HEAVIEST DEFEAT: 0-4 *v.* Swindon Town, 1 September 1937

FA CUP – ROUND ELIMINATED: 3rd

LEAGUE CUP – ROUND ELIMINATED: –

FULL MEMBERS CUP – ROUND ELIMINATED: –

LEADING LEAGUE APPEARANCES (MAX: 42): 42 – L. Lievesley, 40 – G. Walker

LEADING LEAGUE GOALSCORERS: 16 – J. Blackman, 14 – E. Waldron

1938/39

PALACE MISS OUT TO UNFANCIED WELSHMEN

The Palace side put together by manager Tom Bromilow for this season came closer to winning promotion back to the Second Division than any other Palace team between 1929 and 1964. The squad of players that had finished 1937/38 in good form, augmented by the returning stars who had recovered from their long-standing injuries, needed little addition or adjustment as the season progressed.

Eric Steele was signed from Millwall in the autumn and Albert Wilson came from Mansfield in January to increase successfully our threat from the flanks. Bert Robson matured so quickly that he took over as our centre forward in mid-December and hit 11 goals from his 20 appearances. Bob Shanks deputised capably after George Walker incurred a desperate knee injury at the turn of the year, which was sufficient to keep our popular skipper out for the rest of the season.

On 1 October – the end of the week in which Chamberlain returned from Munich to proclaim 'Peace in our time' – Palace chairman, Mr E.T. Truett, called for three cheers for the Premier before Palace's home match with Clapton Orient (4-2) and the band played the national anthem. By the time the proceedings had come to a conclusion, only goal average separated Palace from Aldershot, the unlikely early leaders of the divisional table, and we had a match in hand.

However, this 1938/39 season was to prove the one season of glory for unfancied Newport County. On 8 October Palace travelled down to Monmouthshire, lost 0-2, and Newport leapfrogged over us to the top of the table. Matters always remained close and exciting, with our crucial chance of pulling County back to a position in which we might prove them vulnerable being the return fixture at Selhurst Park in mid-February. After a goal-less first half, in which Newport had demonstrated their class, and with the hour approaching, Les Lievesley swung a magnificent ball over to Albert Dawes. Albert took a heavy tackle, recovered his balance and the ball, then passed sweetly out to Albert Wilson. The winger raced onto it, beat his opposing full-back, then drove it hard and low into the net after closing to some ten yards' range.

For ten minutes or so Palace's forwards were at their best, but were unable to add the killer goal that the big crowd of nearly 30,000 longed to see. But, as our impetus faded, so Newport came back strongly, though our defence played with composure under the mounting pressure. Then, with just three minutes remaining, and it looking as if the battle might well have been won, fate stepped in. County had a free-kick, which was lofted to the edge of our area. Arthur

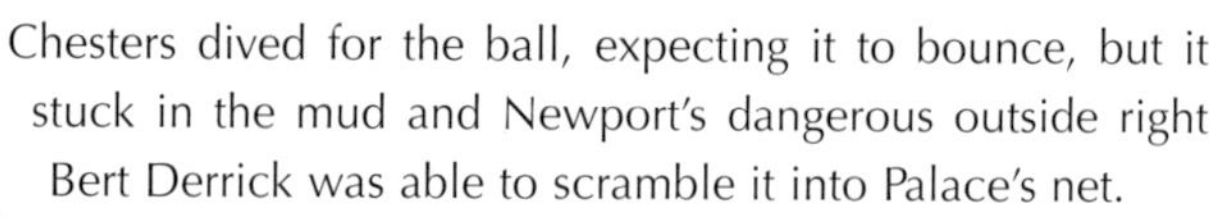

Left: Prolific scorer Albert Dawes.

Chesters dived for the ball, expecting it to bounce, but it stuck in the mud and Newport's dangerous outside right Bert Derrick was able to scramble it into Palace's net.

Despite a terrific assault by the Palace in the closing minutes Newport were able to hold on for their point. Inevitably, Palace were never able to make up the deficit, although the final gap was reduced to three points at the end of the season.

It was small surprise that during the close season of 1939 Mr Bromilow left Selhurst Park to manage Leicester City. He did so on the best of terms and with the knowledge that he had done his job well here. He had resurrected an ailing club and a fading team after returning to us in January 1937 and been unfortunate not to gain promotion two years later.

Tom's natural successor was George Irwin, the former Palace goalkeeper who had served as our trainer under Mr Bromilow for a couple of seasons. He knew the game thoroughly and was well-respected by the players, officials and our fans. The coming war years were going to demand much from everyone, and it was as well for Crystal Palace FC that our fortunes were in the hands of such a capable and well-equipped person.

SEASON: 1938/39

GROUND: Selhurst Park

MANAGER: Tom Bromilow

LEAGUE/DIVISION: Football League Third Division (South)

FINAL POSITION: 2nd

BIGGEST VICTORY: 6-2 *v.* Mansfield Town, 17 December 1938

HEAVIEST DEFEAT: 0-4 *v.* Clapton Orient, 4 February 1939

FA CUP – ROUND ELIMINATED: 1st

LEAGUE CUP – ROUND ELIMINATED: –

FULL MEMBERS CUP – ROUND ELIMINATED: –

LEADING LEAGUE APPEARANCES (MAX: 42): 42 – F. Dawes, 41 – A. Chesters

LEADING LEAGUE GOALSCORERS: 12 – A. Dawes, 11 – A. Robson

1939/40

AN EIGHT-DAY LEAGUE SEASON BUT PALACE CLAIM A WARTIME CHAMPIONSHIP

The portents of war hung ominously over Britain at the dawn of the 1939/40 football season, but all the usual preparations were made at clubs up and down the country and the Football League decided to make the numbering of players a compulsory feature of the game.

After a trial match and a Football League Jubilee Fund game at Brighton (3-3) on the previous Saturdays, the ill-fated League programme for 1939/40 began on Saturday 26 August 1939. Palace were at Mansfield and came back from a 1-3 half-time deficit to win 5-4, largely due to a hat-trick from our diminutive inside left Ernie Waldron. However, the following Wednesday evening we were handed a 0-5 beating by Reading at Elm Park. Palace's last Football League match to be played before the hostilities was on Saturday 2 September when we entertained Bristol Rovers and won 3-0 with goals from Ernie Waldron (2) and Trevor Smith.

It was on the following morning, Sunday 3 September 1939, that war was declared and announced to the nation in the famous radio broadcast by HM King George VI. The Football League tournament was annulled, all players' contracts were suspended and for a while there simply was no football played, of any description.

Towards the end of September the Football League announced that England and Wales would be spilt into eight regional tournaments in which eighty-two of the League clubs would participate. Palace were in a Southern Group (section A) with six other London teams, plus Watford, Southend and Norwich City. Before the regional leagues could get underway most clubs played a series of friendly matches and our first game after the outbreak of the war was at Guildford City on Saturday 23 September 1939 – the result was an humiliation, for we lost 0-5 at the Southern League club!

Palace most definitely saved their best form for the opening match in the new League at West Ham on Saturday 21 October 1939. This was regarded as an awesome task by the contemporary scribes, but Palace played certainly their best game in this section, perhaps of the whole season, and trounced the Irons 6-2! Jack Blackman hit a hat-trick while Billy Bark, Bert Robson and Fred Gregory (from a penalty) were also on target for us. We could not continue in such brilliant style of course, but we performed rather better than most pundits expected of a Third Division club. We ran top-flight Charlton to within a single goal home and away in high-scoring thrillers (3-4,

A section of the modest crowd at Palace's first home wartime game, against Brighton (2-2), on 7 October 1939, on the terracing where the Arthur Wait stand has since been built.

4-5), beat Spurs 3-1 at White Hart Lane, but found Arsenal (the eventual Section winners) much too strong (0-3, 0-5) with Reg Lewis from Purley scoring all the Arsenal goals at the Palace on Boxing Day.

We finished well down the Section table in seventh place, but the competition was dogged by recurrent bad weather and the outstanding matches were played off piecemeal later in the season. Palace finally completed their games on 25 May 1940 with a 2-7 defeat at Millwall.

Nevertheless, the first wartime arrangements had worked well and certainly the fans of the lowlier clubs like our own were delighted at the unexpected opportunities to see their teams taking on clubs from the higher divisions of the League in competitive matches.

For the latter half of 1939/40 a supplementary competition was run, based as much upon Football League status as upon geographical location, and Palace were placed in the 'South D' group with nine other teams from the Third Division (South). Palace soon demonstrated their ability to win this competition: we secured maximum points from the first four games, lapsed briefly when several key players were away, but then powered to the top of the table, scoring 64 goals in the 18 matches, including our biggest ever competitive score, 10-0 against Brighton on 6 April, and won the group with a four-point margin over our closest rivals Queens Park Rangers.

SEASON: 1939/40

GROUND: Selhurst Park

MANAGER: George Irwin

LEAGUE/DIVISION: Football League South 'A' Division, Football League South 'D' Division

FINAL POSITION: 7th and 1st

SEASON'S BIGGEST VICTORY: 10-0 *v.* Brighton & Hove Albion, 6 April 1940, Football League South 'D' Division

SEASON'S HEAVIEST DEFEAT: 2-7 *v.* Millwall, 25 May 1940, Football League South 'A' Division

FA CUP – ROUND ELIMINATED: –

LEAGUE CUP – ROUND ELIMINATED: –

FULL MEMBERS CUP – ROUND ELIMINATED: –

LEADING LEAGUE APPEARANCES (MAX: 36): 35 – A. Hudgell, 34 – F. Gregory

LEADING LEAGUE GOALSCORERS: 25 – A. Robson, 17 – T. Smith

1940/41

PALACE GAIN ANOTHER WARTIME CHAMPIONSHIP

As the followers of Crystal Palace anticipated the second wartime season, they did so with the knowledge that several of the key men from the successful side of the previous spring and early summer, which had won the 'South D' championship, would not often be available. Fred Gregory was a PT instructor in the RAF, Ted Owens and Trevor Smith were already flying in the Air Force, Albert Wilson had been called up, while reliable centre half Joe Millbanks was in the Navy.

Of course most clubs were similarly affected and there grew up a sophisticated system of inviting 'guests' to represent clubs other than their own. Some clubs benefited greatly under this arrangement – Aldershot would be the best southern example, for they could call upon experienced professionals who were stationed at the Army barracks – but others, like the Palace, did not use the 'guest' system greatly to begin with (George Irwin invited only two non-Palace men to play for us in 1939/40 and no more than a handful in 1940/41) preferring to give their own youngsters the opportunity to gain valuable experience by playing.

Although sometimes abused beyond belief, usually the 'guest' system worked sensibly to the benefit of players, fans and clubs alike and, without it, some matches simply could not have been played. Clubs were often willing to allow one of their own players (or more) to turn out for the opposition to make up their numbers and the annals of the war years are full of occasions where players lined up against their own club! Thus, Clapton Orient appear to have had particular difficulty throughout the Second World War in raising a side and twice in 1940/41 a Palace player 'guested' for them. On Saturday 19 October the O's arrived at Selhurst Park a player short and Palace's Fred Gregory was invited to 'guest' for them. Fred duly obliged and when the Orient were awarded a penalty for handball, the Palace crowd advised the visitors to allow Fred to take it for them, for few men have ever been able to hit a dead ball as powerfully as Fred. They did, and Fred scored! Palace won 6-2 with a team that included both Fred and Albert Dawes, along with Fred Gregory's younger brother Mark! A month later our own Ian Gillespie and an amateur, A.E. Waite, played for Orient against us. Palace won 4-2 but Gillespie netted Orient's second goal!

Another curious arrangement at wartime football was that if play was interrupted by an air-raid warning, however early in the game it sounded, the scoreline at the time would stand! Thus we lost 0-1 after half an hour at Millwall on 14 September.

The Football League arranged two regional divisions for 1940/41. Because of the difficulties in travelling at that time, clubs were free to play as many or as few games as they chose. Positions in this tournament were decided purely on goal average, so that it is a great (if rather unexpected!) joy to record that the Palace, who have rarely been among the best goalscorers in the League, were second in the table only to West Ham at the end of 1940 and by the time the extended competition had been completed we were at the head of the table with the best goal average of all! We had scored 86 goals with 44 against, for an average of 1.954. West Ham were second on 1.794 and Arsenal third with l.739.

Perhaps two reasons for this success can be adduced. Firstly, we had two marvellous goalscorers in Albert Dawes and Albert Robson. Albert Dawes was only available until early February and netted 26 goals from his 22 games in this competition, while Albert Robson scored 36 times in his 40 outings. The other reason may have lain in a strange incident when Palace were playing Southend and the visiting 'keeper strode from the pitch in disapproval at a Palace goal. He was followed to the dressing room by the referee, who emerged ten minutes later with the green jersey, and the game resumed with the visitors' centre forward in goal. Palace won 7-0 and that rout at least greatly enhanced our statistics at the head of the table!

Fred Gregory.

SEASON: 1940/41

GROUND: Selhurst Park

MANAGER: George Irwin

LEAGUE/DIVISION: Football League South Regional League

FINAL POSITION: 1st

BIGGEST VICTORY: 7-0 *v.* Southend United, 17 May 1941

HEAVIEST DEFEAT: 1-3 *v.* Norwich City, 5 October 1940, 1-3 *v.* Reading, 2 June 1941

FA CUP – ROUND ELIMINATED: –

LEAGUE CUP – ROUND ELIMINATED: –

FULL MEMBERS CUP – ROUND ELIMINATED: –

LEADING LEAGUE APPEARANCES (MAX: 27): 27 – A. Tootill, M. Gregory, A. Robson, 26 – N. Collins

LEADING LEAGUE GOALSCORERS: 24 – A. Robson, 20 – A. Dawes

1941/42

THE THIRD WARTIME SEASON BEGINS AMID CONTROVERSY

Controversy was in the air before the 1941/42 football season even got under way. When the Football League announced its plans for the third year of the wartime arrangements Palace, along with all the other London clubs, bluntly refused to accept them and announced that they would form a new, independent League, which would obviate any need for long (and sometimes dangerous) journeys, while also regularly providing matches of local interest for the fans.

Predictably the League reacted fiercely and threatened all the clubs involved with expulsion, but the London clubs, plus Aldershot, Brighton, Reading and Watford, decided that they would indeed branch out alone in spite of the opposition from the parent body, and since the Palace made a profit of some £400 on this 1941/42 season, as against losses of very much more in the previous two terms, it must be reckoned that the London clubs' judgement was sound enough.

In the end, everything finished harmoniously enough, and the sixteen who 'erred and strayed' were taken back into the League's fold for 1942/43.

Palace began their London League programme with a home match against Millwall on Saturday 30 August 1941 and won a close-fought match 2-0 with goals from Bert Robson as the hour approached and Ian Gillespie a minute from time. It was interesting that the Palace team for this match had not varied greatly from the one that played our first wartime fixture against West Ham nearly two years before.

In the first half of the 1941/42 season Palace were in absolutely tremendous form. Convincing and sometimes spectacular victories were obtained even against opponents from the First or Second Divisions: Fulham, 3-1 in October; Portsmouth, 3-1, Charlton, 4-0 and West Ham (away) 5-0 in November and, for the delight of modern fans, Brighton 10-1 on 3 January 1942 to enable Palace to challenge even the might of Arsenal at the top of the table.

Thus it was the greatest pity that the match scheduled for the top two clubs to meet at Selhurst Park just before Christmas was prevented from taking place by dense, swirling fog. Palace were at the height of their form at that stage and might just have been able to surprise even the Gunners. The match was eventually staged on 9 May 1942, when a thrilling 3-3 draw resulted.

Had the Palace been able to sustain their form throughout the season, they must have been serious contenders indeed for a further wartime honour, but the absence of key members of the

Skipper Nick Collins.

team such as Michael Gregory, Joe Millbank and Billy Bark disrupted our side and, increasingly, manager George Irwin had to call upon guest players to make up our numbers. Among the more distinguished guests to play for the Palace at this stage of the Second World War were goalkeeper Sam Bartram from Charlton and full-back Sid Tickeridge from Spurs, while Ronnie Rooke of Fulham even returned to his former (and future) club for one friendly at the end of the season.

Palace eventually finished 1941/42 in sixth place with 34 points from their 30-match programme. Arsenal were champions with 48 points, Portsmouth the runners-up with 42.

Had there been a Player of the Year award back in 1941/42, it would certainly have gone to skipper and left half Nick Collins, who played in every match and whose driving, tenacious skills were greatly admired around the grounds at this time. Nick had been with the Palace since August 1934 and made over 150 League and Cup appearances for us before the Second World War came. The first three wartime seasons were Nick's best years in the game and it was a great pity that he was away in the Royal Navy for the remainder of the hostilities, but it is an indication of his worth to the Palace club that we won honours in the first two wartime seasons and were well on course for another tilt at a title in the first half of this one before unavoidable absences began to break up our side.

SEASON:1941/42

GROUND: Selhurst Park

MANAGER: George Irwin

LEAGUE/DIVISION: London League

FINAL POSITION: 6th

BIGGEST VICTORY: 10-1 *v.* Brighton & Hove Albion, 3 January 1942

HEAVIEST DEFEAT: 2-7 *v.* Arsenal, 6 September 1941

FA CUP – ROUND ELIMINATED: –

LEAGUE CUP – ROUND ELIMINATED: –

FULL MEMBERS CUP – ROUND ELIMINATED: –

LEADING LEAGUE APPEARANCES (MAX: 30): 30 – N. Collins, 29 – A. Hudgell

LEADING LEAGUE GOALSCORERS: 21 – A. Robson, 10 – A. Dawes

1942/43

A CHAOTIC SITUATION AS PALACE 'GUESTS' PROLIFERATE

The 1942/43 season saw the most ambitious wartime arrangements so far undertaken by the Football League. An eighteen-club division made up the Football League (South), the Palace among them, and we began the new term in terrific form. With a side composed almost entirely of established Palace favourites we went to White Hart Lane on the season's opening day, Saturday 29 August, and played probably our best game of the entire campaign. After a scoreless first half Spurs went ahead early in the second period, but Palace were soon on terms via Albert Wilson. Two minutes later Bert Robson shot just inside the post to put us ahead. Billy Bark hit the Spurs bar but Palace were not to be denied and Robson clinched the contest twenty minutes from time to complete an excellent Palace victory. Only two members of our winning team at Tottenham were guests, but that situation could not last long and in our first twenty matches in the Football League (South) manager George Irwin fielded no fewer than forty-five different players, twenty-one of them guests from other clubs. In the second half of the season the position became even more chaotic with forty-seven different players appearing in Palace sides in eighteen matches. A total of seventy players actually represented the Palace during 1942/43, yet only eight of them played even fifteen times!

Palace were always, but only, a mid-table side in the Football League (South). To begin with we promised rather more than that, because after the grand opening day success over Tottenham we beat Clapton Orient 5-3, got a 2-2 draw at West Ham, lost 0-1 to Queens Park Rangers then overwhelmed Brighton 8-1 at Hove before gaining another praiseworthy point against top opponents by drawing 4-4 with Charlton at The Valley, thanks to an inspired rally in which we scored three times in the last quarter of an hour.

But any aspirations we may have harboured at that stage (early October) were rudely shattered by a run of six consecutive defeats, including a 1-7 pounding from Arsenal, when Reg Lewis netted five times and scored a first-half hat-trick! It became even more difficult for George Irwin to raise a Palace side and we finally finished in fifteenth place. Arsenal won the League comfortably with a five-point margin over Spurs and Queens Park Rangers.

One of the glorious curios of this 1942/43 season at Crystal Palace was the rare footballing sight of a pair of brothers playing alongside each other at full-back. This happened precisely

Right: Bert Robson was twice on target at Spurs (3-1) on the opening day of the season.

nine times in this campaign with Fred Dawes, our regular left-back, being joined on these occasions by his elder brother Albert in the number two shirt! Albert actually played in eight of the ten outfield positions for the Palace this season and was the epitome of the utility player who can be of such enormous value to his club.

Several Palace men were playing regularly elsewhere throughout the 1942 season. For example, Arthur Hudgell was appearing for Raith Rovers, and Michael Gregory for Doncaster Rovers, but Palace signed one player from Cardiff City who was to render absolutely sterling service to our club in the person of centre half Bill Bassett, while youngster Ted Harding was given his first run-out for the senior side on 24 October as a seventeen-year-old at Chelsea, where we fell to a 1-4 defeat. Ted played 6 times during this season and was to go on to become a highly valued and loyal full-back for the Palace after the Second World War, when he would make over 150 League and Cup appearances in our colours.

SEASON: 1942/43

GROUND: Selhurst Park

MANAGER: George Irwin

LEAGUE/DIVISION: Football League South

FINAL POSITION: 15th

BIGGEST VICTORY: 8-1 *v.* Brighton & Hove Albion, 26 September 1942

HEAVIEST DEFEAT: 0-9 *v.* Arsenal, 6 February 1943

FA CUP – ROUND ELIMINATED: –

LEAGUE CUP – ROUND ELIMINATED: –

FULL MEMBERS CUP – ROUND ELIMINATED: –

LEADING LEAGUE APPEARANCES (MAX: 28): 25 – T. Smith, 22 – A. Dawes, A. Robson

LEADING LEAGUE GOALSCORERS: 10 – A. Dawes, 9 – A. Robson

1943/44

PALACE MAKE A BETTER SHOWING

For the fifth season under the piecemeal and ad hoc arrangements necessitated by the Second World War, the Palace club was again in the Football League (South) with all the other London sides.

Naturally, several of Palace's best and most experienced players were unavailable, though this was a plight common to all clubs and there is no suggestion that we suffered any more than most of the others in this respect. Arthur Hudgell was now serving with the RAF in Iceland and Nick Collins, the club skipper, was away in the Navy. The Gregory brothers were in the north of England: Mick was in Doncaster and assisting the Rovers while Fred was stationed near Crewe and playing for the Alex whenever the chance arose. Ted Owens was in the Westcountry and played regularly for Bath City, where he was later joined by Michael Gregory. With the help of the two Palace men, Bath had a fabulous season and actually won a second championship contrived by the Football League for that area. Fred Dawes was only available for the Palace for the first couple of months of the season, his Royal Artillery service preventing him from playing for us, except once on a rare leave, after mid-November.

However, again like almost every other club, the Palace were regularly strengthened by the inclusion of guest players. Most notable among these were R.C. Mountford, who had made over 100 appearances as Huddersfield Town's quality right-back in the First Division before the Second World War and played in the famous 1938 FA Cup final for the Terriers; centre half Harold Spencer from Burnley (although Spencer had played for us in the last couple of months of 1942/43) and centre forward Bob Ferrier, formerly of Manchester United but now of Oldham.

Like the previous two seasons, team selection was hopelessly difficult. By the end of October, after just ten matches, manager George Irwin had used no fewer than thirty-eight players, twenty-four of them as guests from other clubs! By the end of the season fifty-six different players had represented the Palace, though sharp-minded readers will realise that that figure was actually an improvement on 1942/43!

Palace fans faced an increase in the price of admission to Selhurst Park for 1943/44. The Football League agreed at its 1943 meeting that the match fee to be paid to players should be raised to a maximum of £2 instead of the £1.50 that had previously applied: this increase, coupled with a rise in entertainment tax, compelled the directors of most clubs, including our own, to put up the admission charges. At Selhurst Park it now cost 1*s* 6*d* to stand on the terraces, (members of the forces in uniform and children were admitted for 7*d*) and 2*s* in the enclosure, while a seat in the centre stand cost 3*s* 6*d*. Modern equivalents of those prices are 7.5p, 10p and 17.5p!

Palace fared much better in the Football League (South) than in the previous season and we finished fifth in the table with 37 points from our 30 matches. The winners of the division were Tottenham with 46 points, although on the opening day of the season Albert Wilson scored direct from a corner to equalise a Spurs goal just after the interval, while at Selhurst Park in late November an early Bob Ferrier header and two second-half goals from Albert Wilson accounted for the visitors who were unable even to reply.

Palace's better showing was largely due to Bob Ferrier, who notched 19 goals for us from his 20 appearances in the League. He was certainly a threat to even the best defences, though ironically his own career in the Football League both before and after the Second World War was rather enigmatic.

Two other Palace men should be mentioned here. Albert Dawes played in every outfield position during 1943/44 and missed just four games in our 38-match season, while the club suffered a sad loss on Christmas morning when our secretary, Mr Fred Burrell, collapsed and died at Norwood Junction Station as the team and officials were preparing to journey to Brighton for our match at Goldstone Road.

Palace's pre-war star Ted Owens assisted Bath City to a title this term.

SEASON: 1943/44

GROUND: Selhurst Park

MANAGER: George Irwin

LEAGUE/DIVISION: Football League South

FINAL POSITION: 5th

BIGGEST VICTORY: 6-0 *v.* Aldershot, 29 April 1944

HEAVIEST DEFEAT: 1-6 *v.* West Ham United, 2 October 1943

FA CUP – ROUND ELIMINATED: –

LEAGUE CUP – ROUND ELIMINATED: –

FULL MEMBERS CUP – ROUND ELIMINATED: –

LEADING LEAGUE APPEARANCES (MAX: 30): 27 – A. Dawes, 25 – T. Smith

LEADING LEAGUE GOALSCORERS: 19 – R. Ferrier, 11 – A. Dawes, A. Wilson

1944/45

VICTORY IN EUROPE IS ULTIMATELY SECURED... AND RARE SIGHTS ON THE PALACE WING

The opening of the 1944/45 football season took place in the shadow of events of worldwide importance in the Second World War in Europe, while the Allies' invasion of France on 7 June 1944 inevitably meant that many players who had previously been available to play, either in their own right for their clubs or as guests for other teams, were no longer able to do so. At Crystal Palace Bert Robson, our clever right winger or centre forward, who had been such a prolific scorer in earlier wartime seasons, was the latest player to join up, while there was news that our recently signed centre half Bill Bassett had been wounded while serving with the Fifth Army in its successful Italian campaign.

Trevor Smith and Bob Ferrier, key members of the Palace side that had acquitted itself so competently in 1943, played just a single game for Palace between them in 1944/45, although Ferrier made that one game worth his and Palace's while by netting a hat-trick to help us beat First Division Brentford 6-1 at Selhurst Park on 21 April in the Football League (South).

However, there were contrasting compensations for the Palace. Arthur Hudgell was back in the country and was available for all bar the first month of the season and among several new guest players in the Palace team was Harry Ferrier, a distinguished left-back from Barnsley who made up for the continuing absence of old favourite Fred Dawes. Ferrier was a thoroughbred: after the Second World War he joined Portsmouth and gained Football League championship medals with them in 1949 and 1950. His full-back partnership at the Palace with another guest, R.C. Mountford from Huddersfield Town, became one of the most pleasing Palace features of this 1944/45 season.

Other guests of note were forwards Alf Somerfield of Wolves and Freddie Kurz of Grimsby, both of whom played for Palace in the Football League after the war, who were our leading goalscorers, while among the Palace stars who were able to make occasional appearances for us were those veterans from the pre-war days, Les Lievesley, Jack Blackman, Ian Gillespie, Joe Millbanks and Tommy Reece. More regular were goalkeeper Alf Tootill, Albert Dawes and Albert Wilson, while Jack Lewis showed increasing maturity and real ability after he became available in the second half of this season.

However, the fact that sixty-seven different players made at least one appearance for the Palace in this 1944/45 season, and that fewer than a third of them were actually

Left: Jack Lewis.

Palace-registered players, tells its own story of the inevitably huge disruption that was still characteristic of the nation's life at this stage of the conflict. Nevertheless, it must be admitted that the most unlikely player to don a Palace shirt during this season did have strong links with our club – for he was a director, no less! Mr Leslie Ward, who had recently been elected to the Palace board, played at outside right in our team at Charlton (0-1) in a War Cup sectional match on 3 March! It was considered that he 'had a good first half but', not surprisingly, one must feel, 'faded somewhat in the second'!

Another unusual Palace winger in this 1944/45 season was full-back Fred Dawes! Fred was drafted in for two outings at outside right and another at outside left when he was on leave and available to play for us – and scored for us on the first of these occasions, at Selhurst Park against Chelsea (3-3) on 30 December 1944, perhaps suggesting that he could have made his career as a raiding winger instead of a redoubtable full-back!

SEASON: 1944/45

GROUND: Selhurst Park

MANAGER: George Irwin

LEAGUE/DIVISION: Football League South

FINAL POSITION: 6th

BIGGEST VICTORY: 6-1 *v.* Clapton Orient, 11 November 1944, 6-1 *v.* Brentford, 21 April 1945

HEAVIEST DEFEAT: 1-9 *v.* Portsmouth, 26 December 1944

FA CUP – ROUND ELIMINATED: –

LEAGUE CUP – ROUND ELIMINATED: –

FULL MEMBERS CUP – ROUND ELIMINATED: –

LEADING LEAGUE APPEARANCES (MAX: 30): 25 – R. Mountford, 23 – A. Hudsell

LEADING LEAGUE GOALSCORERS: 14 – F. Kurz, A. Somerfield, 9 – A. Wilson

1945/46

THE FIRST PEACETIME SEASON FOR SEVEN YEARS

By the late summer of 1945, with the worst ravages of the Second World War now passed, our nation was eager to return to normality as quickly as possible. It was clearly demanding far too much of the Football League clubs to implement the League's original suggestion that the full peace-time fixture arrangements be reverted to for 1945/46 though, without any promotion or relegation. Instead, Third Division (South) clubs were divided into two sections, one each for clubs north and south of the Thames. Thus, rather than making the long, arduous and none-too-remunerative journey to Mansfield, Palace played their opening game of the new term on Saturday 25 August at home to Aldershot, although Palace folk were disappointed by the unconvincing 0-0 draw that resulted.

However, if the start to 1945/46 was rather lame, it soon became clear that the Palace did possess a side that had the ability to challenge for the title of this wartime section. From 29 September, when we beat Brighton 5-1 at Selhurst Park, to Christmas morning, Palace won 9 and drew 1 of the 10 League games we played, scoring 29 times and conceding just 6! Indeed, it was the 4-1 victory we secured over Bournemouth at our headquarters on Christmas morning that secured the championship because our sole remaining challengers, Cardiff, were only able to draw 2-2 at Bristol Rovers and were now unable to catch us, even if they were to beat us 6-1 the following afternoon!

This triumph, Palace's third in the wartime competitions, was thoroughly praiseworthy and one in which everyone at the club could take considerable pride.

For Palace fans, another highly pleasing feature of 1945/46 was that, for the first time since the autumn of 1939, a 'proper' programme was produced. Throughout the hostilities Palace, like most clubs, had simply produced a single-sheet programme though the information these flimsy pieces of paper carried was really quite amazing. However, under the editorship of the Palace Supporters' Club secretary, Mr L.W. Davis, an excellent eight-page journal was produced for almost all the home matches, complete with match reports, player profiles, an apposite cartoon, lucky programme number and a half-time scoreboard. That old favourite, the 'Penny On The Ball' was also reintroduced to the delight of many, especially the younger followers of the club, and the loudspeaker system, damaged in an air raid early in the Second World War, was also restored.

Freddie Kurz.

With the dawning of 1946 Palace were presented with their most testing matches of the entire season, for we were drawn to meet Queens Park Rangers over two legs in a third round FA Cup tie. A crowd of over 20,000 was at Shepherds Bush for a match that resulted in a dour 0-0 draw. The following Wednesday saw both clubs make minor adjustments to their sides, but again both defences remained unscathed, so a replay was required, at Fulham a week later. This was staged upon a frozen surface and with a light, bouncing ball. Rangers won with a goal netted soon after half-time by Bert Addinall, who had guested for the Palace a couple of times earlier in the season and who would play for us again after the Second World War.

Two men had signed for the Palace in the midwinter of 1945/46 after previously playing for us as guests. Both would help to form Palace's post-war League sides for several years. Their names were Dick Graham and Freddie Kurz.

Freddie Kurz had been a regular for us through the title-winning campaign of the autumn and early winter of 1945. His impressive striking tally of 20 goals (including two hat-tricks) from 17 outings led the Palace fans to petition the board to buy him outright. Once the FA Cup draw paired us with Queens Park Rangers, the directors hurried the transfer through at a then-club record fee of £5,000 since guests were not allowed to play in FA Cup games.

Dick Graham had been with former Palace boss Tom Bromilow at Leicester but guested with us from mid-November 1945 and played so well that manager George Irwin persuaded him to sign for us a month later. He was an ever-present member of our side in the remainder of 1945/46 and made a total of 155 League appearances for the Palace between 1946 and 1950 before a deep-seated spinal injury necessitated his retirement.

SEASON: 1945/46

GROUND: Selhurst Park

MANAGER: George Irwin

LEAGUE/DIVISION: Football League Third Division (South) South Region

FINAL POSITION: 1st

BIGGEST VICTORY: 10-1 *v.* Swindon Town, 10 November 1945

HEAVIEST DEFEAT: 1-6 *v.* Cardiff City, 29 December 1945

FA CUP – ROUND ELIMINATED: 1st

LEAGUE CUP – ROUND ELIMINATED: –

FULL MEMBERS CUP – ROUND ELIMINATED: –

LEADING LEAGUE APPEARANCES (MAX: 20): 20 – F. Dawes, 18 – A. Hudgell

LEADING LEAGUE GOALSCORERS: 20 – F. Kurz, 6 – J. Blackman

1946/47

PALACE DISAPPOINT IN THE FIRST POSTWAR SEASON

Fully competitive post-war soccer opened on the last day of August 1946 and at Selhurst Park there appeared to be sound grounds for optimism. Manager George Irwin had at his disposal a useful looking squad of men, comprising pre-war stars like Fred Dawes, Bert Robson and Ernie Waldron, wartime signings including Dick Graham, Freddie Kurz and Bill Bassett, plus probably the best footballer on our staff at that time in young Arthur Hudgell, who had developed through the years of the hostilities into a top-quality full-back.

The portents, then, were excellent. Sadly, the actual performance fell very much short of that! Robson rarely produced his sparkling wartime form; Waldron was unsettled and soon signed for Aberdeen. It became difficult to field a settled side – only once could manager Irwin put out the same team for more than two consecutive matches – and in our second match of this 1946/47 season Palace suffered their highest-ever scoring defeat in the League. We had lost 1-3 at Mansfield on the opening day, when Ernie Waldron spent the afternoon in a local hospital rather than assisting his colleagues because he had a fish bone stuck in his throat, and then were at Reading the following Wednesday evening. Three goals in arrears after a quarter of an hour, Palace staged a mini-revival to make the interval scoreline 2-3, but immediately after the break Reading netted five times in a quarter of an hour and proceeded to reach double figures. No other Palace result has reduced your author and chaplain to tears!

However, for the record, in the return fixture at the Palace two weeks later, we won 2-1. Freddie Kurz hit the woodwork three times without the ball going into Reading's net and their goal came right at the end of a match we had dominated throughout.

Certainly, when Palace did play to their full ability, we were able to record some splendid victories. Two away wins in three days at Norwich and Leyton Orient in September and a 6-1 home victory over an admittedly depleted Torquay on Christmas morning provided convincing evidence that we could play attractive and effective football but, in all honesty, we were usually enigmatic and disappointing.

Palace were excused the early rounds of the FA Cup but, when the third round draw was made, we found that we were the only London club required to travel and that it was to Tyneside we had to go to face mighty Newcastle United. There was to be no repetition of the

Dick Graham punches clear during Palace's 2-0 win over Watford on 15 February 1947. Jack Lewis (left) and Bill Bassett are the other Palace players.

1907 giant-killing; we lost 2-6 in a brave performance, with Bill Naylor (formerly Billy Bark) netting our brace of goals. But sitting high up in the Gallowgate stand that afternoon was a scout from neighbouring Sunderland. He was so impressed with Arthur Hudgell's distinguished performance that Roker Park officials were constantly to be seen at Selhurst and, at the end of January, Arthur left us for Wearside at a then-record fee for a Third Division player.

Other players were also soon on the move to First Division clubs as left winger Howard Girling and Bill Naylor travelled across to west London to join top-flight Brentford. In February bitter winter weather closed in and Palace were only able to play a home match against Leyton Orient on 1 February because eighteen German prisoners-of-war had cleared the snow from the pitch that morning, while the game at Swindon on 15 March was played in a blizzard. We beat the O's 2-0, but lost at Swindon to a fiercely disputed penalty five minutes from time. In the end postponements were inevitable and the season had to be extended until the Whitsun bank holiday weekend to accommodate all the rearrangements. Not untypical of the whole season, Palace drew at home with Bristol City on Saturday 24 May (the latest date on which Palace have completed their home matches in an ordinary peace-time season), but lost 2-4 at Port Vale on the bank holiday two days later.

SEASON: 1946/47

GROUND: Selhurst Park

MANAGER: George Irwin

LEAGUE/DIVISION: Football League Third Division (South)

FINAL POSITION: 18th

BIGGEST VICTORY: 6-1 *v.* Torquay United, 25 December 1946

HEAVIEST DEFEAT: 2-10 *v.* Reading, 4 September 1946

FA CUP – ROUND ELIMINATED: 3rd

LEAGUE CUP – ROUND ELIMINATED: –

FULL MEMBERS CUP – ROUND ELIMINATED: –

LEADING LEAGUE APPEARANCES (MAX: 42): 42 – F. Dawes, J. Lewis, 38 – D. Graham, T. Reece

LEADING LEAGUE GOALSCORERS: 9 – W. Naylor, 6 – A. Robson, H.Girling

1947/48

NEW MANAGEMENT TEAM UNABLE TO RAISE PALACE SIGHTS

By the time Crystal Palace played their last matches of the extended 1946/47 season the club was under new management with Jack Butler, formerly of Arsenal and England, put in charge. Jack's impressive pedigree on the pitch was certainly equalled as a coach and manager off it: he had been in charge of the Belgian national side and the Denmark FA, had coached at Leicester City and managed Torquay United. Bob John, another former Arsenal defender and regular Welsh international was the new Palace trainer, and these two men had been contemporaries at Highbury.

These appointments were ambitious ones by the Palace board but, unfortunately, they failed – dismally. Butler and John discovered, as many top-flight players before and since have found, at the Palace and elsewhere, that running a club in a lower division is a very different matter from, and far more demanding than, playing at the highest domestic level.

Actually, and in all honesty, Palace's opening to 1947/48 was encouraging, although none of our early opponents were among the leading clubs in the section. Freddie Kurz had Palace ahead on the hour over at Leyton Orient on the first day of the season, although Jack Lewis had fired an earlier penalty straight at the O's keeper Stan Tolliday, and the home side levelled matters from the other penalty spot with ten minutes or so to go. Aldershot were Palace's first visitors on Wednesday 27 August when Jimmy Russell's early strike separated the sides and then a stooping header from our former Manchester United inside forward Albert Mycock was responded to within a minute by Torquay's Joe Conley, as the hour approached upon the Gulls' visit to Selhurst Park, only for Billy Burrell to net late on to secure Palace's fifth point from the first six available (under the two-points-for-a-win system that operated at that time).

However, Aldershot beat us 2-0 at the Recreation Ground and Palace were only able to secure one more victory before mid-October, so that we were usually a lower-middle-of-the-table side throughout 1947/48, with goals hard to come by at least until the final third of the season. Our defence could rarely be faulted but Jack Butler sought to improve our striking power by signing Jimmy Clough, a raiding winger from Southport, and Alf Somerfield, an inside forward who, it will be remembered, had guested for the Palace during the Second World War from Wolves. Things did improve: Palace scored a remarkable 5-0 win at Watford on 14 February (still our best victory at any of Watford's grounds, secured by a Marcel Gaillard goal on the Belgian's League debut for us, plus a brace from Jimmy Clough and others from Freddie

Palace *v.* Watford again, this time on 27 September 1947 (1-2). Bill Bassett tangles with Bill Dunderdale, with Tommy Reece (left) and Albert Mycock on hand.

Kurz and Glyn Lewis) and gained two splendid 4-0 home wins over Swansea and Bristol City in March and April. But, despite this rally, which actually only revealed itself on sporadic occasions and never against the division's foremost sides, Palace could still only finish in thirteenth position, with goal aggregates of just 49 scored and the same number conceded.

Probably Palace's best players in 1947/48 were our defensive triumvirate of Dick Graham, who played every game, and full-back colleagues Ted Harding and Fred Dawes but Freddie Kurz netted a creditable 18 League goals, with precious little support coming from elsewhere.

The FA Cup brought a little excitement to a rather drab season and lifted morale for a while late in 1947, but even here the Palace flattered to deceive. We defeated Port Vale at Selhurst Park and Bristol City at Ashton Gate after extra time to reach the third round, in which the draw brought Chester to the Palace for their first-ever visit. An eager crowd of some 22,000 turned up hoping to see us dismiss the men from the Northern section, but Chester scored eight minutes before half-time against the run of play and were then able to resist all Palace's efforts to redress the situation.

SEASON: 1947/48

GROUND: Selhurst Park

MANAGER: Jack Butler

LEAGUE/DIVISION: Football League Third Division (South)

FINAL POSITION: 13th

BIGGEST VICTORY: 5-0 *v.* Watford, 14 February 1948

HEAVIEST DEFEAT: 1-4 *v.* Port Vale, 31 January 1948

FA CUP – ROUND ELIMINATED: 3rd

LEAGUE CUP – ROUND ELIMINATED: –

FULL MEMBERS CUP – ROUND ELIMINATED: –

LEADING LEAGUE APPEARANCES (MAX: 42): 42 – R. Graham, 41 – E. Harding

LEADING LEAGUE GOALSCORERS: 18 – F. Kurz, 8 – J. Clough

1948/49

A DISASTROUS SEASON LEADS TO JACK BUTLER'S DEPARTURE

If 'difficult' would sum up Jack Butler's first full season of 1947/48 at Crystal Palace then frankly only 'disastrous' will do to describe 1948/49. The Palace reverted to the club's former and original colours of claret-and-blue shirts and white shorts, which had been dispensed with for a decade, but the change brought no luck and no improvement whatsoever.

The Palace had a lamentable record this term. We leaked goals but could score few ourselves in spite of the noble efforts of Freddie Kurz, who accumulated virtually one-third of our total. The defence toiled earnestly but was always suspect under pressure and prone to mistakes – we let in five goals on no fewer than four occasions and could rarely prevent the opposition from scoring. Jack Butler put out thirty-three different players in a vain attempt to stem the tide, but it was to no avail.

Perhaps fortunately, Palace met the eventual Third Division (South) champions Swansea (still then Swansea Town) home and away in the first two weeks of the season. Having lost 1-5 at Reading on the opening day – a defeat that should certainly have sounded the alarm at Selhurst Park – we hosted the Swans the following Wednesday, and played one of our best games of the term, though it seems doubtful that Swansea were yet showing the quite imperious form that would ultimately see them finish matters with an impressive seven-point margin over the second-placed club Reading. Palace were awarded an early penalty against Swansea but, while Freddie Kurz netted, the referee demanded a retake for an infringement. Freddie's second attempt was brilliantly saved and the Palace striker lashed the rebound wide of the post. The Swans took a twenty-fifth-minute lead but Palace rescued a point ten minutes from the end following a corner, through Ted Broughton. At Vetch Field we conceded an early goal direct from a corner, saw Sammy McCrory thunder a piledriver against our crossbar, conceded twice more and were simply glad to get away without incurring any further damage or embarrassment.

Following two welcome victories at Selhurst Park in early September, Palace failed to win again until 20 November when Jimmy Clough scored the only goal of the game at Southend midway through the second half from Peter Mulheron's pass. But even that success still left us at the foot of the Third Division (South) table – and things worsened at Christmas when we lost 0-5 and 0-1 to Newport in the holiday fixtures.

Left: Marcel Gaillard, a Belgian winger, appeared in Palace's last 11 games of 1948/49 and netted 2 goals.

Ultimately, Palace finished this season six points adrift of Aldershot, the club in twenty-first place in the table. In the FA Cup we were dismissed in the first round, Bristol City gaining speedy revenge for our success in 1947/48 with a single-goal victory at Selhurst Park.

Frankly, at the time it was hard even to imagine that there might just be some light at the end of this extremely long and arduous tunnel. There were a few youngsters coming to the fore, like inside forward Johnny Rainford and left winger Ray Howells, but it seemed that, unless another goalscorer could be found to augment Freddie Kurz's efforts, our prospects were bleak indeed.

Thus, 1948/49 was a tale of one woe after another. Jack Butler was bitterly upset by it all and insisted that his letter of resignation be accepted by the Club. He left Palace with dignity, but that was little or no consolation for our supporters (who remained commendably loyal in spite of it all), for our club had suffered its worst season since joining the Football League and now faced the indignity of having to apply for re-election for the first time.

SEASON: 1948/49

GROUND: Selhurst Park

MANAGER: Jack Butler

LEAGUE/DIVISION: Football League Third Division (South)

FINAL POSITION: 22nd

BIGGEST VICTORY: 4-0 *v.* Bristol City, 19 March 1949

HEAVIEST DEFEAT: 0-5 *v.* Newport County, 25 December 1948

FA CUP – ROUND ELIMINATED: 1st

LEAGUE CUP – ROUND ELIMINATED: –

FULL MEMBERS CUP – ROUND ELIMINATED: –

LEADING LEAGUE APPEARANCES (MAX: 42): 37 – E. Broughton, F. Kurz, 34 – J. Clough

LEADING LEAGUE GOALSCORERS: 12 – F. Kurz, 6 – J. Thomas

1949/50

RONNIE ROOKE AND HIS 'REGIMENT' LIFT PALACE TO SEVENTH

Immediately upon the departure of Jack Butler from Crystal Palace FC the club appointed another former Arsenal personality as our player-manager – Ronnie Rooke. Rooke was no stranger to Selhurst Park. We saw previously that his success here in the 1930s had been limited, but now he came to us as one of the leading lights of London football and the League's top scorer in 1947/48 with 33 goals.

This appointment by the Palace was in line with progressive thinking among some of the ambitious clubs in the lower divisions. Hull City and Notts County had pioneered the way by signing 'big-name' men of the day in Raich Carter and Tommy Lawton respectively. Drawing phenomenal crowds, Hull won the Third Division (North) title in 1948/49 and County were to do so in our section in the 1949/50 season. Rooke, it was hoped, would duly lead the Palace the same way before long.

The new manager made several interesting signings, the best of which turned out to be Jock Watson, a strong centre half who had been with Rooke at Fulham and then played for Real Madrid, and little Wally Hanlon, formerly of Brighton and Bournemouth, a tricky winger who became a firm Palace favourite.

In a pulsating game at Selhurst Park on 10 September, against star-studded Notts County in front of a 30,000 crowd, Jack Lewis scored his last goal for us as Palace ran County close but were unlucky to lose 1-2. Lewis was a grand player, one of our best half-backs to be sure. The London FA called him up for their fixture with the Belgian FA in Brussels and thus Palace's first post-war representative honour, but a few weeks later Bournemouth bought him for the substantial fee for those days of £7,500. He had played 124 League games for us and most of our fans were really sorry to see him leave. Then Fred Dawes came to the end of his playing career at Bournemouth on 1 October when he sustained a nasty head injury. He was to continue to serve Palace faithfully in administrative and managerial capacities, but it was a sad end to an illustrious Palace career.

Jack Edwards (destined to become another great Palace favourite and club skipper) deputised for Fred in the next match – a real roughhouse at Millwall in which Ronnie Rooke eluded some tight marking to score his 101st League goal and was subsequently sent off – but Palace won 3-2.

Ronnie Rooke took over as Palace manager for 1949/50.

For much more salutary reasons, Rooke certainly gained Palace some welcome if unaccustomed publicity. After his return from suspension, we slammed five past Exeter City on 17 December to win 5-3, then drew 4-4 at Ipswich on Christmas Eve with the player-manager scoring twice. The first two months of 1950 saw an excellent playing record of six victories and two draws, including a really fine 1-0 win at Notts County, where Fred Kurz's goal wrecked their unbeaten home record. The press dubbed Palace 'The Rooke Regiment' and there were some big crowds to see them play. Inevitably Rooke was our leading scorer this term with 21 League goals.

Certainly among the most memorable Palace displays in the entire season was the 6-0 rout of visiting Brighton on the second Saturday of February. Rooke had us ahead early on with a classic, long-range low drive from a pass by Ted Harding. A little after half an hour, Fred Kurz controlled a deflected shot by young winger Ray Howells and crashed the ball into the Albion net. Brighton attempted a rally after the break but outside right Billy Blackshaw broke clear and centred for Rooke to score a peach of a goal. With his back to the target, he controlled the cross, spun on his heel and then lobbed the ball over the goalkeeper and into the net. Sublime! It spelt 'finis' for Brighton's hopes and they realised that a rearguard action was required to limit further damage.

Ray Howells raced away and finished well, Rooke himself turned provider for another former Arsenal man, Charlie Chase, to volley home and Rooke completed his hat-trick from a Howells cross with nearly a quarter of an hour still to go.

SEASON: 1949/50

GROUND: Selhurst Park

MANAGER: Ronnie Rooke

LEAGUE/DIVISION: Football League Third Division (South)

FINAL POSITION: 7th

BIGGEST VICTORY: 6-0 *v.* Brighton & Hove Albion, 11 February 1950

HEAVIEST DEFEAT: 0-4 *v.* Northampton Town, 12 November 1949

FA CUP – ROUND ELIMINATED: 1st

LEAGUE CUP – ROUND ELIMINATED: –

FULL MEMBERS CUP – ROUND ELIMINATED: –

LEADING LEAGUE APPEARANCES (MAX: 42): 41 – J. Watson, 39 – R. Rooke

LEADING LEAGUE GOALSCORERS: 21 – R. Rooke, 10 – F. Kurz

1950/51

NEW BOARD, NEW PLAYERS, NEW MANAGERS... BUT PALACE HAVE THEIR WORST EVER SEASON

The origins of the disastrous affairs of Crystal Palace FC in season 1950/51 lay some six months before this term began in the approach in late January 1950 to a specially convened Palace board meeting by seven local businessmen with a view to taking over the already ailing club. They did so but, as 1950/51 would emphatically demonstrate, they 'made a real mess of things through [their] inexperience', to quote the most prominent member of the septet, Mr Arthur Wait, who, of course, was to become a key figure in Palace's climb through the divisions and our exhilarating rise to the top flight.

The summer of 1950 was a busy one at Selhurst Park, quite apart from all the administrative adjustments required by the takeover. First, Ronnie Rooke announced his decision to hang up his boots in order to concentrate upon his managerial role then, with the positive encouragement of the new board of directors, it must be said, he went out and spent the huge sum of nearly £30,000 on new players, invariably experienced men, but as their times at the Palace and later elsewhere would show, almost always past their best. The most expensive import was wing half Bill Whittaker from Huddersfield, who cost us £10,000. Les Stevens, a winger, came from Bradford for £7,000; Morris Jones, formerly a proven goal-scoring inside forward with Swindon, cost £4,000, as did Charlie Rundle, a centre forward from Tottenham, while defender George Smith cost £2,500 from Southampton.

The massive outlay proved utterly to no avail when Palace opened the season at home to Aldershot. We lost 0-2 and Rundle spent most of the game as a passenger after an early ankle injury. Everything continued to go wrong. We lost five of the first six matches, using seventeen players in the process, including Rooke himself, who returned to the side in a vain attempt to stem the tide, and it was obvious that Palace were going to suffer a most difficult season. By mid-November Palace were at the foot of the table with just 4 wins from 18 League matches and nine points: we had just lost six League games on the trot with an aggregate goal difference of 3-21!

Nevertheless, it was hoped that the FA Cup might offer some solace: over 24,000 fans turned up at fog-shrouded Selhurst Park for the first round tie against fourth-placed local rivals Millwall – only to see the game abandoned after little more than half an hour with the score still goal-less. In reality, that was something of a reprieve, because Millwall were clearly the better side.

Right: Arthur Wait, whose consortium took control of Crystal Palace FC in January 1950.

When the match was restaged the following Wednesday afternoon in bleak, wet conditions, all we could offer was a missed penalty and a last-minute consolation goal from Noel Kelly, after the Lions had powered their way to four strikes of their own without undue exertion. Misery was etched on the face of every Palace follower that day, and many of them had left long before we scored our goal. The implications were inevitable and severe: manager Ronnie Rooke was immediately dismissed, but our club continued to struggle for many years to come.

Palace's new board of directors decided to put two men into the manager's office: Fred Dawes, a great Palace favourite, and Charlie Slade, who had done some good work for us on the scouting side and was a respected coach. But both men were in a thankless, impossible situation. The task they had inherited was beyond redemption and things deteriorated in mid-February when it was announced that Dick Graham's back injury would prevent him from playing again.

Thus, Palace never even looked like getting off the bottom of the table. Our fans did not see a single home win in the last ten matches! No club had started 1950 with greater optimism than ours, but no club suffered keener disappointment.

SEASON: 1950/51

GROUND: Selhurst Park

MANAGER: Ronnie Rooke to 29 November 1950, then Fred Dawes and Charlie Slade

LEAGUE/DIVISION: Football League Third Division (South)

FINAL POSITION: 24th

BIGGEST VICTORY: 4-2 *v.* Newport County, 30 September 1950

HEAVIEST DEFEAT: 1-6 *v.* Nottingham Forest, 27 January 1951

FA CUP – ROUND ELIMINATED: 1st

LEAGUE CUP – ROUND ELIMINATED: –

FULL MEMBERS CUP – ROUND ELIMINATED: –

LEADING LEAGUE APPEARANCES (MAX: 46): 39 – W. Hanlon, 36 – E. Harding

LEADING LEAGUE GOALSCORERS: 5 – R. Rooke, 4 – N. Kelly, J. Thomas

1951/52

ANOTHER MANAGERIAL CHANGE BRINGS THIRD DIVISION (SOUTH) RESPECTABILITY

After the dreadful 1950/51 season the summer of 1951 witnessed an air of unease at Selhurst Park – along with a greatly reduced playing staff as the directors sought to recoup some of the massive outlay they had encouraged just twelve months earlier. Two useful new signings were made: these were George McGeachie, a wing half from Rochdale, who skippered the Palace for the first third of the season, and Les Devonshire, a winger from Chester, as Fred Dawes and Charlie Slade sought to steer the club into more settled waters. However, that would have been wishful thinking, for all too soon the Palace were in dire trouble again.

By mid-October we were just two points away from the foot of the table and the board of directors, implicitly admitting that their choice had been a huge mistake, decided that another change of management was necessary. Charlie Slade reverted to the job he did best, that of chief scout, while Fred Dawes' services were dispensed with completely. This was a quite disgraceful decision, certainly among the nastiest ever made at the Palace. It was unworthy of those who made it and so obviously the shabbiest possible treatment to as loyal a club servant as could be found anywhere in the game. It was also needlessly harsh. Thinking Palace fans at the time and subsequently have always recoiled from its bleak severity: after all, the main responsibility for the acute situation in which our club found itself at that time lay with the directors themselves – it was they who had given Ronnie Rooke *carte blanche* in the spending spree of summer 1950 that had backfired so spectacularly.

The man who took up the considerable challenge at Selhurst Park was Laurie Scott who, like Rooke and Butler before him, was a former Arsenal star. Scott was a polished, intelligent right-back and had represented England in seventeen consecutive internationals in the late 1940s. It had taken a five-figure fee to prise him away from Highbury, but he made his Palace debut before a crowd of around 21,000 for our home match against Ipswich Town on Saturday 20 October. Palace played really well, showing a confidence and class well above that expected of a club in the lowly position we occupied in the league table, and won more convincingly than even the 3-1 scoreline suggests, with our goals coming from Cam Burgess, who netted twice in the second half, having previously been involved in Fred Price's early opener.

Palace's star performer against Ipswich was actually the new player-manager's full-back colleague, Harry McDonald, who had joined us from non-league football in September 1950. His appearances in 1950/51 were intermittent, but by now he was an established feature of our defence and only George McGeachie played more League games for Palace than Harry this term. Harry was the perfect model for aspiring youngsters. He was neat and composed, strong and sturdy, but he possessed a turn of pace that could be exhilarating to watch and would frequently surprise his opposing winger. Harry remained Palace's first-choice at left-back for three-and-a-half seasons and made 146 senior appearances for us.

Burgess had arrived a month before Laurie Scott's appointment. He had been with Bolton and Chester but he came to Selhurst Park upon the recommendation of his former Sealand Road colleague Les Devonshire, and was to score some mightily useful goals for Crystal Palace. His most prolific spell this term was in November-December and began three weeks after the new boss made his debut, when he scored our brace in a salutary 2-5 defeat at Northampton. We lost at home to Reading but Cam was again on target for us, then he netted the goal that beat visiting Southend on 1 December. His pair down at fancied Bournemouth, netted with five minutes gone and five minutes to go, brought Mr Scott his first away win with the Palace and Cam hit two more a week later to secure a point from visiting Colchester and, even though Brighton beat us 2-1 at Selhurst Park on Christmas morning, Cam scored our goal. Nine goals from six games! By the end of the season he had equalled Ronnie Rooke's (then) post-war scoring record of 21 League goals – and Cam did so in just 22 matches!

Laurie Scott, Palace manager from October 1951, converses with Ron Brett, who died in a car crash in August 1962.

SEASON: 1951/52

GROUND: Selhurst Park

MANAGER: Fred Dawes and Charlie Slade until 11 October 1951, then Laurie Scott

LEAGUE/DIVISION: Football League Third Division (South)

FINAL POSITION: 19th

BIGGEST VICTORY: 4-0 *v.* Leyton Orient, 15 September 1951

HEAVIEST DEFEAT: 0-5 *v.* Plymouth Argyle, 22 August 1951

FA CUP – ROUND ELIMINATED: 1st

LEAGUE CUP – ROUND ELIMINATED: –

FULL MEMBERS CUP – ROUND ELIMINATED: –

LEADING LEAGUE APPEARANCES (MAX: 46): 46 – G. McGeachie, 40 – H. McDonald, F. Evans

LEADING LEAGUE GOALSCORERS: 21 – C. Burgess, 10 – F. Evans

1952/53

PALACE FIASCO IN THE FINCHLEY FOG

The 1952/53 season eventually turned out a much more positive one than its immediate predecessors. Bill Simpson, an inside left from Aston Villa, was the only new face in the team that crashed 1-4 at Brighton on the opening day, but another summer signing who would render the club valuable service was Cecil (nicknamed 'Archie' after the ventriloquist's doll of the period) Andrews from Portsmouth, a wing half. Soon to arrive were Bob Thomas from Fulham, able to play at centre or inside forward, Les Fell, a right winger from Charlton who had appeared in the Valiants' 1946 FA Cup final side and Colin Grimshaw, an inside forward or wing half from Arsenal.

However, in the early part of this season Palace had another bad time, although after Fell, Thomas and Grimshaw had joined us we began to improve considerably and Cam Burgess embarked upon a terrific run of goalscoring. Cam hit three hat-tricks in four matches and twelve goals in six games in October and November to pull the Palace away from the bottom of the table with a sequence unparalleled in terms of goals scored since the Second World War until Andy Johnson's brilliant efforts in the new millennium. One unique Palace victory in that 1952 run was the 6-3 win at Swindon on 1 November, when both Cam Burgess and Johnny Rainford secured hat-tricks! Unsurprisingly, Palace were twice in arrears and behind at half-time at the County Ground but our second-half display was awesome and of course quite unexpected. The scoreline had reached 3-3 by the hour but a Rainford header completed the youngster's hat-trick and two more from the swarthy little Scouse goalscoring machine wrapped things up perfectly for us.

Regrettably though, Palace's momentum slowed. We had another lean period between December and mid-March and this included the disastrous and now legendary defeat in the FA Cup by non-league Finchley. The original fixture was abandoned because of fog, with Finchley leading 3-1 but poor Palace could take no advantage of this reprieve and were unable to prevent the amateurs from repeating the dose when the match was replayed four days later. It was all hugely embarrassing.

Palace's troubles had begun before the first match had even started! Bob Thomas and Les Devonshire got lost in the north London fog and had to phone the Finchley ground to admit that they were stranded over at Park Royal! Palace fans who were at Finchley were thus startled to hear a broadcast appeal for any of our players who were there to report to our dressing room, and Bob Bishop deputised for Thomas because he was able to wear Devonshire's boots. If that

Bob Thomas.

was farcical, so was the game! Visibility deteriorated so badly that the linesmen had to stand ten yards or more inside the pitch in an attempt to follow the play and the referee had no alternative but to abandon proceedings after sixty-two minutes. Palace and their fans were highly relieved – but not only did poor Bob Bishop never have another chance to play in our first team (though he subsequently became a director at the club), there was to be a final, awful twist when the amateurs despatched us in the second game, taking their chances and repeating the original scoreline.

These were certainly tough times in which to support Crystal Palace, and the spectre of a third application for re-election in five years began to loom, but a splendid revival began at Northampton on a snow-covered pitch on which Cam Burgess hit a twenty-nine-minute hat-trick.

Bill Simpson and Bob Thomas began to score regularly, with Simpson now playing at centre forward and relishing the service provided by Les Fell. Another regular in the side over the last two months of 1952/53 was goalkeeper Roy Bailey, who would go on to earn himself a permanent niche in our annals. By the end of the term Palace were a match for anyone: in the last game of the season, played on the Friday evening before the FA Cup final, we beat the divisional champions Bristol Rovers in the most terrible conditions, after fully twenty-four hours of continuous rain.

Wally Hanlon.

SEASON: 1952/53

GROUND: Selhurst Park

MANAGER: Laurie Scott

LEAGUE/DIVISION: Football League Third Division (South)

FINAL POSITION: 13th

BIGGEST VICTORY: 4-1 *v.* Walsall, 11 October 1952

HEAVIEST DEFEAT: 0-5 *v.* Bristol City, 13 September 1952

FA CUP – ROUND ELIMINATED: 2nd

LEAGUE CUP – ROUND ELIMINATED: –

FULL MEMBERS CUP – ROUND ELIMINATED: –

LEADING LEAGUE APPEARANCES (MAX: 46): 37 – R. Thomas, H. Briggs, 34 – R. George

LEADING LEAGUE GOALSCORERS: 19 – C. Burgess, 11 – W. Simpson

1953/54

ANOTHER LOWLY FINISH BUT FLOODLIGHTS ARE INSTALLED AT SELHURST PARK

Palace carried the excellent form they had shown in the closing stages of 1952/53 over into the first part of 1953/54, which remains unique to this day because we began our fixtures on a Thursday. We drew 2-2 at home to Northampton. Without ever causing the least anxiety to the division's pacesetters at the head of the table, Palace did at least have a modestly successful first half of the season, although even then we had our occasional falls from grace, like the 0-6 defeat at Northampton at the end of October and the humiliation of another FA Cup exit on a non-league ground, this time at Great Yarmouth Town.

But then, in 1954, Palace deteriorated beyond recognition and finished the term only one place above the re-election positions. An important new signing for 1953/54 had been Jess Willard from Brighton, a wing half who occasionally played at centre forward and who became a great servant of the Palace club as coach and scout once his playing days were over. Ernie Randall, a useful centre forward from Chelsea, scored regularly for Palace early in the season, but his career was blighted by a broken leg in the Christmas morning encounter against Norwich City (1-0), and in his absence our decline really set in.

In retrospect, undoubtedly the most interesting feature of the season for Palace fans was the installation of floodlighting at Selhurst Park. Compared with today's sophisticated pylons, those original lighting arrangements had an almost 'Heath Robinson' appearance: they were in clusters of twelve lamps with four groups erected on the main stand roof, and four mounted at the top of poles along the open terrace opposite, where the Arthur Wait Stand now is, with cables looped between them.

Palace arranged an imaginative series of floodlit friendlies against First and Second Division clubs and foreign opposition: these were usually well patronised by Palace fans, for whom the games provided welcome variation from the routine fare of the Third Division (South), from which of course only one club could gain promotion each season and where the fixture lists had begun to have a rather stale look about them.

The new Palace lights were officially opened by the club chairman, Mr David Harris, before the first of the floodlit games. Chelsea travelled over from west London on Monday 28 September 1953 and a superb match delighted a crowd of 17,082. Jim Lewis put Chelsea ahead in the fiftieth minute but midway through the second half Ernie Randall and Albert Foulds

Right: Harry Briggs was the skipper of Palace's 1953/54 side.

got a simultaneous headed touch to a corner from Les Fell to provide Palace with the draw our spirited performance deserved.

Without Ernie Randall to lead our forward line, Palace had to rely heavily upon Bob Thomas and, to his great credit, the veteran did all that was expected of him, finishing with 20 League strikes from his 45 appearances. In early February manager Laurie Scott signed a cultured inside forward, Tommy Tilston, from Wrexham to assist in these matters. It was intriguing how the signing came about: Wrexham had been engaged in an extended second round FA Cup tie with Brighton, which had gone to a second replay – in those days these were invariably staged on neutral territory, and this one was played at Selhurst Park just before Christmas. Wrexham won, Tilston took the eye of the Palace boss and signed for us six weeks later.

Another forward player of interest seen in our colours in the last few weeks of 1953/54 was Keith Morton, who was one of the last amateur players to appear for our club. Keith played at centre forward in the final five games and was on target three times.

SEASON: 1953/54

GROUND: Selhurst Park

MANAGER: Laurie Scott

LEAGUE/DIVISION: Football League Third Division (South)

FINAL POSITION: 22nd

BIGGEST VICTORY: 4-1 *v.* Torquay United, 7 November 1953

HEAVIEST DEFEAT: 0-7 *v.* Exeter City, 9 January 1954

FA CUP – ROUND ELIMINATED: 1st

LEAGUE CUP – ROUND ELIMINATED: –

FULL MEMBERS CUP – ROUND ELIMINATED: –

LEADING LEAGUE APPEARANCES (MAX: 46): 45 – R. Bailey, R. Thomas, 43 – H. Briggs

LEADING LEAGUE GOALSCORERS: 20 – R. Thomas, 10 – E. Randall

1954/55

ANOTHER NEW MANAGER, BUT THIS TIME A NEW POLICY TOO

Palace boss Laurie Scott could probably see his tenure of the managerial position at Selhurst Park slipping away from him in the early weeks of the 1954/55 season, and once Palace had lost 1-7 at Watford in a Tuesday evening game, his departure was virtually inevitable. We lost 0-3 at Aldershot at the end of the following week, then again 1-4 at Bournemouth (where our single goal was from an 'Archie' Andrews penalty). Our opening ten matches had thus yielded one (home) win and just six points. Following a goal-less draw at home to Swindon on Saturday 25 September the board of directors decided to remedy the situation. Mr Scott was relieved of his post and a statement was inserted into the programme for the next match, the return fixture against Bournemouth on Wednesday 29 September, when Palace recorded their second win of the season, with newly signed winger David Grieve and Jimmy Belcher netting for us before half-time. Bournemouth replied ten minutes into the second half but could not force an equaliser.

The managerial vacancy was filled some two weeks later and the new incumbent, Mr Cyril Spiers, was introduced to the supporters via the programme for the floodlit friendly match against Clyde on 13 October. Spiers had been a fine goalkeeper in his day for Aston Villa, Spurs and Wolves, and had a distinguished managerial record at Cardiff City and, briefly, Norwich. He was a quiet, hardworking, fatherly sort of man and his speciality was his ability to spot a youngster, induce him to sign for his League club and then groom him, perhaps over several years, for the limelight. This was a complete shift in the policy of the Palace club, for since the Second World War, and long before it, we had imported most of our players from other outfits of a similar standing to our own.

Obviously, such a policy could not be expected to pay immediate dividends. Nor did it at Selhurst Park. Palace seldom appeared likely to have to apply for re-election but we finished only four points clear of the pair who did. There were a few bright spots to the season to enliven the supporters' hopes for the future and the most praiseworthy among these were a 2-2 draw secured at highly placed Southampton on Saturday 23 April in our last away game, through 'Archie' Andrews and Jimmy Belcher goals either side of half-time, and a single-goal victory over Brighton at Selhurst Park on the Saturday before Easter when Peter Berry beat the Albion 'keeper from twenty-five yards and from a difficult angle in the seventieth minute in a game in which both sides spurned many chances.

Right: Manager Cyril Spiers.

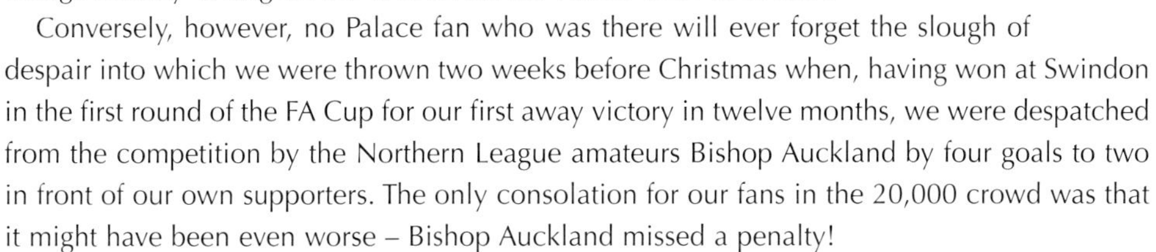

It was Palace's misfortune to have to play champions-elect Bristol City twice in our final five games due to a rearrangement required for the match at Ashton Gate, and the (probably inevitable) two defeats in the last fortnight of the season simply came when City were powering to the title, then extending their considerable advantage at the top of the table.

Our Third Division (South) season did at least finish with a home victory, over Norwich City, to ensure that we avoided having to seek another re-election. An early 'Archie' Andrews penalty helped to settle the Palace side and Jimmy Belcher converted a sweet Tommy Tilston pass soon after the interval: Norwich only rallied late on and though Sammy Chung hit our woodwork the Palace were in control.

Conversely, however, no Palace fan who was there will ever forget the slough of despair into which we were thrown two weeks before Christmas when, having won at Swindon in the first round of the FA Cup for our first away victory in twelve months, we were despatched from the competition by the Northern League amateurs Bishop Auckland by four goals to two in front of our own supporters. The only consolation for our fans in the 20,000 crowd was that it might have been even worse – Bishop Auckland missed a penalty!

SEASON: 1954/55

GROUND: Selhurst Park

MANAGER: Laurie Scott until 25 September 1954, then Cyril Spiers from October 1954

LEAGUE/DIVISION: Football League Third Division (South)

FINAL POSITION: 20th

BIGGEST VICTORY: 4-1 *v.* Walsall, 12 March 1955

HEAVIEST DEFEAT: 1-7 *v.* Watford, 7 September 1954

FA CUP – ROUND ELIMINATED: 2nd

LEAGUE CUP – ROUND ELIMINATED: –

FULL MEMBERS CUP – ROUND ELIMINATED: –

LEADING LEAGUE APPEARANCES (MAX: 46): 41 – C. Andrews, 37 – R. Bailey

LEADING LEAGUE GOALSCORERS: 12 – J. Belcher, 7 – C. Andrews

1955/56

ANOTHER RE-ELECTION SEASON

The shift in policy towards a youth-orientated playing staff continued at Crystal Palace in 1955/56, but this season was a really trying one for the club and its fans because, while the youngsters in our colours could play most attractively at times, we finished the season next to bottom and had to seek re-election for the third time.

The contrast in the level of our performances could be highlighted in the first three months of the season. It is doubtful whether a Cyril Spiers Palace side ever performed better than the one that travelled over to Loftus Road to play Queens Park Rangers on Monday evening 5 September. Perhaps playing away from Selhurst Park actually helped our lads; maybe Rangers were over-confident. But whatever the catalyst was, that Palace team was quite superb and far too good for Rangers, so that, under captain Tommy Tilston's inspirational direction, we romped to a 3-0 victory. Of course Palace have won at that venue since then – but never by such a margin! To this day it remains statistically our best ever showing at Rangers' headquarters. The skipper had us ahead in only the third minute after Ron Brett and Mike Deakin had opened up the home defence. Jimmy Belcher hit a post and Peter Berry had a shot chested off the line with the goalkeeper beaten. It was all over early in the second half when Brett himself slammed home a Tilston cross on the half-volley then, four minutes later and with Rangers still reeling, Brett fired in again after a similar combination.

Yet, in direct contrast to that wonderful show, we were quite woeful in our first round FA Cup tie against Southampton. A dreary scoreless draw at Selhurst Park required a replay at The Dell, where we lost without so much as looking as if we might seriously contest the matter.

Such frustrations were extremely hard to bear at the time, but in retrospect it is possible to see that Mr Spiers' efforts were beginning to come to fruition, even if there was no tangible evidence there and then. By the conclusion of this season Mr Spiers had produced useful strikers in Mike Deakin, Barry Pierce, George Cooper, flame-haired Jimmy Murray and the ill-fated Ron Brett. He had moulded Jimmy Belcher into a mature and cultured wing half alongside another fabulous discovery in Terry Long, and had found two promising wingers who really should have made more of their careers, Bernard Harrison and Harry Gunning. Best of all, Johnny Byrne, one of the finest players produced at the Palace, was already on the club books and appearing for the reserves.

But, invaluable as the combined contribution of these young men to Crystal Palace was ultimately to prove, that was in the future. The actuality of the last two months of 1955/56 was grim. We began March with a four-point margin over the bottom two clubs and produced

Right: 'Archie' Andrews made 19 appearances for Palace in the Third Division (South) in 1955/56.

another fine away performance to beat Coventry 3-1 at Highfield Road, but we then lost four matches in a row before winning at Colchester on Easter Saturday. But, by the time Reading had completed a holiday double over us on Easter Monday our lead had shrunk to two points and Millwall had a game in hand.

We contrived to beat Norwich at Selhurst Park with late goals from George Cooper and Peter Berry lighting up a dour, scrambling affair, but then lost three more matches in a row, so that even after beating Newport County 1-0 in our last home game our prospects were far from clear. In the end a two-goal defeat at Shrewsbury in our rearranged final match ensured that our fate was sealed and that it would be necessary for us to join Swindon in the dispiriting re-election process.

SEASON: 1955/56

GROUND: Selhurst Park

MANAGER: Cyril Spiers

LEAGUE/DIVISION: Football League Third Division (South)

FINAL POSITION: 23rd

BIGGEST VICTORY: 3-0 *v.* Torquay United, 31 August 1955, 3-0 *v.* QPR, 5 September 1955

HEAVIEST DEFEAT: 0-8 *v.* Leyton Orient, 12 November 1955

FA CUP – ROUND ELIMINATED: 1st

LEAGUE CUP – ROUND ELIMINATED: –

FULL MEMBERS CUP – ROUND ELIMINATED: –

LEADING LEAGUE APPEARANCES (MAX: 46): 41 – P. Berry, 38 – M. Deakin

LEADING LEAGUE GOALSCORERS: 8 – M. Deakin, 7 – T. Tilston

1956/57

PALACE SHOW MODEST LEAGUE IMPROVEMENT AND HOST A THRILLING CUP-TIE

Palace fans of the mid-1950s were a stoical bunch! The frustrations and disappointments of 1955/56 certainly carried over into 1956/57. It took us eight games before we recorded our first win of the season and we were always in the bottom third of the divisional table although, as in the previous term, the young Palace side proved its potential on isolated occasions, like the 4-1 win secured at Watford on Saturday 3 November.

This victory was certainly Palace's best League performance of 1956/57 and was owed in large part to our wingers, Peter Berry and Bernard Harrison, who were repeatedly able to turn the Hornets' defence from their flanks. Jimmy Murray netted twice in the first half and Jimmy Belcher and Barry Pierce scored in the second period for a convincing win — but, typically at this time, Palace lost their next match, 0-1 at home to Shrewsbury.

A further hint of the profitable outworking of Cyril Spiers' long-term policy was seen when two noteworthy debuts were made on the same afternoon by youthful players who were to have important roles in Palace's future destiny. Vic Rouse in goal and Johnny Byrne at centre forward lined up in a Palace League side for the first time on Saturday 13 October when Palace hosted a match against Swindon Town (0-0).

Palace's biggest gate for a League game (22,627) was at the final match of the season. This brought Torquay United to Selhurst Park on Wednesday evening 1 May, with a large contingent of their own fans for, if they could win, they would gain promotion to the Second Division. The supporters of both sides witnessed a splendid game, with a draw a fair result. Barry Pierce put Palace ahead seven minutes after half-time but the men from Devon equalised eight minutes later.

As this 1956/57 season progressed, Palace utilised an interesting attacking policy that was many years ahead of its time, by deploying Pierce and Mike Deakin as twin centre forwards. It was probably seen at its most effective when Barry notched a hat-trick in a Selhurst Park FA Cup replay against Brentford to take us into the third round for the first time in nine years. Indeed, the club and its fans were extremely relieved to have reached even the second round! A first round pairing with Walthamstow Avenue caused no little anxiety, even though we had the benefit of home advantage, given our previous three seasons' defeats by non-league opponents! However, the amateurs were safely overcome and our young team played extremely well to

Peter Berry is about to net Palace's opening goal in our 2-0 win over Plymouth on 26 January 1957.

bring Brentford to Selhurst Park for the replay, since the Bees were among the strongest teams in our division at that time.

So appealing was the match that it drew a crowd of 23,137 – among Palace's post-war best at that time – and the thrill-packed clash lives in the memory to this day. Brentford grabbed an early lead when Jimmy Towers converted a Ron Peplow cross but Palace were on terms midway through the first half when Barry Pierce headed home a centre from Peter Berry. The Bees were ahead again twelve minutes later when Towers became the supplier for George Francis, but Palace responded well and levelled again, three minutes before half-time.

The second half may have been goal-less, but the action was thrilling and intense as Ray Potter and Gerry Cakebread made magnificent and athletic saves. In extra time Brentford pressed strongly and drew two more fine saves from Potter early in those proceedings, but the contest was won and lost in the 102nd minute. Bernard Harrison collected a loose ball, in the middle of the park and streaked away down his flank. He beat Croydon-born Ian Dargie and centred to where Barry Pierce was waiting unmarked to deliver a perfect, fierce, downward header into the bottom corner of the net for a classic finale.

SEASON: 1956/57

GROUND: Selhurst Park

MANAGER: Cyril Spiers

LEAGUE/DIVISION: Football League Third Division (South)

FINAL POSITION: 20th

BIGGEST VICTORY: 4-1 *v.* Watford, 3 November 1956, 4-1 *v.* Norwich City, 15 December 1956

HEAVIEST DEFEAT: 1-4 *v.* Gillingham, 6 October 1956

FA CUP – ROUND ELIMINATED: 3rd

LEAGUE CUP – ROUND ELIMINATED: –

FULL MEMBERS CUP – ROUND ELIMINATED: –

LEADING LEAGUE APPEARANCES (MAX: 46): 46 – L. Choules, 45 – J. Edwards

LEADING LEAGUE GOALSCORERS: 16 – M. Deakin, 10 – B. Pierce

1957/58

PALACE BECOME FOUNDER MEMBERS OF THE FOURTH DIVISION

There had been initiatives since the early 1950s for the formation of national Third and Fourth Divisions from the then-existing northern and southern sections of the Third Division, and it was eventually decided to implement this at the end of 1957/58. The Palace club had been to the fore of these initiatives and our chairman in 1956, Mr John Dunster, had put the case on behalf of the lower-division sides to the Football League at its annual meeting in the summer of that year. The means of determining which clubs would form the new Fourth Division was brutally clear: those who finished 1957/58 in the upper half of their regional section would play the following term in the Third Division – and those who did not would found the new league basement, the Fourth Division.

Like all the Third Division clubs Palace faced this prospect with high hopes of finishing above halfway, but it was an all-too-familiar tale that evolved. In spite of occasional excellent results – there was none better this season than the 3-0 whipping of Plymouth, who were complete with the expensive Jimmy Gauld from Everton (later jailed for four years as a ringleader of a match-fixing betting syndicate in 1964) on 26 October, which took the Palace into the upper half of the table for the first and only time – we could never string together more than two consecutive victories in the whole season. Similarly, in the FA Cup two meritorious wins, at Margate (3-2) and at home to Southampton (1-0) put us all in good humour for a third round tie when Ipswich would come to Selhurst Park, but our poor finishing and a superb display by our former goalkeeper Roy Bailey nullified our chances of further progress and we lost 0-1.

By the middle of March 1958 the situation confronting the Palace was starkly clear: there were six weeks of the season remaining and we had a dozen games left to play, but we were down in sixteenth place with considerable leeway to be made up if we were to avoid becoming founder members of the Fourth Division. Manager Spiers had broken his youth-policy rules and brought additional experience to leaven his squad of young men when he acquired winger Tony Collins from Watford, but it was now obvious that something else was needed. Mr Spiers sought to supply that elusive ingredient with one more signing, his last for the club.

He obtained the distinguished, cultured expertise of Johnny McNichol, the Scottish inside left from Chelsea's championship winning side of three years earlier. Johnny's arrival was a master stroke, yet it made a compelling argument for a much earlier blending of youth and experience. He scored upon his debut against Port Vale at Selhurst Park on 13 March to secure our first win

Johnny McNichol scores on his Palace debut against Port Vale on 15 March 1958.

in six games and altogether he found the net on seven occasions in those last twelve matches. It seemed as if we might still manage to creep into the top half of the table by the final reckoning – but Johnny's signing had been delayed just that little bit too long. Palace lost the next two matches, at Brighton (one of Johnny's former clubs) and at Watford, only to win the next home game, against Exeter City. But two Easter draws against Colchester followed by home and away defeats by Queens Park Rangers within the space of rather less than seventy-two hours – and that in spite of being in front on each occasion – made it certain that we were doomed.

Time had run out for manager Cyril Spiers. It was his misfortune that the time at his disposal was foreshortened by the coming of the make-or-break season of 1957/58, for perhaps another twelve months would have produced a different outcome. However, the hard fact was that another post-war manager had failed to bring the Palace any success and we were in the new Fourth Division. Mr Spiers saw the situation for what it was and left soon after the season ended.

SEASON: 1957/58

GROUND: Selhurst Park

MANAGER: Cyril Spiers

LEAGUE/DIVISION: Football League Third Division (South)

FINAL POSITION: 14th

BIGGEST VICTORY: 4-1 *v.* Swindon Town, 12 October 1957, 4-1 *v.* Walsall, 11 February 1958

HEAVIEST DEFEAT: 0-4 *v.* Port Vale, 2 November 1957

FA CUP – ROUND ELIMINATED: 3rd

LEAGUE CUP – ROUND ELIMINATED: –

FULL MEMBERS CUP – ROUND ELIMINATED: –

LEADING LEAGUE APPEARANCES (MAX: 46): 46 – T. Long, 42 – V. Rouse

LEADING LEAGUE GOALSCORERS: 17 – G. Cooper, 9 – P. Berry

1958/59

NEW MANAGER, NEW OPPONENTS... BUT NO PROGRESS

The appearance of Crystal Palace FC in the new national Fourth Division for 1958/59 was admittedly a disappointment to everyone who had the club's well-being at heart, but it was not without its interest too, for the club and the fans were meeting new opponents, visiting new grounds and renewing old rivalries. Crystal Palace met nine clubs for the first time under League auspices in the new Fourth Division in 1958/59: Barrow, Carlisle, Chester, Crewe, Darlington, Hartlepool, Southport, Workington and York. We renewed acquaintances with Port Vale, who had left the southern section of the Third Division back in 1951 to play in the north, Oldham and Gateshead, whom we had last met in 1924/25 in the Second Division (the latter as South Shields) and, longest of all, Bradford Park Avenue, whom we had played in just one Football League season in 1921/22.

George Smith was Palace's new manager. He had been appointed in the summer of 1958, charged with the task of lifting Palace out of the new basement division. He was a tough disciplinarian, who had gained a reputation as a player and a coach, having previously been in charge of Eastbourne and Sutton United before accepting the position at Selhurst Park, and he vowed before matters got underway for 1958/59 that if he did not gain promotion for the Palace within two years, he would resign. It quickly became apparent that it was not going to happen at the first try! That said, Palace began the season in handsome and comprehensive style!

Season 1958/59 began on Saturday 23 August when we were favoured with a home match against Crewe Alexandra, and the visitors gave most of the crowd of 13,551 a blast of healthy reality within two minutes by opening the scoring! Thankfully however, from that point and apart from a few brief, isolated moments, the Palace dominated the proceedings and were able to romp to a 6-2 win. The game became a personal triumph for the Palace centre forward Mike Deakin, who was making his first appearance for nine months after a major cartilage operation, and he notched a superb first-half hat-trick in considerably less than half an hour. And there was another hat-trick for the Palace fans to savour that afternoon. This one was provided by Johnny Byrne, still only nineteen years old, but already beginning to demonstrate the prowess that would lead him to stardom and help lift the Palace out of the Fourth Division.

Mike Deakin watches Johnny Byrne tangle with Crewe goalkeeper Jerry Lowery during Palace's first ever Fourth Division game (6-2).

Unfortunately, despite such a rampant start, Palace seldom threatened to take one of the four promotion places that are offered from the bottom division and we finished seventh, six points adrift of Shrewsbury Town, the club in the fourth promotion place.

An important addition to Palace's playing strength had been made in mid-season when Roy Summersby signed for us from neighbouring Millwall. Roy netted on his Palace debut, at Walsall on 13 December where Palace won 2-0. Our other scorer that day was Johnny Byrne, and the pair would develop an invaluable, intuitive partnership that would yield a rich dividend for Palace in the years ahead. However, in this 1958/59 season, while Roy scored 9 goals from his 25 Fourth Division appearances for us, he was playing more as a provider for Byrne and Mike Deakin, who established a new Palace post-war scoring record with his 23 strikes, which surpassed the efforts of Ronnie Rooke and Cam Burgess earlier in the decade.

Palace's best performances were reserved for cup competitions. In the FA Cup we reached the third round, but lost bravely to Second Division promotion candidates Sheffield United at Bramall Lane, while in the Southern Floodlit Cup we had a stirring final tie at Selhurst Park against Arsenal on Monday 27 April 1959. A crowd of 32,384 saw Mel Charles score a fine winning goal after Johnny Byrne had hit a marvellous equaliser with ten minutes to go.

There was honour and distinction for one Palace player in this season when goalkeeper Vic Rouse was selected to play for the full Welsh international side in their Home International Championship match against Northern Ireland in Belfast on 22 April 1959, and thus became the first international player from the Fourth Division. Wales lost 1-4 but Vic performed creditably, producing several fine saves and preventing his side from taking a really heavy beating.

SEASON: 1958/59

GROUND: Selhurst Park

MANAGER: George Smith

LEAGUE/DIVISION: Football League Fourth Division

FINAL POSITION: 7th

BIGGEST VICTORY: 6-2 *v.* Crewe Alexandra, 23 August 1958

HEAVIEST DEFEAT: 0-5 *v.* Bradford Park Avenue, 7 February 1959

FA CUP – ROUND ELIMINATED: 3rd

LEAGUE CUP – ROUND ELIMINATED: –

FULL MEMBERS CUP – ROUND ELIMINATED: –

LEADING LEAGUE APPEARANCES (MAX: 46): 46 – T. Long, J. McNichol, 45 – J. Byrne, A. Noakes

LEADING LEAGUE GOALSCORERS: 23 – M. Deakin, 17 – J. Byrne

1959/60

ONE HUGE VICTORY BUT SEVERAL EMBARRASSING DEFEATS AND STILL NO PROGRESS

George Smith found 1959/60 no more rewarding than his first season in charge at Selhurst Park, 1958/59, had been, and our overall progress was very similar to that of twelve months before. In fairness to Mr Smith it should be pointed out that potentially his best signing for Crystal Palace, that of Dave Sexton, formerly of West Ham and Brighton, was prevented by injury from appearing in little more than half the games due to injury. However, even with Dave in the Palace side we had lost the four matches prior to the only truly memorable feature of this season, which was the 9-0 annihilation of Barrow on Saturday 10 October 1959.

The match itself drew a modest crowd of some 9,500 and, writing as one of them, none of us had the least inkling that we might be about to witness Palace's biggest-ever victory in League or major cup matches. The occasion was obviously a personal triumph for Palace forward Roy Summersby, who notched four of our goals – the first time since the Second World War that a Palace man had hit more than three goals in a game.

However, the scoring was opened by left winger Ray Colfar, a 1958 signing from Sutton United and a clever, wily character whose displays gained the respect of the Palace fans of the time but, surprisingly, is an often forgotten former player at our club. Ray netted midway through the first half with a twenty-yard drive following a sweeping, incisive long pass from Dave Sexton, and it became apparent a quarter of an hour later that Barrow could be in for a torrid afternoon when Palace's Eire star, right winger Johnny Gavin, netted direct from a corner. Roy Summersby then collected his first two goals within a couple of minutes of each other as half-time approached, and when Ray Colfar hit his second early in the second half, it was clear to everyone that Barrow's defences had not only been breached but were on the point of being overrun. After the hour Summersby scored two more goals in quick succession, the first going in off a post, the second from a penalty for handball. Johnny Byrne had an effort disallowed before he converted an unselfish pass from Colfar and then rounded matters off in the penultimate minute with a low drive past the dispirited goalkeeper.

It actually got even better for the Palace and their fans. Four days later we played a floodlit friendly against a Caribbean XI and won 11-1! But then we contrived to put the season into true

Right: Manager George Smith.

perspective by losing at Aldershot the following Saturday afternoon. Thus, it will come as no surprise to any modern-day reader to learn that Palace actually spent most of this 1959/60 season hovering around the middle of the table. True, we did manage to improve somewhat in the early spring, but while we gained 1-0 victories at Chester in mid-February and in the Barrow return two weeks later, we were also held to draws at Selhurst Park by Southport, Aldershot and Gateshead to put our prospects into true perspective. Then Palace went to Rochdale on 26 March and lost 0-4 to a side that included our former skipper Jack Edwards and winger Tony Collins. Frank Lord, later to be a Palace coach under Malcolm Allison, was at centre forward for the 'Dale and scored two of their goals. And then that Spotland defeat was immediately followed by a 0-1 home reverse by Workington, so it is not difficult, even all these years later, to understand why the closing weeks of 1959/60 were pretty low-key ones at Selhurst Park.

As the term wound its way to its inglorious conclusion and it became apparent that Palace were doomed to spend at least one more season in the League basement, manager George Smith kept his word and quietly departed from the Palace scene.

SEASON: 1959/60

GROUND: Selhurst Park

MANAGER: George Smith

LEAGUE/DIVISION: Football League Fourth Division

FINAL POSITION: 8th

BIGGEST VICTORY: 9-0 *v.* Barrow, 10 October 1959

HEAVIEST DEFEAT: 1-7 *v.* Notts County, 2 January 1960

FA CUP – ROUND ELIMINATED: 3rd

LEAGUE CUP – ROUND ELIMINATED: –

FULL MEMBERS CUP – ROUND ELIMINATED: –

LEADING LEAGUE APPEARANCES (MAX: 46): 46 – T. Long, J. McNichol, R. Summersby, 45 – V. Rouse

LEADING LEAGUE GOALSCORERS: 16 – J. Byrne, 15 – R. Summersby

1960/61

PALACE GAIN PROMOTION AT LAST

The Palace directors did not have far to search for a successor to outgoing manager George Smith. Smith's assistant since 1958 had been Arthur Rowe, the former and famous Tottenham and England centre half and one of the top thinkers in the game. He was an experienced manager too, for in the late 1940s and early 1950s he had transformed Spurs from Second Division mediocrity to champions of that division and followed up by immediately winning the Football League title in 1950/51 with cultured, flowing football.

The Palace board had sought Rowe's services in 1958, but he had not been physically strong enough at that time to accept full responsibility. Now, on 15 April 1960, Arthur took up the challenge presented at Selhurst Park – and took the Palace to promotion for the first time in forty years with attractive, polished play, thus setting the Club on the road to glory.

The only close-season signing was that of Ron Heckman, a blond, fast-raiding winger from Millwall, well known to London soccer fans. Palace's 110 League goals in 1960/61 were due in no small part to the efforts of this man, whose 14 goals from 42 appearances set up a post-war scoring record for a winger at our Club (that only David Hopkin has bettered) and those of Johnny Gavin over at outside right. However, Mr Rowe also made an astute signing early in October when, with several Palace forwards injured, he secured his former Spur Dennis Uphill from Watford. Uphill was a strong, burly centre forward, well suited to life in the lower divisions, and took a lot of the physical pressure off Johnny Byrne to play a laudable part in the Palace success.

Our first match of the 1960/61 season had the Palace patrons positively purring with satisfaction as our side, adopting Rowe's famous 'push and run' tactic, put on a fabulous display to smash visiting Accrington Stanley 9-2. This stunning success was immediately followed by a double over Darlington and a 5-1 win from a rain-interrupted match at Doncaster. Palace thus had a superb base from which to launch a promotion bid, but lowly Hartlepool pulled a surprise by holding us 2-2 at Selhurst Park – and then we came up against Peterborough United, in their first season in the League, home and away inside five days. They trimmed us to size 0-2 at Selhurst to push us off the top of the table and at London Road we were well beaten 1-4 in a terrific match, which left us outside the top four promotion places altogether.

It was in the late autumn that Palace responded. Between 28 September, when Palace walloped Southport 5-0 at Selhurst Park and Johnny Byrne hit a second four-goal haul of the season, and 29 October, when we returned with both points from Northampton (who were strong promotion contenders themselves and finished the term just one place below the Palace) after beating the Cobblers 2-1 in a stirring encounter, Palace secured six victories with only one defeat.

Len Choules had come into the side for the Southport game, but it was after the Monday evening 2-5 crushing at tearaway Stockport County that Mr Rowe signed Dennis Uphill, and the burly striker netted a brace on his Palace debut when we beat Barrow 4-2 at Selhurst Park. Then a 2-1 success at Gillingham in a rare southern away game put us back on the top of the table with just over a third of the season's fixtures completed.

Our run came to an end in November at Oldham, which has seldom proved a happy ground for Palace teams, although Palace had scorched to a two-goal interval lead at Boundary Park with Ron Heckman on target both times. Oldham roared back in the second half and were winning 4-2 before Johnny Byrne scored a late but unavailing third. However, the Palace did not allow this defeat to deflect them from their intentions and perhaps their most important away victory of the season was secured when they travelled to York on 10 December to meet the highly placed and aspiring Minstermen, who were the only club in our division with an unbeaten home record. Coming after three goal-less Palace games, including our two FA Cup ties with Watford, this was a particularly testing fixture against dangerous opponents. The game was somewhat dour and certainly tense until we broke the deadlock when George Petchey chipped a delightful opener. Then, with Roy Summersby playing as a man inspired throughout the second half, and after York had hit our crossbar, Johnny Byrne sent Dennis Uphill away. The big man bustled his way to the byline, then crossed for Ron Heckman to crack home our second goal.

The great Arthur Rowe, who set Crystal Palace on the road to glory.

Jim Mercer's celebrated cartoon depicting Palace's 9-2 rout of Accrington Stanley on the opening day of 1960/61.

Palace then stroked their sophisticated way through the rest of December with three more wins and a draw, but received a nasty jolt upon their visit to Chester (whose former Sealand Road ground often proved a graveyard for our teams) on 7 January. We appeared a little overconfident, spurned several early chances, fell behind and eventually disintegrated to lose 0-3 in some disarray. But, as previously, Palace responded well. We won the next game, another away match, this time at distant Hartlepool, and showed some character in doing so, for we trailed after twenty-five minutes before eventually running out 4-2 winners.

Our next four home fixtures all yielded full reward, as did away matches at Mansfield and Barrow, but in early March we really did begin to falter and cause our fans no little anxiety. The precise reasons for this are not discernible but, by now, Palace were very much a team in the public eye and perhaps the clamour even then of the media had begun to turn a few of the players' heads or to distract them. We lost four games in a row in March for the only time in the entire campaign, going down at third-placed and promotion-bound Bradford Park Avenue, at home to a bogey side in fourth-placed Northampton, at humble Aldershot and then, in front of a massive 37,774 crowd – the highest ever in the League's lowest division, and surely never to be exceeded – 0-2 on Good Friday afternoon to Millwall at Selhurst Park.

These lapses allowed Peterborough to skip in front of us again but, twenty-four hours after the Millwall defeat, we got back to winning ways with a 2-1 victory over visiting Oldham, with Johnny Byrne our inspiration and the scorer of two sweet goals. We avenged the Millwall result precisely at The Den, when Ron Heckman notched what he described as 'the best goal I've ever scored' against his former club on the half hour; then, seven minutes later, he supplied the cross from which outside right Tom Barnett netted the second.

We slipped to a single penalty-goal defeat at Workington but by mid-April three of our remaining four games were at home and it was only necessary to secure a point from one of them to ensure at least promotion, even though the bigger prize of the championship was beyond our reach. Nearly 20,000 fans turned out for the first of these, against Aldershot, piquancy being added because the Shots included Alan Woan and another former Palace goalscorer in Mike Deakin, and of course we wanted revenge for the defeat in Hampshire the previous month. However, Aldershot ran us close: they led after a quarter of an hour and hustled us out of our measured style, before Roy Summersby equalised with a searing shot after thirty-five minutes. It looked as if we would have to settle for just the single point we needed until Tom Barnett headed home from George Petchey's cross just three minutes from time.

Up at Crewe for the last away game, with a somewhat depleted team, we came through 2-1 via an early own goal and a late winner from Roy Summersby, who was having a marvellous finale. Roy notched both Palace goals against Stockport on the following Wednesday evening, when nearly 19,000 supporters braved a dreadful night of rain, thunder and lightning in order to cheer their side to an assured and thoroughly deserved second place in the table. That brace took Palace's goal total to a new peak, passing the previous season's-best of 107, set up thirty years before, and it was the same player who despatched visiting York City on the hour with what is still our Club record 110th League goal of the season in the final match.

There were individual scoring records established too. Johnny Byrne, with 30 League goals, created a post-war tally that remains unbeaten to this day, while Roy Summersby, our second-highest scorer with 25 League strikes, also broke the previous best of 23, held by Mike Deakin.

Other heroes of this 1960/61 promotion season were skipper Johnny McNichol, who had begun the term at wing half but finished it as our right-back, Vic Rouse in goal, towering Gwyn

Evans and Len Choules who sewed up the centre of our defence most effectively and wing halves George Petchey and Terry Long, who both rendered the Club grand service after their playing days were over, as we shall see.

It was also the inaugural season of the Football League Cup in 1960/61. Palace's exploits do not take long to relate, for we lost our first match in the new competition 0-2 at Darlington. Laurie Scott, the former Palace manager, returned to Selhurst Park with Hitchin Town in the first round of the FA Cup, but Palace saw off the amateurs 6-2, only to lose to Watford in a thrilling Vicarage Road replay in the next round, going down to a very late goal indeed, in injury time at the end of the extra half hour.

Since it came a full forty years after the last one, the promotion season of 1960/61 was a new experience for the vast majority of folk connected with the Crystal Palace club, but what was so particularly pleasing about this triumph was that it had been achieved in such an attractive manner. The Club's waning fortunes, certainly since the Second World War, had been restored to a substantial degree, and a base had been prepared from which, given continued astute leadership both on and off the park, further progress might reasonably be expected.

SEASON: 1960/61

GROUND: Selhurst Park

MANAGER: Arthur Rowe

LEAGUE/DIVISION: Football League Fourth Division

FINAL POSITION: 2nd

BIGGEST VICTORY: 9-2 *v.* Accrington Stanley, 20 August 1960

HEAVIEST DEFEAT: 2-5 *v.* Stockport County, 3 October 1960

FA CUP – ROUND ELIMINATED: 2nd

LEAGUE CUP – ROUND ELIMINATED: 1st

FULL MEMBERS CUP – ROUND ELIMINATED: –

LEADING LEAGUE APPEARANCES (MAX: 46): 46 – J. McNichol, V. Rouse, G. Petchey, R. Summersby, 43 – T. Long

LEADING LEAGUE GOALSCORERS: 30 – J. Byrne, 25 – R. Summersby

1961/62

IMPRESSIVE OPENING IN MORE SENIOR SURROUNDINGS

Palace paraded three new players when they opened their first season in the Third Division in August 1961. Full-back Ray Little, who had joined us from Brighton, had appeared in the 1955 and 1956 FA Cup finals with Manchester City, Ronnie Allen, the famous West Bromwich Albion and England centre forward or winger and Andy Smillie, a talented little fellow from West Ham who based his game upon that of the brilliant Hungarian Ferenc Puskas and finished this season as Palace's top League goalscorer with 16 strikes, all joined us.

Palace started well. Continuing to play the stylish 'push and run' game, they were top of the table in September and remained in the top six places throughout the autumn, while further honours came to the club when Johnny Byrne became our first full England international since May 1923 when he lined up against Northern Ireland at Wembley on 22 November.

Our first game after winning promotion was at Torquay and, with Byrne and Allen blending perfectly from the start, we were much the better side throughout the first half and some Palace fans came to think that this first forty-five minutes of the season was actually our side's best 'half' on an away ground of the entire League term. Johnny Byrne hit a post early but was on target after quarter of an hour, rounding the centre half then thumping the ball past the exposed goalkeeper. Roy Summersby added our second with a quarter of an hour to go and, although the Gulls were able to reduce the arrears, Palace's victory was fully deserved.

However, our impetus faded. We were back in tenth place after the 3 March defeat at Peterborough (1-4), in which Byrne played his last game for us before signing for West Ham at the then-record fee between two British clubs of £60,000 plus the return to Selhurst Park of Ron Brett, and we ultimately finished the season down in fifteenth place.

Probably our best performance of the entire campaign was in a third round FA Cup tie at Aston Villa on the cold first Saturday of the new year, when we were so outstanding that regular Palace fans of the day remain convinced that our display at Villa Park represented the peak that Palace reached under manager Arthur Rowe. We came so close not just to embarrassing Villa but to defeating them that no fair-minded onlooker would have begrudged us the replay we so patently deserved. Villa swaggered through the opening quarter of an hour, clearly believing that victory was theirs for the taking, and when they scored the first goal it seemed that this

Left: Ronnie Allen joined the Palace for the 1961/62 season.

might be so, although Palace fans who were present will confirm my own certainty that the scorer, Harry Burrows, was blatantly offside.

But what followed was wonderful: Byrne soon levelled for us and then Dennis Uphill had us ahead. Villa equalised but Byrne restored our lead, only for Derek Dougan to put Villa back on terms again. Palace were quite clearly at least the equals of their top-flight hosts and the game had reached its dying moments when Palace conceded a killer goal. A drifting cross-cum-centre eluded the groping hands of Vic Rouse and then ended up in the far corner of our net with barely time to restart the contest.

Another supremely important event in the annals of Crystal Palace FC took place at Selhurst Park on the night of 18 April 1962 when the crack Spanish side Real Madrid, came to celebrate the opening of the new floodlighting system. The occasion was masterminded by the then-Palace chairman Arthur Wait, and it is to his eternal credit that he inspired such a momentous evening. It was cold, wet and raw, but we forgot all about the weather as Real paraded their fabulous skills, and we will always remember Puskas, Di Stefano and Ghento as well as Palace's fabulous fight back from two down in eight minutes to 3-4 with a wonderful goal from Terry Long, and the Spanish señors clearly apprehensive as to the outcome right to the end.

SEASON: 1961/62

GROUND: Selhurst Park

MANAGER: Arthur Rowe

LEAGUE/DIVISION: Football League Third Division

FINAL POSITION: 15th

BIGGEST VICTORY: 7-2 *v.* Torquay United, 16 December 1961

HEAVIEST DEFEAT: 0-5 *v.* Swindon Town, 23 December 1961

FA CUP – ROUND ELIMINATED: 3rd

LEAGUE CUP – ROUND ELIMINATED: 1st

FULL MEMBERS CUP – ROUND ELIMINATED: –

LEADING LEAGUE APPEARANCES (MAX: 46): 45 – T. Long, 42 – R. Summersby

LEADING LEAGUE GOALSCORERS: 16 – A. Smillie, 14 – J. Byrne

1962/63

DICK GRAHAM AVERTS DISASTER

Between March and September 1962 Crystal Palace played twenty consecutive League games without recording a victory – our worst sequence in the entire history of the club and one we do not ever want to see challenged! By Christmas 1962 we were inevitably next to bottom in the Third Division and in acute danger of dropping back into the oblivion of the Fourth Division. The club's decline should not solely be attributed to the absence of Johnny Byrne – that was merely one factor in a thoroughly depressing time. The club and the players, but particularly manager Arthur Rowe, were badly affected by the tragic death of Ron Brett in a traffic accident at the end of August and then, with problems enough besides, Arthur Rowe himself was struck down by illness and forced to drop his responsibilities.

Dick Graham, our former goalkeeper and assistant to Mr Rowe since January 1961, took over at the Palace helm. He immediately changed the style of play and made two masterly signings. Palace began to adopt a much more direct game, which involved less close passing and greater use of the long ball, and it paid immediate dividends. Graham's first signings were those of Cliff Holton, a striker of vast experience with Arsenal, Northampton and Watford, and 'Dickie' Dowsett, another proven goalscorer, from Bournemouth. Big Cliff added power to a diminutive if skilful forward line while Dowsett provided the ideal foil and was a clever header of the ball.

The players' first match together in the Palace colours was a Boxing Day derby at Selhurst Park against Millwall and it is no exaggeration to claim that the whole future of Crystal Palace hung upon this game. Millwall sought to mark Holton out of the contest upon his Palace debut, but in attempting to do so the Lions' defence left the way open for Palace's other forwards to cleave their way through and net three goals, something they had not previously accomplished all season.

Palace adopted a classic Dick Graham attitude – one with which our fans grew increasingly familiar over the ensuing years, and our tough, man-for-man marking soon gained control. The most important duel was on Palace's left flank where Millwall's flying winger Joey Broadfoot was a constant menace, but Bert Howe gradually cut off the danger there and subsequently shadowed the Lions' star as he roamed all over the park. In the end, the Palace defence finished with a clean sheet – our first in eight games and more than welcome to everyone.

The conditions were bitterly cold and it was icy underfoot but, on that tricky surface, it was the Palace who looked the more assured. Speedy and confident, our side gained the ascendancy a little after a quarter of an hour when Peter Burridge netted against his former club following

Left: Dick Graham took over as Palace's boss in December 1962.

a Bert Howe free-kick. Early in the second half Dickie Dowsett scored his first Palace goal. Reacting quickly to a Ronnie Allen through ball, he raced past a defender to turn it past Reg Davies in the Millwall goal. For the finale in the closing minutes, Millwall's toiling defence brought down Peter Burridge in the penalty area and although the fans called for a Cliff Holton 'special', Ronnie Allen stepped up to clip a deft shot past the goalkeeper's left hand.

Palace simply progressed from there and the transformation was quite amazing to watch. Our forwards became a real striking force, one that cast doubt in the minds of opponents even before a match began, and the second half of the season, protracted until nearly the end of May because of the long winter freeze, was a much healthier, happier one. It included 6-0 and 5-0 routs of Bradford Park Avenue and Wrexham here at Selhurst Park and a fabulous, highly memorable 4-1 victory at Watford where Cliff Holton netted a hat-trick against his former club and the Watford patrons rose at the finish to acclaim their erstwhile hero.

Palace finished the term on 23 May with a 4-0 win up at Barnsley to finish in the top half of the table in eleventh place. In view of the disastrous start, that was an achievement of high merit of which Dick Graham and his men could be justly proud.

SEASON: 1962/63

GROUND: Selhurst Park

MANAGER: Arthur Rowe until November 1962, then Dick Graham

LEAGUE/DIVISION: Football League Third Division

FINAL POSITION: 11th

BIGGEST VICTORY: 6-0 *v.* Bradford Park Avenue, 30 March 1963

HEAVIEST DEFEAT: 1-4 *v.* QPR, 3 September 1962, 1-4 *v.* Port Vale, 8 December 1962

FA CUP – ROUND ELIMINATED: 2nd

LEAGUE CUP – ROUND ELIMINATED: 2nd

FULL MEMBERS CUP – ROUND ELIMINATED: –

LEADING LEAGUE APPEARANCES (MAX: 46): 44 – B. Wood, 39 – T. Long

LEADING LEAGUE GOALSCORERS: 14 – P. Burridge, 12 – D. Dowsett

1963/64

PALACE WIN ANOTHER PROMOTION

Palace began 1963/64 with just one close-season signing, that of tough little midfielder or winger Bobby Kellard from Southend. Later in the term manager Dick Graham secured two more experienced men to augment our squad – immaculate full-back John Sewell from Charlton late in October, although John's contribution this season was restricted by injury, and former West Bromwich Albion forward Brian Whitehouse, who netted on his debut and hit 6 goals in Palace's final 9 games.

The Glaziers were a strong Third Division outfit. We played an aggressive, abrasive style, but we played with discipline and there were quality performances in the side, especially from the aptly named goalkeeper Bill Glazier and captain Ronnie Allen. Glazier was a formidable opponent and, although he reached his prime after he left Selhurst Park, he was always safe and dependable. The defence in front of Bill was notoriously tight: that was never better shown than in four consecutive matches in January and February when the forwards netted just a single goal per game, but the defence conceded just one to enable us to take seven points out of the eight available under the two-points-for-a-win system that operated then.

Skipper Ronnie Allen was the former West Bromwich Albion and England winger or centre forward. His experience and guile ideally qualified him to marshal Palace on the field although we were denied his presence in the last nine matches because of a dislocated knee.

This glorious season actually began with a dreadful beating, 1-5 at Jimmy Hill's Coventry City, but precisely the same side gained a scoreless draw at Reading in midweek, then produced a 3-1 win over Mansfield. Nine matches without defeat in the early autumn took us into second place but then we lost twice, both by 1-3 margins at Watford and Oldham. However, by the end of the year we had regained the number two position. We lost an unforgettable match at Bournemouth 3-4, but then put together fourteen undefeated matches, including ten victories, so that by Easter we were on top of the table. In spite of massive support Palace could only finish with five draws and two defeats but the fifth of those draws, at Wrexham on Wednesday 22 April was enough to ensure that we won promotion.

A midweek clash at Wrexham is rarely likely to pull a large contingent of Palace fans because of the relatively difficult journey and, in April 1964, that trip was much more time-consuming than it would be today. However, our supporters were at the Racecourse in commendable force and were rewarded with a well-fought, exciting match, in which both sides led before half-time. Having fallen behind early on, Palace equalised when Brian Whitehouse netted against one of

Safe and dependable goalkeeper Bill Glazier played every game for Palace in the 1963/64 promotion season.

his former clubs with a thirty-yard drive in the twenty-seventh minute, and Cliff Holton drove home a penalty six minutes later, but relegation-bound Wrexham were themselves successful from the spot five minutes before half-time. The score remained unaltered in the second half and at the final whistle some of our less inhibited fans ran onto the pitch to congratulate the players upon the certainty of promotion. There was dancing and singing and it was all good-natured fun and delight among our supporters, some of whom remain to this day among our Club's most respected patrons!

Thus, it was no surprise when a crowd of almost 28,000, our best for nearly three seasons, came to Selhurst Park for the last match of this triumphant season. They came not just to celebrate promotion, but also because the fate of the championship itself was in Palace's own keeping – a single point would ensure that we would return to the Second Division as the Third Division champions.

In retrospect it is difficult to think of potentially more troublesome home opponents for this occasion than Oldham. Always in the promotion race themselves and one-time leaders of the table, their own hopes of progress had only been quite recently dashed. The Latics needed no inspired pre-match team talk to lift them to one of their best performances of the season and the big, expectant Palace crowd provided precisely the atmosphere for them to produce it.

It was soon apparent that both sides had a healthy respect for each other. The exchanges were tight, dour and, in one sense, almost uneventful, except that, for the Palace, every minute that passed without a goal brought us that much closer to the championship. Then, as the interval approached there occurred a moment that appeared to indicate that the tide was turning in Palace's favour. A forty-fourth-minute penalty was awarded to us for handball and the ever-reliable Cliff Holton banged the ball home to the delight and relief of the assembly. But our jubilation was premature, for soon after the break our advantage was snatched from our grasp.

The major perpetrator of Palace's downfall was an unlikely looking fellow by the name of Bob Ledger. Balding, modestly built and slightly tubby, Ledger was almost goblin-like in his appearance, but the visitors' outside right certainly had Palace in thrall for the first quarter of an hour immediately upon the resumption for, during that brief period, he helped himself to an amazing, clever and inevitably match-winning hat-trick in the space of just eleven minutes. It was also ironic: it was the only hat-trick seen at Selhurst Park all season; and the first one scored here in over a year, and it cost Palace the title.

Our fans watching this unfold could scarcely believe their eyes and, even with so many supporters in the ground, the atmosphere had become hushed and restrained. It soon became clear that there would be no way back for us, particularly after a Cliff Holton free-kick that ripped into the net was disallowed for encroachment by an Oldham player, so our thoughts were inevitably winging to Coventry's match against Colchester for, if they could win it, our two-goal deficit would present the Sky Blues with the title by the slenderest of margins, on goal-average. Twice before Palace had forfeited championships in this manner and that was what happened this time. Coventry scrapped out a 1-0 victory and, as Palace's big crowd waited anxiously after the final whistle, this result and its implications were announced to them.

However, even though there was a feeling of anti-climax about, the wonderful fact was that Palace had still won promotion and it was entirely fitting to celebrate it. On to the pitch came all the players who had contributed to the tremendous success of the season and bouquets of flowers in the Club colours were thrown to the fans in appreciation for their support. It was a memorable occasion for everyone present, but it was poignant too for those who had witnessed our relegation from the Second Division back in 1925 for, amazingly, the team that had won at Selhurst Park on the last day of that season to consign us to the lower reaches of the League for thirty-nine years had been none other than... Oldham Athletic.

It may seem surprising to modern-day readers, but some people complained about Dick Graham! Some supporters and parts of the sporting press decided that Dick's tactics were dour and dull, while his habit of announcing his team as late as possible and making several positional changes was allegedly annoying and confusing. Palace fans would defend Dick on both charges!

There was no doubt that our defence was easily the best in the division and that it was adept at soaking up pressure. Dick was deploying Alan Stephenson and Brian Wood in an early but highly effective dual centre half role, and Bert Howe, Don Townsend and John Sewell were all at their best at the time – but with forwards of such proven goalscoring skill as Cliff Holton, Ronnie Allen and Peter Burridge in the side Palace could never be fairly described as 'dull' and, by the time we were finding scoring difficult, we had become one of the sides that all the others in the division wanted, planned and strove (but usually failed) to beat, so that perhaps their frustrations led to outbursts of unreasoned criticism. Dick Graham's 'numbers game' could be rather perplexing, but whether it actually assisted the Palace against their opponents must be debatable. However, it should be remembered that in those days most programmes still persisted in laying out the team in the formation of two full-backs, three half-backs and five forwards, so Dick was also chipping away at the old thinking of the game, which decreed that a player with a certain number had a pre-ordained role to fulfil on the field.

Finally, it is worth noting that Palace's prospects of success in this 1963/64 season were probably enhanced by the manner in which our hopes of progress in the Cup competitions were extinguished early in both tournaments in the Westcountry. Bristol Rovers put us out of the League Cup (0-2) at the first hurdle, leaving us still without a victory in the new competition.

Then, in the FA Cup, after we had disposed of visiting Harwich & Parkestone in the first round, notching up our highest-ever score in that competition with an 8-2 win, we fell where many more distinguished clubs had fallen before, on Yeovil's former 'Slopes of Huish' in early December (1-3).

SEASON: 1963/64

GROUND: Selhurst Park

MANAGER: Dick Graham

LEAGUE/DIVISION: Football League Third Division

FINAL POSITION: 2nd

BIGGEST VICTORY: 4-0 *v.* Luton Town, 18 September 1963

HEAVIEST DEFEAT: 1-5 *v.* Coventry City, 24 August 1963

FA CUP – ROUND ELIMINATED: 2nd

LEAGUE CUP – ROUND ELIMINATED: 2nd

FULL MEMBERS CUP – ROUND ELIMINATED: –

LEADING LEAGUE APPEARANCES (MAX: 46): 46 – W. Glazier, A. Howe, 45 – B. Wood

LEADING LEAGUE GOALSCORERS: 20 – P. Burridge, C. Holton, 7 – R. Allen, B. Whitehouse

1964/65

A SUCCESSFUL SECOND DIVISION RETURN AND A GLORIOUS CUP VICTORY

Season 1964/65, Palace's first in the higher divisions of the League for forty years, developed into a thoroughly successful one. That said, at the start at least, there were one or two setbacks to overcome!

Palace's first match was against Derby County at Selhurst Park on Saturday 22 August 1964. Dick Graham was content to rely entirely upon men who had been closely involved in gaining promotion the previous April and most of the 22,935 crowd were delighted when Peter Burridge gave us an early lead. But, with Bill Glazier and his colleagues clearly out of touch, Derby equalised before the half hour and then after the break scored twice in five minutes, so that despite a late Cliff Holton reply, there was no doubt that the Palace had received a nasty lesson.

Mr Graham decided that no fewer than six changes were required for the midweek visit to Swindon, including the debut of John Jackson in goal. But it was to prove no story-book debut for 'Jacko' and we were well beaten, then we lost again in the third match of the season, with Bill Glazier back in goal, at Swansea.

But Palace recovered quickly and well. We recorded our first victory when Swindon came up for the return and then proceeded to win no fewer than five consecutive matches. Indeed, during September we played eight League games and won seven of them!

Dick Graham retained Palace's high work-rate of the previous season-and-a-half, but he gradually adjusted his tactics to include greater skill, through the signings of Keith Smith from Peterborough in November and David Burnside just before Christmas. Burnside was a tremendous ball-artist and scored twice on his Boxing Day debut to enable Palace to come from behind to beat Portsmouth 4-2 at Selhurst Park. Smith became the scorer of one the fastest-ever goals in the history of football, and certainly the fastest in the annals of our club, when he netted in just six seconds in the reverse fixture of the opening match of the season, at Derby on Saturday 12 December, where Palace gained a 3-3 draw.

Another indication of manager Dick Graham's skilful manipulation of the transfer market was shown when Bill Glazier moved to Coventry City in October for the then-record fee for a goalkeeper of £35,000. Graham immediately purchased Welsh international Tony Millington from West Bromwich Albion to make Palace a profit of some £30,000 in the week! However,

Goalkeeper Tony Millington and defender Bert Howe ensure that Newcastle's Ron McGarry finds no way to reach the ball during our match at St James' Park on 24 October 1964 (0-2).

the emergence of John Jackson was to be one of the features of 1964/65 and, by the end of the year, Jacko was earning high praise for his performances. By the season's end he was in undisputed possession of the Palace 'keeper's jersey.

In March Ronnie Allen left the Palace to return to the Midlands as senior coach at Wolves after playing exactly 100 League games for us, but it was at this time that there began to emerge a new wing half/midfield player named David Payne, who was to become a great Palace favourite and a quality player for us in the top flight.

Palace's FA Cup progress illustrates most effectively the fine balance Dick Graham and his team had attained. To overcome Bury (then a vigorous Second Division club) in the third round, to the tune of 5-1, with only ten men after losing Brian Wood with a badly broken leg, was a triumph for the Palace stormtroopers.

Southampton were then dismissed at The Dell in much the same style, but Palace then outplayed Nottingham Forest, the renowned footballers from the top flight, at their own game to win by a convincing 3-1 margin and reach the last eight for the first time since 1907. This superb performance on a heavy snow-flecked pitch was the peak of Palace finesse and achievement under Dick Graham. The tie had created a new record crowd of 41,667, but within three weeks that was eclipsed by the 45,384 who came to see the sixth round tie against mighty Leeds United, although the match itself was something of an anti-climax and Palace were never able to equal the tough Yorkshiremen, going down 0-3 in a bruising encounter.

SEASON: 1964/65

GROUND: Selhurst Park

MANAGER: Dick Graham

LEAGUE/DIVISION: Football League Second Division

FINAL POSITION: 7th

BIGGEST VICTORY: 3-0 *v.* Hudderfield Town, 14 November 1964

HEAVIEST DEFEAT: 0-3 *v.* Bolton Wanderers, 10 October 1964

FA CUP – ROUND ELIMINATED: 6th

LEAGUE CUP – ROUND ELIMINATED: 4th

FULL MEMBERS CUP – ROUND ELIMINATED: –

LEADING LEAGUE APPEARANCES (MAX: 42): 40 – A. Stephenson, R. Kellard, 39 – A. Howe, B. Whitehouse

LEADING LEAGUE GOALSCORERS: 11 – C. Holton, 9 – K. Smith

1965/66

DICK GRAHAM LEAVES, BERT HEAD TAKES OVER AND STEVE KEMBER MAKES HIS DEBUT

Dick Graham's first move towards improving the Palace squad for the 1965/66 season was a bitter disappointment to most Palace fans because he allowed Cliff Holton to leave Selhurst Park. Cliff had undoubtedly been Dick Graham's best signing and had done a terrific job since his arrival in the midwinter of 1962/63. He had gained a huge following at the Palace and, even if he was beginning to slow up a little and spend more time in defence than formerly, his sheer presence in our side added power and experience, while his arrival in opponents' penalty areas for Palace set pieces still caused utter chaos. Cliff moved back to Watford from the Palace and then on to Charlton in February 1966.

Dick's aim had been to replace Cliff with big Derek Kevan, the former West Bromwich Albion and Chelsea centre forward and ex-England international. Alongside Kevan was another new striker, Ian Lawson, an England Youth international who joined us from Leeds, having previously been with Burnley. On paper it should have worked out well enough, but unfortunately neither Kevan nor Lawson proved at all successful with Palace and inevitably both players and the manager came in for strident criticism from the fans.

In fairness to Dick Graham it must be pointed out that, even if his flair in the transfer market had deserted him, he was still capable of making useful signings on Palace's behalf. During the summer of 1965 Dick brought in two experienced players who were to serve our club most usefully – Ernie Yard, a versatile player who joined us from Bury and was the only Scot on the Palace books, and Jack Bannister, a strong competitive midfield man, who arrived from Scunthorpe but was well known to Mr Graham from their days together at West Bromwich and made over 100 League appearances for the Palace.

Leaving at this stage were Peter Burridge, who added yet another London club to his career list by joining Charlton in November, while Bobby Kellard went to Ipswich. Later in the term Brian Whitehouse joined Burridge and Holton at The Valley, but by then Stewart Imlach had returned to Selhurst Park as player-coach – and there had been a managerial change as well.

Just three days into the New Year it was announced that Dick Graham himself was leaving Crystal Palace – sacked, with two years of his contract still to run – and that Arthur Rowe would take temporary charge. Within a few hours of the news breaking Graham was handed a letter signed by his twenty-one senior professionals, regretting his departure and thanking him for what

Left: Derek Kevan.

he had done for the club. This was perhaps surprising, because Graham had had his disagreements with many of the players and several of them were on the transfer list! The most publicised tiff between the tough, uncompromising Graham and his players had been on Euston Station as the team prepared to journey to Carlisle for the Second Division fixture on 11 December, which culminated in twenty-one-year-old Alan Stephenson being sent home. The incident appeared to have blown over, but the tensions obviously continued and three weeks later Graham was dismissed. His contribution to the Palace between December 1962 and January 1966 can scarcely be overestimated, for he took us from almost certain relegation to the Fourth Division to a respected place in the Second Division.

However, in the light of subsequent Palace history, not even the dismissal of Dick Graham was the most significant event in the 1965/66 season at Selhurst Park. Rather, it was the debut, first goal and early career of a man who was to have the unique distinction of playing in both Palace teams that gained promotion to the top flight in 1969 and 1979, of captaining our First Division side in 1971 and of serving several times as Palace's manager, Steve Kember.

Towards the end of the season on 18 April 1966, Palace announced the appointment of their new chief, Bert Head, who joined us from Bury. At the time of this appointment the Shakers' chairman was heard to remark 'We've lost and you've got the best manager in the business,' and few Palace fans of that period would argue that he was wrong.

SEASON: 1965/66

GROUND: Selhurst Park

MANAGER: Dick Graham to 3 January 1966, then Arthur Rowe (caretaker manager) to 14 April 1966, then Bert Head

LEAGUE/DIVISION: Football League Second Division

FINAL POSITION: 11th

BIGGEST VICTORY: 4-1 *v.* Portsmouth, 8 September 1965

HEAVIEST DEFEAT: 0-4 *v.* Derby County, 27 November 1965

FA CUP – ROUND ELIMINATED: 3rd

LEAGUE CUP – ROUND ELIMINATED: 2nd

FULL MEMBERS CUP – ROUND ELIMINATED: –

LEADING LEAGUE APPEARANCES (MAX: 42): 40 – A. Stephenson, 38 – J. Jackson

LEADING LEAGUE GOALSCORERS: 7 – B. Whitehouse, 6 – I. Lawson

1966/67

BERT HEAD'S FIRST SEASON IN CHARGE AT THE PALACE

The 1966/67 season opened on Saturday 20 August, an afternoon of tropical heat. Palace's opponents were Carlisle at Selhurst Park and we played well in the torrid conditions to win 4-2. Two new players each scored a brace that afternoon, Tom White and Bobby Woodruff.

Tom was a stocky, robust but extremely skilful centre forward who joined Palace from Aberdeen. He did not have much luck with injuries while he was with us, but his presence early in this season helped Palace ease to within a point of the top of the Second Division by the second week of September. Bobby Woodruff had been discovered by Bert Head at Swindon, but he joined the Palace from Wolves. He was renowned in football for his phenomenal long throw, which gave his side the equivalent of a corner whenever they gained a throw-in within twenty yards of the corner flag. But Bobby was also a fine header of the ball and a mean goalscorer. His 18 League goals for us in this 1966/67 season, which he equalled in 1967/68, was easily our best in the higher divisions until the days of Mark Bright and Ian Wright.

Two other important signings by Bert Head were those of John McCormick, who joined us with Tom White from Aberdeen, and Cliff Jackson from Plymouth. There were departures too of course, and a most unusual one took place early in September 1966. Palace were due at Molineux for a Second Division fixture on Wednesday 7 September and in the team line-ups in the match programme we had David Burnside listed to play. However, during the very day of the match Burnside was transferred to Wolves, actually played against us and scored Wolves' goal in a 1-1 draw.

Unquestionably Palace's most popular signing of 1966/67 took place in mid-February when Bert Head persuaded Johnny Byrne to return to us from West Ham. By coincidence a friendly match against Leicester had been arranged for the following evening and the Palace fans welcomed their former favourite back to the Selhurst Park fold by singing 'Hello Johnny, Welcome home, Johnny' to the theme tune of the hit musical of the period, *Hello Dolly*. It was an emotional night and Johnny hit Palace's goal to demonstrate the potential wisdom of the manager's decision.

Regrettably though, it never worked out and Johnny moved on to Fulham on the day of the transfer deadline in the following season, 16 March 1968. Negotiations for this move took place almost entirely on the Manchester-London train, on which the two teams were returning from

Right: Tom White.

defeats in fixtures in the North-West. Byrne's Palace career had embraced 259 League and Cup games. He scored 101 goals for us and was the first post-war player to net over a century of goals for our club, while his 30 League goals in 1960/61 remains the post-war record for a single season.

In spite of a run of misfortune with injuries, Palace had a really good season in Mr Head's first full term. Although Tom White and John Sewell broke their collarbones in consecutive matches in early September, we were second in the table in mid-November after an excellent 2-1 win at Coventry, the eventual champions, where our goalscorers were Cliff Jackson and Steve Kember.

The other promoted side was Wolves and we took three points out of the four from them, as we did from Coventry, actually saving our best performance of the whole season for Wolves and the final game. They came to Selhurst Park on Saturday 13 May with Ronnie Allen as their manager and with former Palace men David Burnside and John Holsgrove in their side. They already knew that they would be promoted but, if they could gain a draw at our expense, they would go up as champions. A splendid crowd of 26,930 saw Palace sweep the visitors imperiously aside with a powerful and confident display. We were three goals ahead after little more than an hour, finished 4-1 winners and could have had another two or three goals!

SEASON: 1966/67

GROUND: Selhurst Park

MANAGER: Bert Head

LEAGUE/DIVISION: Football League Second Division

FINAL POSITION: 7th

BIGGEST VICTORY: 5-1 *v.* Northampton Town, 8 October 1966

HEAVIEST DEFEAT: 1-6 *v.* Hull City, 10 December 1966

FA CUP – ROUND ELIMINATED: 3rd

LEAGUE CUP – ROUND ELIMINATED: 2nd

FULL MEMBERS CUP – ROUND ELIMINATED: –

LEADING LEAGUE APPEARANCES (MAX: 42): 42 – A. Stephenson, J. Bannister, R. Woodruff, 40 – D. Payne

LEADING LEAGUE GOALSCORERS: 18 – R. Woodruff, 10 – S. Kember

1967/68

PALACE GO TOP OF THE TABLE BRIEFLY AND THE PROMOTION SIDE ASSEMBLES

Palace paraded a new strip for 1967/68. The all-white one favoured since 1964 was replaced by claret jerseys with a thin light-blue stripe, white shorts and light-blue socks with a claret turnover.

We began the season with no significant additions to the staff and made a brilliant start to the new term by winning at Rotherham 3-0, easily our best result there. Our first home game was against Derby County who had just appointed a new manager, Brian Clough no less. However, the Palace won with a twenty-ninth-minute header from Bobby Woodruff.

Palace continued to progress and, by the evening of Saturday 30 September after our 1-0 defeat of Queen Park Rangers at Selhurst Park, we were sitting, for the first time in our history, at the top of the Second Division table. A record crowd for a Football League fixture of 38,006 saw Terry Long strike the thirty-eighth-minute goal that put Palace there. Terry had joined us in May 1955 from Wycombe Wanderers and had played most of his games for us as a wing half-back or full-back. He made his debut against Walsall at Selhurst Park on 28 September 1955 when Palace won 2-0 with goals from another debutant, Jimmy Murray. Terry missed just four matches in the 1956/57 season, then played every game in each of the next three seasons so that between 5 September 1956 and 4 March 1961 he made 214 consecutive League appearances, a figure only ever improved upon by John Jackson, who amassed 222.

Terry was a model professional and a great club man, and received a richly deserved testimonial on 11 October 1966. He was a steady defender, though he could play as an inside forward too, and a clever footballer. He did not often score goals but, when he did, they were important or spectacular affairs, like the one against Rangers or the one that brought the crowd to its feet against Real Madrid. Like Johnny Byrne, Terry played for the Palace in four divisions of the League, (Third (South), Fourth, Third and Second) and his 442 League appearances for us have only been exceeded by the great Jim Cannon.

With Palace riding high in the Second Division it was an ideal time for another great club servant, George Petchey, to play his testimonial and on 15 November 1967 the Palace side faced a team of stars, largely from the bigger London clubs, called an 'International XI' for George's benefit. Palace won 6-3 and our last three, from Bobby Woodruff, Cliff Jackson and Tom White, were all scored in a cracking blitz in the last five minutes. George had come to the Palace in the summer of 1960 to play under Arthur Rowe. He helped Palace to gain promotion and continued as a regular first-team man

Right: Colin Taylor.

with Dick Graham, making 24 appearances in the side that won its way into the Second Division in 1963/64. His career was blighted by a troublesome eye complaint, but George assisted Arthur Rowe after Dick Graham's departure, helped to mould the side that took us to the top flight for the first time and was an integral part of our set-up in that division until he became the Orient manager in 1971.

Palace remained at the head of the Second Division for just two weeks but were deposed by a 0-2 defeat at Blackpool in pouring rain. After Christmas we were sixth and we finished in eleventh place. During this period of relative decline Palace were knocked out of the FA Cup in a Selhurst Park replay by Walsall, whose goal in the 1-1 draw at Fellows Park was a thunderous free-kick from Colin Taylor that so impressed Bert Head that he signed Taylor in May 1968. Colin's 8 League goals for us in 1968/69 were to be invaluable as we surged to promotion.

Palace received three big fees around the time of the spring transfer deadline. As well as Johnny Byrne's departure, Tom White left us for Blackpool and Alan Stephenson got his wish for First Division football by joining West Ham for a club-record fee in the region of £75,000. Upon Alan's departure the club captaincy was awarded to John Sewell and now the scene was set for an epic season.

SEASON: 1967/68

GROUND: Selhurst Park

MANAGER: Bert Head

LEAGUE/DIVISION: Football League Second Division

FINAL POSITION: 11th

BIGGEST VICTORY: 6-0 *v.* Norwich City, 16 April 1968

HEAVIEST DEFEAT: 1-5 *v.* Millwall, 13 April 1968

FA CUP – ROUND ELIMINATED: 3rd

LEAGUE CUP – ROUND ELIMINATED: 2nd

FULL MEMBERS CUP – ROUND ELIMINATED: –

LEADING LEAGUE APPEARANCES (MAX: 42): 42 – J. Jackson, R. Woodruff, 41 – J. Bannister, S. Kember

LEADING LEAGUE GOALSCORERS: 18 – R. Woodruff, 7 – S. Kember, T. White

1968/69

PALACE REACH THE TOP FLIGHT FOR THE FIRST TIME

Palace boss Bert Head made two summer signings in the 1968 close-season, and then augmented his playing squad by bringing in three more men during the early autumn.

First to join was Colin Taylor, nicknamed 'Cannonball' for his fearsome shooting, who arrived from Walsall in May and was to contribute 8 invaluable goals from the left flank. Then came Mel Blyth from Scunthorpe United towards the end of June. Mel became a key component in several Palace sides: he was tall, strong and fair-haired, and began as a wing half or inside forward but developed into a magnificent back-four man, where his stature made him a natural central defender. His partnership with John McCormick became a feature of this promotion season and of Palace's subsequent four-year tenure in the old First Division, while over that period only John Jackson appeared more times for the Palace than Mel.

Three autumn signings completed Mr Head's assembly of the team that was to crown his management with success. The first of these was in September, when tough Roger Hoy joined us from Spurs to add defensive and midfield strength, then in October Mr Head made the first of a series of highly successful sorties across the border for players from the Scottish League. On this occasion he brought back John Loughlan, a talented left-back, and Tony Taylor, a winger at the time, but soon to become a mighty midfield man for us, from Greenock Morton.

Thus Mr Head's team was moulded to his satisfaction and usually to the delight of Palace patrons. Each member of it was a gifted footballer, and under Bert's expert, shrewd guidance they were blended into a formidable unit. The magnificent John Jackson was in goal with the immaculate John Sewell at number two (now the club captain), and John Loughlan at left-back. Our central defensive pillars were John McCormick and Mel Blyth. In front of them were the talented local boys David Payne and Steve Kember with midfield dynamo Tony Taylor. Roger Hoy filled in at full-back or in midfield. The front runners were the enormously popular Mark Lazarus, Cliff Jackson and Colin Taylor with Bobby Woodruff, who played either as a striker or in midfield, but had the misfortune to break his collarbone as the season approached its climax.

Palace's opening fixture in the Second Division was on Saturday 10 August down at Cardiff, who were always a tough proposition on their own soil in those days, but Palace romped to as fine an opening day away victory as has ever been witnessed by our fans. In front of a partisan

16,359 crowd we took a sixth-minute lead through debutant Mel Blyth, who played at inside forward in the early season games and was on hand to slide the ball home when the Bluebirds' goalkeeper could only parry an effort from Cliff Jackson. Cliff himself cracked a second for us midway through the half and then provided the pass from which David Payne rifled a third five minutes before the break. Only two minutes after the restart Mark Lazarus rounded the left-back and slipped a perfect ball for Cliff Jackson to emphasise our superiority in the best possible manner, with a fierce shot to ensure that there was no way back for the Welshmen. There were certainly some beaming faces among our supporters as we made our way home on that warm summer's evening!

Two home games followed during the next week. Mark Lazarus was in sparkling form against visiting Huddersfield on Wednesday 14 August and his brace of goals, one a close-range shot, the second a terrific header, were just enough to account for the Terriers. But Birmingham showed a high degree of tenacity and, despite trailing by three goals a little after the hour and having been reduced to ten men midway through the first half, notched two late goals to save some degree of face.

The complacency we had shown in the closing stages against Birmingham now became our complete undoing in two testing away games. At Middlesbrough we were trounced 0-4, then at Bury we lost 1-2 despite taking a nineteenth-minute lead through Mel Blyth.

Palace had topped the table after our opening three victories but we only once, and then most briefly, regained one of the two promotion places before the run-in to the end of the season. Nevertheless we were always in contention and never far away from the top two, so the season retained an edge to it throughout both for our players and the fans. A marvellous match against our neighbours and close rivals Charlton, which drew an attendance of 22,991 to Selhurst Park, took place at the end of August. Both sides produced attractive, flowing football and found the net frequently, so that the big crowd was rewarded with a wonderful 3-3 draw. The Valiants raced into a two-goal lead in the opening nine minutes, but Palace scored twice within a minute as half-time approached: Colin Taylor cracked the first, while the equaliser was the first of the season to come from one of Bobby Woodruff's phenomenal long throws. He sent the ball some forty-five to fifty yards into Charlton's goalmouth for an unmarked Mel Blyth to take full advantage. Just after the hour Cliff Jackson put Palace ahead for the first time in the game, only for Alan Campbell to ensure that Charlton gained the point they deserved five minutes later.

As the fixture list approached its halfway point in late November, Palace won two important victories. A single goal from Cliff Jackson, three minutes before the break when he burst through to capitalise upon a shrewd pass from David Payne, secured both points from visiting Blackburn to take the Palace up to third, and this was followed by a quite magnificent performance in the local derby at table-topping Millwall, where we swept into a two-goal lead by the interval, then held the Lions at bay throughout the second half. John McCormick flicked on a Cliff Jackson corner for Mark Lazarus to open our account in the nineteenth minute, then Bobby Woodruff headed a glorious second just before half-time after a John Sewell overlap and cross from the right that had Palace fans purring with delight. Millwall put us under relentless pressure after this but we refused to yield and John Jackson even saved a late penalty from Keith Weller to ensure that we went second behind the Lions in the table.

Third-placed Derby County, the eventual champions, were our visitors for the next game on 30 November, but strong-man Dave Mackay inspired his men to a deserved victory after we had wasted early chances. Derby scored twice in ninety seconds on the hour and, although John

Steve Kember reduces Palace's arrears against Fulham.

Cliff Jackson nets the winner against Fulham.

McCormick quickly replied, the Rams showed all the hallmarks of their pedigree by shutting us out for the rest of the game. So tight were the proceedings at the top of the table that this loss pushed us back into fourth place.

By the end of January, and with the programme interrupted for most of the clubs by postponements caused by bad weather, Palace were back in sixth place with a couple of games in hand. However, Palace were four and eight points away from the promotion places and an abandonment at Blackburn simply compounded our problems. But now Palace received a helping hand from on high when it became necessary, for the entire fixture list had be put on hold by the dreadful winter.

Palace's first match upon the resumption was on 22 February at home to Hull. We came through 2-0 and never lost another match in the League until we were in the top flight! Including that Hull victory, Palace played sixteen matches and won ten of them. The game that told Palace supporters that there was a real chance of what in those days seemed to be the almost unbelievable actually coming true was when Palace went to table-toppers and championship favourites Derby County on Wednesday 5 March, and won a sparkling encounter with a goal from Bobby Woodruff. Palace actually netted five times in this game – and Bobby Woodruff also hit the bar!

Palace followed up this terrific win three days later with another majestic performance, this time at Birmingham, who were another club well to the fore in the push for promotion. Steve Kember slid in our goal from an acute angle in only the sixteenth minute, and we were only denied another just before half-time because the referee had not signalled for a Palace free-kick, from which it ensued, to be taken!

Palace beat Millwall 4-2 on 19 March to slip neatly into second place, although Middlesbrough pushed us back at the end of that week by pasting Hull 5-3 while we could only draw with Charlton at The Valley. Roger Hoy scored our goal and was our outstanding player.

Discerning fans had already realised that the crucial fixture during the run in to the end of the season was going to be the Good Friday 4 April visit of Middlesbrough to Selhurst Park. This clash drew a 41,381 crowd to our headquarters, but both defences were supreme and unquestionably a 0-0 draw was the proper result. Palace, however, had the superior goal average so stayed ahead of Boro, beat Portsmouth 3-1 the following afternoon and then secured two confident 0-0 draws at Huddersfield and Preston. Boro unaccountably lost at home to relegation-bound Bury and were thus unable to catch us, while Charlton were four points behind, with both clubs having two matches left to play.

A crowd of 36,126 fans were present for Palace's last home match, against Fulham, to acclaim the side. We made statistically certain of promotion by winning 3-2, but only after Fulham had led 2-0 and George Petchey had had a few meaningful words with the side during the interval – but Charlton lost at home anyway. The scenes of jubilation at Selhurst Park after the final whistle almost defy description. It was wonderful! Although of course Palace have reached the top flight on several subsequent occasions, this was the one where the Club first reached the First Division, so perhaps the emotions that accompany such a success were felt most sharply then.

One match remained to be played, the rearranged fixture at Blackburn. Our hosts graciously applauded us onto the field, Palace won 2-1 but more comfortably than that scoreline might suggest, while John McCormick and Rovers' Frank Kopel were sent off in some tense exchanges near the end.

Palace fans invade the pitch after victory over Fulham secures promotion.

SEASON: 1968/69

GROUND: Selhurst Park

MANAGER: Bert Head

LEAGUE/DIVISION: Football League Second Division

FINAL POSITION: 2nd

BIGGEST VICTORY: 5-0 *v.* Carlisle United, 7 September 1968

HEAVIEST DEFEAT: 0-4 *v.* Middlesbrough, 20 August 1968

FA CUP – ROUND ELIMINATED: 3rd

LEAGUE CUP – ROUND ELIMINATED: 5th

FULL MEMBERS CUP – ROUND ELIMINATED: –

LEADING LEAGUE APPEARANCES (MAX: 42): 42 – J. Jackson, S. Kember, J. McCormick, 38 – M. Lazarus

LEADING LEAGUE GOALSCORERS: 14 – C. Jackson, 11 – M. Lazarus, R. Woodruff

1969/70

PALACE SURVIVE THEIR FIRST SEASON AT THE TOP

The summer of 1969 saw extensive activity in the form of ground improvements at Selhurst Park, the most significant since its opening in 1924, primarily in the erection of the new, handsome Arthur Wait Stand. Work had begun during the spring of 1969 and the last half dozen or so matches of 1968/69 had been played against the backdrop of earth movement and newly driven piles. It continued apace during the close season under the personal direction (and with the personal involvement) of the chairman himself, who was determined that it should be ready to open in time for Palace's top-flight debut. It was, though it was not officially opened until Wednesday 26 November 1969 when Sir Alf Ramsey did the honours prior to Arthur Rowe's testimonial match. The stand remains a fitting memorial to a devoted Palace servant and a remarkable man.

Bert Head looked largely to Scotland, where the transfer fees were less inflated, to augment his playing strength for the challenge of the First Division. Roger Hynd came from Rangers to play alongside John McCormick while Gerry Queen, a stylish striker from Kilmarnock was probably Mr Head's best signing for Palace over the four years we spent among the elite between 1969 and 1973. Gerry's value to the Palace is best measured by the fact that he was easily our leading scorer at this level between 1969 and 1973 with 24 top-flight goals, while his tally of 18 strikes in the first two seasons represented precisely one quarter of our total.

Conversely, it was inevitably not long before the promotion-winning side began to break up: Colin 'Cannonball' Taylor returned to Walsall in mid-September without playing in the top flight, and by Christmas those two great favourites Mark Lazarus and Bobby Woodruff had gone to Orient and Cardiff respectively.

Palace's first match at the most senior level could not have created greater interest if we had been able to choose our opponents: it was at Selhurst Park and against Manchester United! A record crowd of 48,610 paid record receipts of £16,250 for that unique occasion on 9 August 1969 and was treated to an exciting afternoon's entertainment even if the match fell some way short of being a classic. It was surprising for some fans to see a team of United's calibre fall for Palace's long-throw routine, but Mel Blyth's header from Roger Hoy's delivery dipped over Jimmy Rimmer to give Palace the lead and secure our first-ever goal in the top flight. Bobby

John Jackson claims the ball from a Manchester United cross despite pressure from Willie Morgan and Denis Law during Palace's first-ever top-flight match on 9 August 1969.

Charlton levelled but Palace went ahead again when Gerry Queen evaded David Sadler then fired past Rimmer, but Willie Morgan popped up to equalise again for United. Frankly, Palace fans were quite content that afternoon with the draw their favourites had gained in competition with one of the leading clubs in the land.

Palace then beat Sunderland four days later with goals from Tony Taylor and Cliff Jackson to extend our unbeaten run to 18 matches, then led Everton at Goodison Park with an early goal scored from twenty yards by Mel Blyth, only to go down 1-2 in unfortunate circumstances to a fluke equaliser and a controversial penalty.

But as the season progressed Palace began to struggle and sustained some heavy home defeats. Arsenal won 1-5 at Selhurst Park and Chelsea repeated the lesson in the match on 27 December 1969 at which a new attendance record of 49,498 was established. In order to add some striking power to our side manager Bert Head took Chelsea's deposed striker Bobby Tambling on loan for three matches, then signed Jim Scott, a Scottish international winger or centre forward, from Newcastle for £20,000.

Palace's best away performance had been to win 1-0 at Manchester City and we did the 'double' over them by winning the Selhurst Park return. This was Palace's final match of the season, even though it was played as early as Monday 6 April, and Palace took the points with a twenty-first-minute goal from Roger Hoy. Palace's continued top-flight status would now depend upon whether either Sunderland or Sheffield Wednesday could gain three points from their remaining two games. Thankfully they both failed and Palace were safe.

Mel Blyth netted Palace's first goal against the Red Devils.

SEASON: 1969/70

GROUND: Selhurst Park

MANAGER: Bert Head

LEAGUE/DIVISION: Football League First Division

FINAL POSITION: 20th

BIGGEST VICTORY: 3-1 *v.* Stoke City, 6 September 1969

HEAVIEST DEFEAT: 1-5 *v.* Arsenal, 1 November 1969, 1-5 *v.* Chelsea, 27 December 1969

FA CUP – ROUND ELIMINATED: 5th

LEAGUE CUP – ROUND ELIMINATED: 4th

FULL MEMBERS CUP – ROUND ELIMINATED: –

LEADING LEAGUE APPEARANCES (MAX: 42): 42 – J. Jackson, 41 – J. McCormick

LEADING LEAGUE GOALSCORERS: 9 – G. Queen, 5 – C. Jackson

1970/71

MUCH-IMPROVED START TO THE TERM ENSURES LEAGUE SECURITY

Palace manager Bert Head moved early in the summer of 1970 to secure three men with considerable top-flight experience to strengthen his back four and striking line for the season that lay ahead. The first was stylish, intelligent left-back Peter Wall who joined us for £25,000 from Liverpool. A little later Mr Head obtained two accomplished strikers from Chelsea: Bobby Tambling moved to Selhurst Park on a permanent basis along with blond six-footer Alan Birchenall for a joint-club-record fee of £140,000. Meanwhile, leaving the club were Cliff Jackson and Roger Hoy from the 1968/69 promotion team to Torquay and Luton Town respectively while Roger Hynd went to Birmingham for £25,000 at the end of July.

Although the Palace managed only a single point from our opening pair of matches, for the rest of the first half of the season and a little beyond we gave every appearance of having learned the necessary lessons from the previous term's narrow escape. Gerry Queen and Alan Birchenall quickly came to an effective understanding and several good, even impressive, results were secured. Newcastle and Blackpool were both beaten 1-0 at Selhurst Park and an outstanding 1-1 draw was gained at Anfield when a Gerry Queen header stunned the Kop and Liverpool only managed to stutter to a second-half equaliser, while the single-goal victory earned by Bobby Tambling's 'special' over Manchester United at Old Trafford certainly turned Bobby Charlton's 500th appearance for United sour, and provided huge cause for celebration among the Palace fans who had made the trip!

At one stage the Palace were actually in third place in the top flight table! This followed a 2-0 win at Huddersfield, secured by goals from Gerry Queen and Steve Kember in quick succession around the hour. We were behind Leeds and Manchester City but ahead of Arsenal on goal average.

Perhaps the most memorable First Division match during the autumn of 1970 was the visit of Leeds on Saturday 7 November. The Peacocks netted a fine opener in the fifty-second minute but Palace responded well and put the Northerners under intense pressure. But the breakthrough would not come, and when we were denied what appeared to be a clear-cut penalty with some seven minutes left, matters looked ominous for Bert Head's team. But, with just three minutes remaining, John Sewell hoisted another cross into Leeds' packed goalmouth. Lazily it arched up, over, then down towards the big Leeds 'keeper, Gary Sprake, who stretched upwards to collect it, only for the ball to slip from his grasp, over his shoulder and into the net in front of the Holmesdale Road fans. Jack Charlton pounded the wet turf in fury, but Palace and their supporters were jubilant and justice had been seen to be done.

At Christmas, Palace were still among the top ten and a wonderful home victory over Liverpool on Saturday 16 January was secured by Gerry Queen on the hour but, following another success three weeks later, over Ipswich, there followed a miserable run of eight matches for only one point and a rapid slide down the table. We finished in eighteenth place after losing the last match of the season 0-6 in a shock rout at Southampton, our worst defeat for over a decade.

However, no record of 1970/71 would be complete without reference to Palace's exploits in the League Cup and to one success in particular. We reached the quarter-finals before an injury depleted side went out 2-4 to Manchester United at Old Trafford, in a match that was hollow after Alan Birchenall had been hurt and substituted after only a few minutes' play.

The highlight of the run had been in the previous round when a rousing if goal-less initial match at Selhurst Park sent Palace and Arsenal to a replay at Highbury on 9 November. Palace put on their best display of the season and Gerry Queen put us ahead after goalkeeper Bob Wilson had failed to hold a shot from Jim Scott. Then Bobby Tambling powered home a penalty with a quarter of an hour to go to record an historic Palace win, for this was Arsenal's only defeat on their own ground throughout their entire 'double' season – and Palace returned the following Saturday to take a point from the First Division clash between the sides.

The incomparable Steve Kember.

SEASON: 1970/71

GROUND: Selhurst Park

MANAGER: Bert Head

LEAGUE/DIVISION: Football League First Division

FINAL POSITION: 18th

BIGGEST VICTORY: 3-0 *v.* West Bromwich Albion, 17 October 1970

HEAVIEST DEFEAT: 0-6 *v.* Southampton, 4 May 1971

FA CUP – ROUND ELIMINATED: 3rd

LEAGUE CUP – ROUND ELIMINATED: 5th

FULL MEMBERS CUP – ROUND ELIMINATED: –

LEADING LEAGUE APPEARANCES (MAX: 42): 42 – J. Jackson, 40 – P. Wall

LEADING LEAGUE GOALSCORERS: 10 – A. Birchenall, 9 – G. Queen

1971/72

BERT HEAD MAKES CHANGES TO ENSURE PALACE SURVIVAL

The only change in the staff at Selhurst for the start of 1971/72 was the chief coach. George Petchey left on 12 July to manage Orient and was replaced by the former Manchester City centre half Dave Ewing. The playing staff remained unaltered too, but David Payne was deputed to slot in at right-back in place of John Sewell. Now parading in white shirts with a broad claret and blue stripe, Palace won their opening match of the season for the first time in the top flight on 14 August. Newcastle were despatched 2-0 with goals from Bobby Tambling and Tony Taylor. But Palace then lost seven of the next eight matches and with the new term just five weeks old we were clearly in dire trouble with just three points and five goals to our credit. Drastic action was necessary and Bert Head took it in breathtaking style.

Within a week in mid-September Alan Birchenall had gone to Leicester City for £100,000 and Steve Kember had left us for Chelsea at a fee variously reported as between £150,000 and £170,000. Bobby Kellard (£50,000) arrived back at the Palace from Leicester; striker John Craven (£35,000) joined from Blackpool; Bobby Bell, a central defender, came from Blackburn for £60,000 and Sammy Goodwin (£40,000) moved in from Airdrie. Much to Mr Head's credit the upheaval worked and immediately Palace beat Everton at Selhurst Park then gained away points at Leicester (0-0), Newcastle (2-1) and Coventry (1-1). By early December the team had moved out of the two relegation places, John Craven's arrival was being seen as significant while the return of the twenty-eight-year-old Kellard was considered by many to be a major factor in the praiseworthy Palace revival.

To replace the gifted and popular Steve Kember was no easy task, but Kellard was always a man for a tough job and no mean footballer. Bobby was now deployed in midfield: his industry and skill were amply demonstrated again and he soon became Palace's team captain. He missed only one match in the remainder of that tense season and contributed three goals from the penalty spot at a crucial stage. Palace recouped £12,000 of their investment in him when he moved to Portsmouth just after Christmas 1972, having fulfilled in the most testing circumstances all the hopes that had been pinned upon him by manager Bert Head and the Palace fans.

There was another factor in Palace's recovery. Taking advantage of a virtual media blackout caused by a strike in the newspaper industry in October 1971, Bert Head persuaded Celtic to

Palace forwards John Hughes (left) and Gerry Queen lead a Palace attack at Highbury on 27 September 1971. No goal was forthcoming and Palace lost 1-2.

part with international forwards Willie Wallace and John Hughes for a bargain fee of £55,000. Wallace was a clever, intelligent player while Hughes might have become a prolific scorer for us, but he was badly injured in the game against Sheffield United here at Selhurst Park on Saturday 4 December, for which he will always be remembered by the Palace fans who were there to witness it. John was our inspiration behind a convincing 5-1 victory as, in what proved to be the turning point in our season, he scored twice himself, ran riot in the Sheffield defence and virtually made himself a Palace legend in a single game – but he was never the same player after the injury.

That morale-boosting victory over a leading top-flight club took Palace out of the relegation spots and we continued to play ourselves clear of the danger zone with a side that had again become a team with fight, determination, character and skill, and those qualities eventually saw us to safety with a four-point margin over the relegated clubs.

One of the most contentious matches ever played at Selhurst Park was in January 1972. Palace were drawn to meet Everton in a third round FA Cup tie on Saturday 15 January and trouble began early with a spiteful foul by Joe Royle on 'keeper John Jackson. Matters were soon out of hand and ill-disciplined players and a weak referee brought something approaching a riot to our ground. Twice the crowd invaded the pitch and there was a real threat to the safety of certain culprits and the referee. The result was a 2-2 draw, but fortunately Bert Head and Harry Catterick, together with their players and aided by a different official, produced a splendid Goodison Park replay that ended 2-3 to Everton and with handshakes and smiles all round.

SEASON: 1971/72

GROUND: Selhurst Park

MANAGER: Bert Head

LEAGUE/DIVISION: Football League First Division

FINAL POSITION: 20th

BIGGEST VICTORY: 5-1 *v.* Sheffield United, 4 December 1971

HEAVIEST DEFEAT: 0-4 *v.* Manchester City, 18 August 1971, 0-4 *v.* Manchester United, 25 March 1972

FA CUP – ROUND ELIMINATED: 3rd

LEAGUE CUP – ROUND ELIMINATED: 3rd

FULL MEMBERS CUP – ROUND ELIMINATED: –

LEADING LEAGUE APPEARANCES (MAX: 42): 42 – J. Jackson, 41 – D. Payne, M. Blyth, T. Taylor

LEADING LEAGUE GOALSCORERS: 8 – R. Tambling, 7 – J. Craven

1972/73

PALACE RECRUIT MALCOLM ALLISON BUT STILL LOSE SENIOR STATUS

Although this season was to end in disaster, it started optimistically enough for Crystal Palace for, in September Raymond Bloye became club chairman with Arthur Wait becoming life-president. On the playing side there was a well-deserved promotion when Terry Long became assistant manager, a just reward for a likeable, loyal Palace servant who had joined us from Wycombe Wanderers back in May 1955.

However, as early as only the third match of the season, against Liverpool at Selhurst Park, there was a stern warning of the difficulties ahead when Peter Wall broke his leg in a tackle with his former teammate Tommy Smith, the 'Anfield Iron'. This necessitated a reshuffle in Palace's defence that eventually led to Tony Taylor taking over at left-back. Tony had already starred for Palace in several other positions, but he now proved to be a most effective full-back – and gained the longest sobriquet in the Palace annals: he became known as the 'Play-me-anywhere-as-long-as-you-play-me' man, and over four seasons in the top flight only John Jackson and Mel Blyth bettered his 150 appearances.

Martin Hinshelwood made a successful debut at Southampton in September, but Palace had already been ousted from the League Cup by Fourth Division Stockport in front of our own fans, so another reorganisation via the transfer market was clearly essential. Regrettably though, this time Bert Head's efforts were doomed to failure. Within a week, over a quarter of a million pounds was paid to secure Charlie Cooke (£85,000) and full-back Paddy Mulligan (£75,000) from Chelsea, as well as Iain Philip, a strong midfield or back-four man, from Dundee for £105,000. To offset this partially Gerry Queen joined the Palace 'old boys' at Orient for £70,000 and Willie Wallace moved back to Scotland to Dumbarton.

By mid-October Palace were bottom of the First Division table with only two wins and eight goals from our opening thirteen fixtures, but on Saturday 4 November we at last gained our third win of the season and moved off the foot of the division. That victory was over Everton at Selhurst Park and was the stage for the story-book debut of Don Rogers, who joined his former manager from Swindon and scored the single goal of the game. At a cost of £150,000, Rogers, of the cultivated, lethal left foot, phenomenal acceleration and supreme control, revitalised Palace for a while and the next victory was an amazing 5-0 rout of Manchester United on 16 December, which was the occasion of £100,000 Alan Whittle's debut.

Incredibly, it was Palace's right-back Paddy Mulligan who began the downfall of the Old Trafford sophisticates, hitting a ninth-minute opener and another three minutes before the break. Rogers himself netted our third a minute after the interval and a grandstand finale provided by a Whittle rocket and Rogers rounding Alex Stepney to net the fifth calmly left Palace fans almost delirious with joy.

But, while that victory lifted Palace to nineteenth, we never improved enough to climb clear of the relegation struggle and, after an appalling March, when we gained just two points from six games, we were obviously locked in a titanic struggle for survival. Thus, on Friday 30 March the board of directors appointed the ebullient Malcolm Allison as our team manager, with Bert Head moving upstairs as general manager. The following afternoon, Allison strode to the centre circle before our home match against Chelsea flanked by Ray Bloye and Bert Head to be hailed by the Palace fans, and Palace went on to beat Chelsea 2-0 to record our first win over London opponents in thirty-two top-flight matches. Jim Cannon, making his debut, headed Palace's decisive second goal just before the hour had elapsed.

But Palace gained just one more point from the next five games and our only hope was to beat fellow strugglers Norwich at Carrow Road on Easter Tuesday evening. The tension was almost unbearable but deep into injury time we were holding on at 1-1. Then Norwich were awarded a free-kick on our right. It seared into our goalmouth and in the ensuing melee the Canaries scored. Heartbreak!

Ironically, Palace won our final match of the season at Malcolm Allison's former club Manchester City 3-2, but it was a lost cause and Crystal Palace FC was about to embark upon some of the most testing years in its history.

Peter Wall.

SEASON: 1972/73

GROUND: Selhurst Park

MANAGER: Bert Head to 30 March 1973, then Malcolm Allison

LEAGUE/DIVISION: Football League First Division

FINAL POSITION: 21st

BIGGEST VICTORY: 5-0 *v.* Manchester United, 16 December 1972

HEAVIEST DEFEAT: 0-4 *v.* West Ham United, 28 October 1972, 0-4 *v.* Leeds United, 21 April 1973

FA CUP – ROUND ELIMINATED: 4th

LEAGUE CUP – ROUND ELIMINATED: 2nd

FULL MEMBERS CUP – ROUND ELIMINATED: –

LEADING LEAGUE APPEARANCES (MAX: 42): 40 – T. Taylor, 39+1 – D. Payne, 39 – M. Blyth

LEADING LEAGUE GOALSCORERS: 13 – D. Rogers, 7 – J. Craven

1973/74

MALCOLM ALLISON'S EAGLES ARE RELEGATED AGAIN

The summer of 1973 was a time of substantial change at Crystal Palace FC and not without controversy. Bert Head resigned quietly and with typical dignity, then left the club on 3 May after seven years. It was farewell too to 'The Glaziers', Palace's nickname since 1905, and all hail to the proud 'Eagles' as Malcolm Allison sought a more aggressive, assertive image at our club.

On the playing side John Craven joined Coventry for £60,000 and manager Allison made it clear that other players might also be on the move. Terry Long severed his long connections with the Palace and teamed up with George Petchey at Orient. David Payne also made the move to east London for a fee of £20,000.

With high hopes of a speedy return to the top flight, Palace began 1973/74 with a home match against Notts County, just promoted from the Third Division. A crushing 1-4 defeat showed that a swift return to the First Division was not going to be a mere formality. Far from it!

In fact the 1973/74 season turned out to be the most traumatic in the history of the Palace up to that date, and a thoroughly miserable one from the playing point of view. Many fans were deeply disappointed when the invincible John Jackson left in mid-October for Orient at a bargain fee of £30,000 to conclude a Palace career that dated back to August 1964 and embraced 388 first-class matches: his testimonial match against Chelsea later in the year was a highly emotional occasion. Meanwhile Charlie Cooke and Don Rogers lost their lustre, Stockport knocked us out of the League Cup for the second year running and Bobby Tambling departed for a post in Cork.

Poor Palace got just one point from the first six matches and went the first fifteen games without a win. It was our worst ever start to a season. Eventually we beat Bristol City 1-0 at Ashton Gate on 19 November with an Alan Whittle goal but by then confidence had totally evaporated and it was more a question of survival for the second term running, rather than of a glorious return to the First Division.

At last, as the new year of 1974 came in, Palace found new heart and some vestige of form. We beat West Bromwich on New Year's Day (1-0), drew at home to fancied Bolton (0-0) then, in our first Sunday fixture, brought about by the power crisis and the three-day working week, won at Notts County 3-1 on 20 January. In fact Palace lost just twice between then and Easter and two fine away victories, 2-1 at Nottingham Forest plus a great 3-1 success at Fulham on

John Jackson left the Eagles for Orient in October 1973.

Good Friday before massed Palace support really did give solid grounds for hope of escape from the predicament in which we found ourselves.

On Easter Saturday, however, we lost 2-3 at Millwall and then Fulham gained sweet revenge on the Tuesday to leave us third from bottom – and, of course, 1973/74 was the season in which 'three up and three down' was introduced, so that when we lost 0-2 at home to Hull five days later the signs were distinctly ominous.

In front of a massive Palace contingent, the Eagles won their penultimate match 1-0 on a hard, dusty pitch at Swindon, who were themselves already doomed to relegation, but the issue was now starkly clear. Palace had to beat Cardiff on 30 April at Ninian Park. For Cardiff a draw would ensure safety.

What a night that was! Around four to five thousand Palace fans in a 26,781 crowd saw the away side take a deserved lead in the twenty-ninth minute when Stewart Jump touched home Peter Taylor's corner, only for elation to become frustration when Cardiff equalised five minutes before half-time. After the break there was only one team in it! Peter Taylor hit the base of a post; a Mel Blyth drive from thirty yards was hit with such ferocious power that it threatened to take the 'keeper into the net with it: and so it went on. Ten minutes remained and the home crowd was already whistling for time! Whittle, Possee and Mulligan all went close, but to no avail. And then the final whistle: Cardiff jubilant at yet another narrow escape, Palace despondent yet cheered from the arena by their loyal fans... but the question now to be pondered was whether that loyalty would stretch into the Third Division.

SEASON: 1973/74

GROUND: Selhurst Park

MANAGER: Malcolm Allison

LEAGUE/DIVISION: Football League Second Division

FINAL POSITION: 20th

BIGGEST VICTORY: 3-0 *v.* Sunderland, 9 March 1974

HEAVIEST DEFEAT: 0-4 *v.* Sheffield Wednesday, 29 September 1973

FA CUP – ROUND ELIMINATED: 3rd

LEAGUE CUP – ROUND ELIMINATED: 2nd

FULL MEMBERS CUP – ROUND ELIMINATED: –

LEADING LEAGUE APPEARANCES (MAX: 42): 41 – Don Rogers, 37 – P. Hammond

LEADING LEAGUE GOALSCORERS: 15 – D. Rogers, 9 – D. Possee

1974/75

A RATHER ORDINARY THIRD DIVISION SEASON

So rapid had been Palace's fall from the top division that many of our players were still being paid First Division wages when the 1974/75 season opened and, with an inevitable drop in club income and an over-large playing squad, an urgent reappraisal was needed by manager Malcolm Allison. Thus, before the new season started, two men were on their way: Derek Possee left in July for Orient for £55,000, less than half the figure we had paid for him eighteen months earlier, and in mid-August Tony Taylor went to Southend for £20,000. Incidentally someone worked out that Taylor was the twenty-eighth professional player to leave Selhurst Park in just seventeen months!

Perhaps understandably, Palace opened 1974/75 with some diffidence and in the early matches there were several disappointing performances, particularly away from home. However, these were balanced by some excellent play at Selhurst Park where Watford were beaten 5-1 in a League Cup replay and Swindon trounced 6-2.

Once Palace's away form improved we climbed the table and moved into second place on 6 November after a well-earned point from an evening game at Blackburn.

There was an important flurry of activity in the transfer market in September when Mel Blyth (the final link with the 1968/69 promotion squad) and Don Rogers left for Southampton and Queens Park Rangers respectively. Mel went on to great things with Saints, but Rogers' career was now in decline. On his day he been everything any fan could ever ask from a goalscoring winger or striker. His glorious goal on his debut against Everton in November 1972 was an absolute delight and he rattled 13 goals from his 26 League games that season. But not even his mercurial skills were sufficient to save us from relegation and, like a number of Palace players at that time, his form deserted him badly in the Second Division. As part of the Rogers transfer deal, Terry Venables and Ian Evans arrived from Queens Park Rangers and both made their debuts for us at Hereford on the evening of 18 September but Palace lost 0-2.

On 29 October 1974 Crystal Palace were hosts to the England Under-23 side who were playing Czechoslovakia in the UEFA competition. Palace winger Peter Taylor, now rapidly

Opposite: Palace winger Peter Taylor starred for England Under-23s on his international debut at Selhurst Park.

becoming the darling of Selhurst Park and certainly Malcolm Allison's best signing for our club, was selected for his first international honour by England manager Don Revie, and had a marvellous opening half hour. He scored England's first goal in only the third minute, then flighted the ninth-minute free-kick from which Mick Mills put England two up and firmly on the way to a 3-1 victory.

By Boxing Day Palace were again in second place, despite having won only two League games in two months, but then three consecutive away defeats at Gillingham, Charlton and Aldershot suggested our side was a spent force. But Malcolm Allison drove his men forward again and the Eagles responded with a commendable run of twelve matches without defeat that brought us back to the brink of the promotion pool. The run ended with two 1-2 away defeats, at Grimsby (an ill-tempered battle, with three players sent off) and Chesterfield, which virtually extinguished Palace's hopes. Promotion rivals Charlton faltered, however, on the run in, and Palace were not actually doomed to a further season in the lower reaches until after our penultimate match. We beat Gillingham 4-0 at Selhurst Park in a rearranged game but Charlton beat Preston 3-1 on the same evening to clinch finally their promotion.

In retrospect, the most important features of this 1974/75 season at the Palace were Terry Venables' decision to retire from playing to become the club coach, and Kenny Sansom's debut at Tranmere (0-2) in the last game of the term on 7 May, but other items of interest had been our first League fixtures with Hereford, Tranmere and Chesterfield and the unusual appearance of a pair of brothers on opposing sides when Palace met Wrexham. In both games Graham Whittle played for the Welsh club while Alan Whittle appeared for the Palace.

SEASON: 1974/75

GROUND: Selhurst Park

MANAGER: Malcolm Allison

LEAGUE/DIVISION: Football League Third Division

FINAL POSITION: 5th

BIGGEST VICTORY: 6-2 *v.* Swindon Town, 7 September 1974

HEAVIEST DEFEAT: 0-4 *v.* Bournemouth, 12 October 1974

FA CUP – ROUND ELIMINATED: 2nd

LEAGUE CUP – ROUND ELIMINATED: 2nd

FULL MEMBERS CUP – ROUND ELIMINATED: –

LEADING LEAGUE APPEARANCES (MAX: 46): 43 – P. Taylor, 41 – D. Jeffries, A. Whittle

LEADING LEAGUE GOALSCORERS: 14 – D. Swindlehurst, P. Taylor, 12 – A. Whittle

1975/76

THIRD DIVISION PALACE REACH THE FA CUP SEMI-FINALS FOR THE FIRST TIME

There were persistent rumours throughout the summer of 1975 that Palace boss Malcolm Allison was going back north to manage Stockport County, but these all came to nothing and the 1975/76 season got underway. It fell into two distinct parts. From August until January Palace set a scorching pace in the League, including the creation of a new Club record as we won the first five Third Division matches, opening up a lead of seven points at one stage while remaining unbeaten away from home until 20 December.

Leading goalscorer at this time was a determined, tousle-haired young striker named David Kemp. Small he was in physical stature but he could certainly tuck away the goals and in this, his first season as a League footballer after joining us from Slough Town, he was something of a sensation. Ian Evans too was among the goals – he scored Palace's first hat-trick since October 1966 when he netted all three in our 3-2 victory over Colchester on 30 August, our Club's first ever hat-trick by a defender in fully competitive times. Meanwhile, Eire international Paddy Mulligan (who commanded a regular place in the Republic line-up, yet only featured in the Palace reserves) left on a free transfer to West Bromwich Albion.

After January it was in the FA Cup that Palace excelled, but at the same time we fell away badly in the League, so that after looking favourites for promotion and the divisional championship, we only finished in a disappointing fifth place, although we retained a slim chance of slipping into the third promotion place right up to our final match of the season, at Chester (1-2) on 4 May.

But in the FA Cup we were quite sensational and it is for those exploits that the 1975/76 season retains a lustre among our fans to this day, as the Eagles set a new Club record and became only the fifth Third Division side to reach the semi-finals. By comparison with what was to follow, our early season FA Cup victories were almost mundane, but we knocked out Walton & Hersham and Millwall before Christmas and non-league Scarborough in the third round in early January to set up a visit to Elland Road, home of Leeds United, who were standing in third place in the top flight, as proud as the Peacocks that provide their nickname.

If ever there was a match that was tailor-made for the charismatic Malcolm Allison to spring a shock result on behalf of an underdog, this one was it. In fact, so superb were Allison's Eagles on this chilly West Yorkshire afternoon that not only were Leeds outplayed on their own pitch,

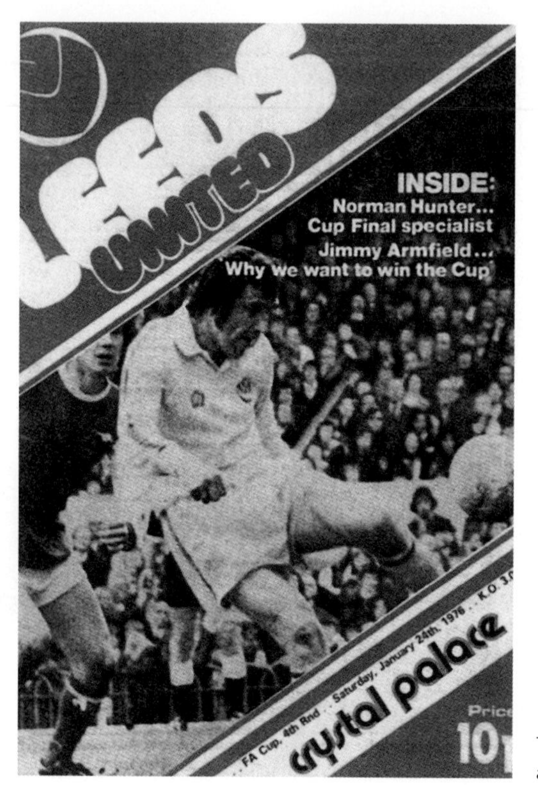

The programme for Palace's fourth round FA Cup victory, at First Division Leeds United.

but it is possible in retrospect to see that it was at this stage of Malcolm's managerial tenure at Selhurst Park that his side was reaching its peak. Certainly the subsequent victories at Chelsea and Sunderland were equally splendid ones and inevitably, as the competition progressed, gained greater media coverage, but it should be noted that both those opponents were 'only' Second Division sides whereas Leeds were one of the top sides in the country at that time. Their team was packed with international players, they were the FA Cup favourites and were regarded by the pundits as certainties for victory against the Palace. Only the enclave of fans who had travelled up from south London thought otherwise.

In the event Leeds were completely bemused tactically by Palace's sweeper system, in which Stewart Jump played as the extra man at the back and Leeds' danger men were closely marked by Palace's other outstanding defenders. The outcome of a single-goal Eagles triumph might mislead modern readers, because the reality was that a four-goal margin would not have flattered the Palace on the day and but for Leeds' Scottish international goalkeeper David Harvey we might have had it. But even Harvey was helpless when Palace were awarded a free-kick midway through the first half, towards the left flank but in front of our supporters. Peter Taylor offered the perfect delivery and Palace's popular, powerful striker Dave Swindlehurst soared to head stylishly into the net past Harvey's right hand. Jim Cannon and skipper Ian Evans were outstanding, Derek Jeffries had probably his best game in our colours and the youthful Nick Chatterton and Martin Hinshelwood dominated midfield in spite of the presence of Billy Bremner and Terry Yorath, so that Leeds' response scarcely ever looked likely to cause the Palace any serious difficulties.

Alan Whittle's goal at Sunderland put Palace into the FA Cup semi-finals for the first time.

Because the Eagles' fifth round clash at Chelsea was the one that allowed most Palace fans to attend, it has inevitably become the match of that fabulous FA Cup run that in retrospect epitomises the glory of it. The big Stamford Bridge arena was packed to see Palace beat the Blues at their headquarters for the first time and claim the full spotlight of the London-based media. It was also the occasion when the sheer character and prodigious talents of Peter Taylor shone at their brightest for the Eagles. Of course, Chelsea knew how dangerous he might be and contained him for long periods, while Taylor himself admitted that he had played many better games, but, ably supported by every one of his teammates, Peter was the game's outstanding star.

Palace paraded a new, all-white strip with a red-and-blue diagonal sash, and struck twice in three minutes after half an hour. Peter Taylor beat two defenders and whacked a shot against the crossbar for Nick Chatterton to convert from close range. Then Taylor speared a left-foot drive past Peter Bonetti. Chelsea responded in the third quarter of the game with goals from their teenage skipper Ray Wilkins and Steve Wicks but, with the initiative now with the home side, Bill Garner recklessly fouled Alan Whittle some twenty yards out from goal. Dave Swindlehurst shaped to take the free-kick but ran over the ball and Peter Taylor delicately and artistically chipped it over the advanced Bonetti and into the roof of the net for the winning goal.

By the time of Palace's sixth round tie at Sunderland's Roker Park there were quite simply no opponents in the land whom the Eagles feared and the Club took an amazing number of fans to Wearside for this contest against the best team and champions elect of the Second Division, although many of them missed the first half hour because delays on the railways meant that the special trains were late in arriving (no surprise there then!).

If the victories over Leeds and Chelsea were brilliant, this one surpassed them. Seventeen previous visitors to Roker Park had retired unsuccessfully that season and the North-Eastern cauldron had exposed several of them as unworthy opponents, but Palace were so disciplined and professional that once they had demonstrated to the Wearside players and their fans in the capacity crowd that we were neither overawed or lacking the required ability, everyone realised that a Palace victory was a distinct possibility.

Peter Wall played his best ever game for Palace as sweeper on this afternoon, but the whole defence was in excellent, composed form, particularly in the first half when Sunderland, with the benefit of a fierce wind at their backs, dominated matters, but the balance of play became more even after the break. The crucial moment came fourteen minutes from time when the inspirational Peter Taylor received a throw-out from goalkeeper Paul Hammond ten yards inside the Palace half. He sped away, coasted past the challenges of Joe Bolton and Bobby Moncur, then cut over a cross from the by-line that Alan Whittle met in glorious style, bringing the ball under control with his right boot then swivelling and cracking it into the net. We might even have had another goal or two to emphasise the moral extent of the victory, but there was absolutely no question in the last quarter of an hour which team had won the day, so that, even if many Palace fans had missed the start, we left the home team and supporters in no doubt that we were there in numbers at the glorious finale!

The semi-final, at Stamford Bridge, was a total anti-climax that requires no more than this single sentence for it was a dour, lacklustre encounter in which Palace completely failed to do themselves justice, and many of our fans left the ground long before the end. However this had been Palace's first major cup run in years, and it was now that the world saw Malcolm Allison at his flamboyant best, with his 'lucky' fedora (that became an instant south London fashion) as well as the champagne and outsize cigars. The younger fans in particular relished every moment of it all and at least there was a substantial success to enthuse over, even if we did fail to reach the final itself. Malcolm Allison's Eagles, born three years before and bruised and battered by two relegations, could preen their feathers at long last.

However, Big Mal took the failure to reach Wembley really hard and, when Palace threw away the promotion that had appeared to be so certain, it became too much for him. He resigned and left Selhurst Park on 19 May 1976.

To provide a reasoned evaluation of Malcolm's contribution to Crystal Palace FC is a complicated and complex matter. To begin with it must take into account two factors that will never appear to his credit in any book of football records. Firstly, it was Allison who brought Ian Evans and Terry Venables to Selhurst Park and, although injury was to reduce Ian's input to our cause, he was a fine skipper and a mighty asset in defence. Terry Venables' own contribution was to prove most valuable even if it was eventually to turn sour. Secondly, it was under Malcolm Allison that a revitalised Palace scouting team was developed, which was able to spot and attract to the Club young men of such outstanding ability that they would win the FA Youth Cup two years in succession, a feat no club had achieved since 1961, many of them going on to become household names in the game although, regrettably, they usually did so with other clubs. But, even though the mid-1970s will always be remembered by Palace fans for the famous FA Cup run, which Malcolm inspired, it is difficult to regard this, his main period in control of Crystal Palace FC, as being successful, even though some seeds for later progress were sown.

SEASON: 1975/76

GROUND: Selhurst Park

MANAGER: Malcolm Allison

LEAGUE/DIVISION: Football League Third Division

FINAL POSITION: 5th

BIGGEST VICTORY: 4-1 *v.* Mansfield Town, 29 November 1975

HEAVIEST DEFEAT: 1-4 *v.* Rotherham, 3 February 1976

FA CUP – ROUND ELIMINATED: Semi-final

LEAGUE CUP – ROUND ELIMINATED: 2nd

FULL MEMBERS CUP – ROUND ELIMINATED: –

LEADING LEAGUE APPEARANCES (MAX: 46): 45 – I. Evans, 43 – D. Swindlehurst, P. Hammond

LEADING LEAGUE GOALSCORERS: 16 – D. Swindlehurst, 12 – P. Taylor

1976/77

TERRY VENABLES LEADS PALACE TO PROMOTION IN HIS FIRST SEASON

It was on 1 June 1976 that Terry Venables was first appointed manager at Crystal Palace FC and the ensuing three or four years were to prove dramatic and successful. With Terry at the Palace helm we were seldom headline news and gone were the breathtaking ventures into the transfer market. Instead, he ushered in an era of steady, positive hard work in fashioning first a team that could battle its way with skill and style out of the Third Division, and then another one from the young, aspiring stars in the Youth squad that would, it was hoped and expected, be capable of bringing even greater success.

The extraordinary feature of Palace's 1976/77 promotion campaign was that we were never actually in the promotion bracket until after the final match of the season. And such an outcome appeared highly unlikely early in the term when Terry had plenty of problems. The playing side was unsettled and in the first two months of the season Terry called upon no fewer than twenty different players. His major dilemma, whether to use the unsettled Peter Taylor (now a highly prized footballer who obviously would not remain with the Palace for much longer) or not, was only resolved when Peter moved across London to Tottenham for a £200,000 fee at the end of September.

A rising star in the Palace firmament at this time was twenty-year-old striker Rachid Harkouk. Chelsea born of an Algerian father and Yorkshire mother, Rachid joined the Eagles late in June 1976 and demonstrated his ability and value by becoming our leading goalscorer this season. Tall, pale and slim and appearing to be all arms and legs when moving at speed, Rachid was quickly nicknamed 'Spider' by his teammates, adopted by the fans, and carried a shot like a bullet.

Palace held three trump cards that were eventually to produce the craved-for return to the upper half of the Football League in 1976/77. We had a core of players who knew each other now by instinct – defenders Jim Cannon and Ian Evans, midfielder Nick Chatterton and striker Dave Swindlehurst all made their 100th League appearance for the Club during this season. Cannon and Evans formed a thoroughly dependable partnership in the middle of our back four, Chatterton was tenacious, skilful and hard-running, precisely the sort of driving energetic dynamo that is needed in a side striving to get out of the lower divisions and Swindlehurst was a big, strong centre forward, brave, good in the air and a consistent goalscorer.

Secondly, Venables' expertise created a new pairing at full-back. Paul Hinshelwood was transformed during the term – initially towards the end of November — from a rather ordinary midfield player, who had formerly been a striker, into a magnificent right full-back, and his partnership with Kenny Sansom was to be an important and invaluable feature of Palace defences throughout the later 1970s. Kenny was the first tangible product of the youth policy instituted by Malcolm Allison from which Terry Venables was to benefit enormously. Kenny was unquestionably Palace's best ever left-back and became quite brilliant. He was a class above the Third Division – and this was at the tender age of just seventeen and eighteen years! His rapid rise to maturity meant that it was possible for the new manager to move big Jim Cannon from the left-back berth, where he had starred in the previous season, to the centre of the Palace defence and this was a considerable bonus.

Thirdly George Graham, vastly experienced from his days with Chelsea, Arsenal and Manchester United, arrived from Portsmouth on 8 November when Palace completed an exchange deal with our now somewhat fading scorer David Kemp moving in the other direction. Once George had settled down with us he became Palace's midfield director.

Palace's defence was quite superb throughout this season. With Cannon, Evans and Sansom all playing every game we conceded only 40 goals in the entire programme of 46 matches. At the time this was a post-war Club record and in fact has only ever been improved upon by the Championship-winning sides of 1920/21 and 1978/79. It is impossible to exaggerate the quality of Palace's back four at this time and the fact that Sansom and Evans were either soon to

Paul Hinshelwood was transformed into a magnificent full-back.

become, or already were international defenders speaks for itself – and Jim Cannon's non-selection for Scotland has always remained a mystery to Palace fans. Evans was also the Club captain and could always be relied upon to get several goals a season in addition to his defensive duties, while his height and heading ability at our set pieces made him an invaluable performer. Palace's last line of defence, Paul Hammond, also made his 100th appearance for us this season. He had been with us since September 1971, but probably only came to the attention of most Palace fans when he deputised ably enough for John Jackson three times in the autumn of 1972. Malcolm Allison made Paul his number-one choice in preference to Jackson and it speaks highly for Paul that he was, eventually, able to justify that decision. He was safe and agile and, certainly at Third Division level, an excellent goalkeeper, until he chose to move across the Atlantic in February to play for Tampa Bay Rowdies. Veteran Tony Burns was reinstated upon Hammond's departure and the seasoned professional added his vast experience to our defence as we sought to force our way into the top three places to gain promotion.

Actually, Palace would never have been able to achieve that objective had it not been for the belated signing of a goal-getting striker at a crucial time. Steve Perrin had augmented Swindlehurst and Harkouk usefully enough throughout the middle months of the season, but the man Terry Venables wanted, and was eventually able to secure in early March, was Jeff Bourne of Derby County. Suddenly the Palace became a free-scoring outfit and Bourne contributed 9 vital goals in our last 15 matches.

Out on the pitch, 1976/77 is remembered for two matches in particular – the first one an FA Cup tie. After the fabulous run to the semi-finals the previous season, our achievements in the Cup this term were rather more mundane. The first round draw pitted Palace against fellow Third Division opponents Brighton, whose manager Alan Mullery had been with Terry Venables at Tottenham. Nearly 30,000 fans were at Albion's headquarters to see a late Rachid Harkouk equaliser necessitate a Selhurst Park replay. Rachid hit Palace's goal in that game too, but the 1-1 outcome required another rematch and it took place thirteen days later at Stamford Bridge in dreadful weather, which kept the attendance down to barely half the crowds that had seen the previous episodes of the tie.

Palace's goal came early, before the sodden pitch became badly cut up, Brighton 'keeper Peter Grummitt fumbling a long shot from Phil Holder. Brighton responded positively but the match is recalled for two late incidents that determined the outcome. Firstly a Brighton equaliser was denied when the referee awarded Palace a free-kick for an obscure reason, then Barry Silkman conceded a penalty. Brian Horton put the kick away, only for a retake to be ordered. Horton's second effort was parried by Paul Hammond and Kenny Sansom completed the Palace escape.

Albion were livid. Their manager expressed himself in vehement terms at the close to the official and then responded to the goading of the Palace fans by offering them a V-sign as he disappeared down the tunnel. If modern Palace fans want to know where the intense feelings we all have towards the Seagulls and their followers originated, they should look no further than a wet night on a neutral ground in west London towards the end of 1976.

The other match that encapsulates 1976/77 for Palace fans of the period will always remain the one at the climax of the campaign. With Jeff Bourne now blended into the side and scoring regularly we were able to claw our way towards the promotion places. A narrow win over Wrexham at Selhurst Park (2-1) was followed four days later by a comprehensive one (4-1) over Lincoln City in which Chatterton had to deputise for Tony Burns as our goalkeeper throughout

Ever-dependable Jim Cannon.

the second half. That left the Palace a single point behind Wrexham when we travelled to the Racecourse for our re-arranged and final match of the season on Wednesday 11 May 1977.

George Graham was suspended and Burns' injury required twenty-year-old Peter Caswell to make his debut. But Palace had enormous support for a midweek game at such a distant venue, although we were largely on the defensive in the first quarter of the game. However, we then snatched the lead. Kenny Sansom possessed a hugely powerful long throw and he used it to great effect that night. In the twenty-seventh minute he sent the ball downfield to Nick Chatterton, whose low drive ricocheted off a defender's heel to David Swindlehurst, who forced it home from close range. Five minutes after half-time it was 2-0 and again it was our young left-back who was the instigator. Kenny made a fine run down the left flank, sent Barry Silkman clear and then ran towards the Wrexham goal for the cross. He put in a header that spun to Steve Perrin, who despatched it with aplomb.

But now Wrexham were desperate and dangerous. So close were the two clubs' goal differences that a Palace win by two goals would require the Welshmen to win their outstanding game, so they rallied and to their credit surged back with two quick replies that would have made their Saturday fixture a formality. Palace's chance seemed to have gone – but with ninety seconds left, we produced a sensational finale.

Kenny Sansom hurled a long throw from the right-side corner and substitute Rachid Harkouk hooked the ball home, just under the bar and above the groping fingers of goalkeeper Barry Lloyd. Wrexham were stunned and Palace came again! Harkouk slipped a perfect pass through to Jeff Bourne and the number nine rammed it into the corner of the net for 4-2. There was barely time for Wrexham to kick-off again before the final whistle blew to produce great jubilation among our players on the pitch and wherever Palace supporters were gathered around the ground.

SEASON: 1976/77

GROUND: Selhurst Park

MANAGER: Terry Venables

LEAGUE/DIVISION: Football League Third Division

FINAL POSITION: 3rd

BIGGEST VICTORY: 5-0 *v.* Swindon Town, 12 April 1977

HEAVIEST DEFEAT: 1-4 *v.* Port Vale, 26 April 1977

FA CUP – ROUND ELIMINATED: 3rd

LEAGUE CUP – ROUND ELIMINATED: 2nd

FULL MEMBERS CUP – ROUND ELIMINATED: –

LEADING LEAGUE APPEARANCES (MAX: 46): 46 – K. Sansom, J. Cannon, I. Evans, 42+1 – P. Hinshelwood

LEADING LEAGUE GOALSCORERS: 11 – R. Harkouk, 10 – D. Swindlehurst

1977/78

A SEASON OF ENCOURAGEMENT IN THE ABSENCE OF CRUELLY INJURED SKIPPER

Back in the Second Division, Palace's attainments in 1977/78 were encouragingly high. The newly promoted club finished the season in ninth place with a side that, by the end of the campaign, regularly included six members of the FA Youth Cup-winning squad from the previous term, while the Youth team won that competition again by beating First Division opponents Aston Villa in the one-off final at Highbury, for the second successive year.

But 1977/78 also had its disappointments. Firstly there was the complete inability of striker Jeff Bourne to recover his goal-scoring touch after the summer recess, and he left the Palace in February 1978 for Dallas USA, after playing 17 Second Division matches for us, which produced just one goal for him. Then, there was never a more sickening occurrence than the serious break sustained by club captain and central defender Ian Evans to his right leg, in a tackle with George Best in the home match with Fulham, on 1 October. That injury threw Palace right out of gear and the loss of the accomplished Welsh international defender could scarcely be overestimated.

Evans had captained the 1975/76 Palace side that had done so well to reach the FA Cup semi-finals as a Third Division outfit, but his best season was undoubtedly 1976/77 when he skippered Palace to promotion to the Second Division, playing every game, while his international career blossomed. He became the regular central defender for Wales and was part of their most successful side for many years. They gained some impressive results against continental opposition but probably their finest achievement during Ian's time was the 1-0 win they secured at Wembley on 31 May 1977. This was the Principality's first victory over England since 1955 and their first on English soil for over forty years. Altogether, Ian had gained 13 full caps for Wales and of course he had made an invaluable, unique contribution to Crystal Palace as a player. The injury was severe: Ian was unable to play again for virtually two years and he was never able to play for his country or for the Palace senior side again.

It was partly in response to Ian's absence that Billy Gilbert came into the Palace team but, besides him,1977/78 saw the League debuts of Peter Nicholas and Terry Fenwick too, the triumvirate having been talented and powerfully effective members of the Youth Cup-winning side of the previous term. These three, plus Ian Walsh and Jerry Murphy (who had each made a single League appearance in 1976/77) and Vince Hilaire (a real veteran with 3 previous

Vince Hilaire, seen here scoring at Coventry in April 1980, became a first-team regular in 1977/78.

appearances!) became regular and impressive members of the first team while David Fry, the former Youth team goalkeeper, also made his debut in the final match of the season.

Meanwhile Peter Wall had taken a contract in Los Angeles with California Surfs after making 177 League appearances for Palace and acting as captain on occasions, both in the First Division and after Ian Evans' injury.

It was a 'beat the transfer deadline' move that brought the ebullient John Burridge to Selhurst Park from Aston Villa for a £40,000 fee on 9 March 1978 and it came twenty-four hours after Steve Perrin had gone to Plymouth for £30,000. Burridge was already an experienced goalkeeper with an extrovert personality who had played for Workington and Blackpool before his spell at Villa Park. He came straight into the Palace side and became a huge favourite with Palace fans, whom he would delight with his energetic pre-match warm-ups out on the pitch.

As the season progressed, so the Palace defence tightened its ranks. Kenny Sansom, mature beyond his years; Paul Hinshelwood, unsung but improving all the time; Billy Gilbert, settling in at number six and learning restraint while developing into a top-quality defender and big Jim Cannon, upon whom the mantle of captain had now fallen. Jim had been spotted for the Palace in Glasgow and to most supporters at Selhurst Park it was simply incredible that the Scottish selectors could not recognise his potential value to their national side.

SEASON: 1977/78

GROUND: Selhurst Park

MANAGER: Terry Venables

LEAGUE/DIVISION: Football League Second Division

FINAL POSITION: 9th

BIGGEST VICTORY: 5-0 *v.* Blackburn Rovers, 29 April 1978

HEAVIEST DEFEAT: 0-3 *v.* Blackburn Rovers, 3 December 1977, 0-3 *v.* Bristol Rovers, 27 December 1977

FA CUP – ROUND ELIMINATED: 3rd

LEAGUE CUP – ROUND ELIMINATED: 2nd

FULL MEMBERS CUP – ROUND ELIMINATED: –

LEADING LEAGUE APPEARANCES (MAX: 42): 41 – K. Sansom, 40 – P. Hinshelwood

LEADING LEAGUE GOALSCORERS: 12 – D. Swindlehurst, 9 – N. Chatterton, R. Harkouk

1978/79

BEST EVER PALACE DEFENCE BRINGS EAGLES ANOTHER TITLE

There were a couple of important transfer moves in mid-summer 1978 that were to affect the destiny of Crystal Palace in the forthcoming season. Queens Park Rangers had shown interest, all through the previous term, in Rachid Harkouk and at the end of June he took his scoring talents to Loftus Road, Palace receiving a £90,000 cheque. A few days later, after Terry Venables had sought him out on the beaches of southern Spain, Palace paid a Club record fee of £200,000 to Preston North End for the skipper at Deepdale, Mike Elwiss. Now the scene was set for an historic season.

The early results of 1978/79, including a 1-1 draw at fancied Blackburn Rovers on the opening day, and, most notably, the 3-1 defeat of another highly rated side, Luton Town, at Selhurst Park in our first home game, when Vince Hilaire demonstrated his immaculate skills so effectively, gave indications that Palace were going to be a force in the promotion stakes. A stunning 3-0 win at Millwall in great heat on 16 September upon Kenny Sansom's 100th League appearance, took Palace to the top of the table.

The Eagles had a profitable encounter with Aston Villa in the League Cup, taking the top-flight club to a second replay staged at Coventry before, in the absence of Jim Cannon, going out to the power of Scottish international striker Andy Gray, who scored twice in a 0-3 Palace defeat. It was with the proceeds from that third round tie that Palace brought Steve Kember back to his old home on 24 October 1978. Kember had played 130 League games for Chelsea before moving on to Leicester City, and now the Foxes required a £40,000 fee to release him. But this was a gilt-edged investment for Palace, who undoubtedly benefited from the experience and skill of their old favourite, who was himself clearly pleased to return.

Terry Venables elected not to use Steve in our extraordinary home game against Fulham the following Saturday, when the result, a shock single-goal victory for the Cottagers and disappointing enough for our fans, was the secondary issue among some amazing happenings. The referee appeared to blow for time a little prematurely, but the Palace had never looked like opening the visitors' solid defence on this afternoon so no-one really queried the matter. Not, that is, until the referee discovered his error and called the sides back from the dressing rooms to play another five-and-a-half minutes to the consternation of everyone present. Whether such a thing has ever happened in the League before or since simply is not known – but it is certainly unique at our Club, and long may it remain so.

For the only time this season Palace lost a second game in succession, at Burnley (1-2), in Steve Kember's first match after returning to us. Our goalscorer was Nick Chatterton in his 151st League game for us, but when Nick was left out for the 3-0 victory over Blackburn Rovers on Armistice Day he requested a transfer and moved quickly to Millwall. Nick had served the Palace well for more than five seasons, scoring 31 times for us, and his subsequent career with Millwall where he became club captain, and Colchester, was a distinguished one.

At the halfway stage of the season, just before Christmas, Palace were two points clear of Stoke at the top of the Second Division table, with Brighton and West Ham another two points behind. In a goal-less draw in our first-ever visit to Cambridge United, Palace suffered a cruel loss when Mike Elwiss limped off with cartilage trouble and was unable to play another first-team match for us, his career in ruins. It took Palace a long while to adjust to Mike's absence and we scored only 2 goals in the next 6 League games.

However, just when it became absolutely essential, Palace's young defence began to break the hearts of opposition strikers. In the first half of the season they had not been exactly generous with the goals conceded, but in the second half they conceded only 8! True, Palace were knocked off their proud perch at the top of the table, but in the last third of the season they came back to snatch the honours, beginning with a crucial and magnificent 2-1 victory over promotion rivals Sunderland in a midweek game at Roker Park on 14 March. Early goals from Vince Hilaire and Jim Cannon inside the first ten minutes silenced the big Wearside crowd and sealed the home team's fate.

Another postponement followed, this time against Burnley, and Palace were therefore always a point or two behind the top clubs for the run in to the end of the season. But in retrospect this seems likely to have helped to ease the pressure that was beginning to build and which could have affected the younger, less experienced members of the side while, of course, we still had the game in hand to play. Despite their youth, the Palace team coped with the tension that was affecting all the leaders as well as any of the top teams and in the twelve games that remained after the win at Sunderland we were never less than impressive. In that sequence we conceded just four goals and continued to secure some invaluable away victories as well as winning all but one of the home games.

For example, on Easter Saturday Palace were down at Bristol Rovers. The match was tense and dour throughout, but it turned on the need to replace Dave Swindlehurst, who had incurred a knee injury early in the second half. Terry Fenwick came on, Jerry Murphy took up a more adventurous role and Palace began to assume control. With less than two minutes to go, matters remained goal-less but then Ian Walsh broke the deadlock with a wickedly angled drive that gave the Rovers 'keeper no chance, and Palace joy and relief knew no bounds.

Easter Tuesday brought Charlton to Selhurst Park with a 30,000 crowd in attendance. Six minutes into the second half Jerry Murphy fastened onto a low cross from Steve Kember and fired expertly past Nicky Johns. Palace might have extended their lead but in the end were content enough with their narrow victory, for it left us in third place, a point behind Stoke and Brighton but still with our game in hand.

A late Paul Hinshelwood equaliser salvaged Palace's pride as well as a point at Leicester in a Friday evening game, then we edged past Notts County in our penultimate home match. County included our former favourite Alan Birchenall but Palace won 2-0 in a sparkling encounter in which the visitors hit our crossbar and goalpost just before half-time and only finally succumbed when Jerry Murphy notched our second goal just four minutes from time.

It was now apparent that if the Eagles could win our last two games we would be promotion bound.

The final Saturday of the season took the Palace to Orient's Brisbane Road, where two of the most popular men ever to play for us were in the opposition line-up – that superb goalkeeper John Jackson and the clever former Everton goalscorer Alan Whittle, now in the twilight of his career.

Steve Kember was suspended for this game, but Terry Fenwick deputised ably as always. The occasion was inevitably fraught and tense, yet there was plenty of flowing football and Orient were posing threats to us as we were to them. In the end a goal of supreme class settled it all in the sixty-eighth minute. Vince Hilaire collected a loose ball, jinked towards goal, then swept it wide to the marauding Kenny Sansom. Kenny crossed right-footed, picking out Dave Swindlehurst at the far post with precision for the big striker to despatch a top-corner goal with devastating accuracy.

The final game, against Burnley, held Palace's destiny. All the other challengers had finished their programmes and the outcome was so close that the issue lay entirely in our own hands. If we gained a first-ever victory over the Clarets we'd go up as Second Division champions. A draw would see us promoted at Sunderland's expense. If we lost we would be as good as nowhere.

The match with Burnley had been rearranged for the Friday evening, 11 May, before the cup final and drew a crowd of staggering proportions to Selhurst Park – 51,482 of us – and obviously never to be surpassed here. The gates were closed a full hour before the kick-off, there were scenes redolent of the first Wembley cup final as fans found unofficial means of entry and the atmosphere fairly sizzled with tension.

On the night Burnley proved no mean opponents, resisting Palace pressure, somewhat fortuitously at times, for seventy-six minutes. Alan Stevenson made a string of fine saves, beginning

Ian Walsh put Palace on the way to the Second Division championship with this goal against Burnley on 11 May 1979.

Walsh was ready to party afterwards!

in only the third minute when he collected a cheeky lob from Vince Hilaire. Jim Cannon scraped the crossbar and there was a profusion of other near-misses. With Palace failing to score, Burnley themselves began to threaten, led by the experienced Welsh international Leighton James and Steve Kindon. A shot from the former was headed off the line by Kenny Sansom.

But with fourteen minutes remaining, Vince Hilaire delivered a perfect cross for young Ian Walsh to rise above his marker and head the ball like an arrow into the top right-hand corner of the net. It was a goal fit to win a championship and the pitch was immediately invaded by delighted, excited fans. Order was restored, the match proceeded and it seemed as if victory would be secured by this narrowest of margins. However, with two minutes left and the great crowd heaving and swaying ecstatically in a manner that would send modern-day police and safety officers into a state of absolute apoplexy, Dave Swindlehurst clinched the title with a right-footed drive to a roaring crescendo.

The scenes at the final whistle were quite amazing. The players fled to the sanctuary of the tunnel as fully 20,000 fans poured onto the pitch. It was pandemonium. The seething mass of fans was good-natured yet, in the super-charged atmosphere, there was an underlying anxiety as to what might possibly happen.

To the delight of the huge throng, Jim Cannon led his men up to the directors' box to receive and acknowledge the riotous cheers of their admirers – and why not? Palace were back in the First Division. We were going up as champions and there was every reason to celebrate, so that everywhere there was jubilation at Selhurst Park!

SEASON: 1978/79

GROUND: Selhurst Park

MANAGER: Terry Venables

LEAGUE/DIVISION: Football League Second Division

FINAL POSITION: 1st

BIGGEST VICTORY: 3-0 *v.* Millwall, 16 September 1978, 3-0 *v.* Blackburn Rovers, 11 November 1978

HEAVIEST DEFEAT: 1-2 *v.* Burnley, 4 November 1978

FA CUP – ROUND ELIMINATED: 5th

LEAGUE CUP – ROUND ELIMINATED: 3rd

FULL MEMBERS CUP – ROUND ELIMINATED: –

LEADING LEAGUE APPEARANCES (MAX: 42): 42 – J. Burridge, K. Sansom, 41 – J. Cannon, W. Gilbert, 40+1 – J. Murphy

LEADING LEAGUE GOALSCORERS: 14 – D. Swindlehurst, 8 – I. Walsh

1979/80

RECORD SIGNINGS, TABLE TOPPERS... BUT PALACE END THE TERM IN DECLINE

Palace made two major transfer signings in the aftermath of promotion, each of which raised the level of our record transfer fee. First to arrive was former England skipper Gerry Francis, who cost us £465,000 from Queens Park Rangers. Then came England 'B' international striker Mike Flanagan for £650,000 from Charlton.

Thus augmented, Palace's first season back among the elite began in extremely encouraging fashion and, as the end of September approached, Palace were lying second in the table after three wins and four draws. Their fourth top-flight encounter at Selhurst Park was against Ipswich Town, managed by Bobby Robson and by this time a firmly established (old) First Division outfit after eleven seasons there. But Palace had dismissed the feeble, bad-tempered challenge of Derby County 4-0 and that of Aston Villa 2-0 in their previous two League games at our headquarters and our fans knew that, even if the Palace were regarded as underdogs, they would certainly make the Suffolk club realise that there was a new force in English football's senior division this season.

The occasion matched the glorious weather and by the end poor Ipswich had been played off the park. In fact, Palace's first half display was absolutely outstanding. Palace fans were in rhapsodies of delight as their youthful favourites demonstrated their talent and superiority with what was quite simply one of the best sustained spells of attacking football the Club has ever produced, then emphasised it with three goals before Ipswich regained a little credibility just as the interval approached.

But Town had no answer to Palace's inspired opening. Dave Swindlehurst rifled Palace's opening goal from a Vince Hilaire cross in the seventeenth minute, then Paul Hinshelwood headed in from a Gerry Francis free-kick on the half hour. The match was over as a contest shortly afterwards. Swindlehurst burst through the middle but was clumsily halted by Russell Osman. The inevitable penalty was taken by Gerry Francis but, with the one flawed moment of the entire Palace performance, he lifted the ball over the bar... only to receive another opportunity because goalkeeper Paul Cooper had moved too soon. This time Francis drilled the ball low into the net.

Yet, for all the near-perfection of the Eagles' first-half display, most fans who were present best recall the single goal of the second half, scored by Palace skipper Jim Cannon right on

Jim Cannon nets Palace's fourth goal against Ipswich to put the Eagles top of the First Division on 29 September 1979.

the hour. In three moves the ball travelled the entire length of the field. Vince Hilaire broke up a poor Ipswich corner and found Mike Flanagan drifting free down the left. Cannon spotted the opening and began an eighty-yard run down the middle. Flanagan saw Cannon's burst and delivered a long, dropping cross that the skipper met with an angled volley into the left-hand side of the goal netting. It brought everyone to their feet, including manager Terry Venables from the bench, who raised two clenched fists to the heavens in salute and, though no-one knew it at that precise time, Jim's strike was the goal that put the Palace on the top of the entire Football League, on goal difference, ahead of Manchester United and Nottingham Forest.

Regrettably of course, such brilliance was all too short-lived, and Palace slipped from the heights, particularly after Christmas, and we finished 1979/80 in mid-table, but it was at this time that some of the media pundits dubbed the Palace as 'the team of the eighties'. Although not a title the Club either initiated or desired, it appeared in retrospect to have had a harmful effect, because our performances never again reached this level of sophistication or effectiveness. In the end of course the sobriquet became a hurtful jibe.

As the season advanced two former Palace favourites moved elsewhere. Dave Swindlehurst joined Derby County in the spring for the Rams' record fee of £400,000 although he still finished the term as the Eagles' top scorer with 7 League goals from his 25 outings. Also leaving Selhurst Park was Ian Evans, who had made a courageous recovery from his broken leg but was unable to force his way back into our senior side. In December he joined Barnsley, where he helped the Tykes win promotion from the Third Division.

SEASON: 1979/80

GROUND: Selhurst Park

MANAGER: Terry Venables

LEAGUE/DIVISION: Football League First Division

FINAL POSITION: 13th

BIGGEST VICTORY: 4-0 *v.* Derby County, 1 September 1979

HEAVIEST DEFEAT: 0-4 *v.* Nottingham Forest, 3 May 1980

FA CUP – ROUND ELIMINATED: 3rd

LEAGUE CUP – ROUND ELIMINATED: 3rd

FULL MEMBERS CUP – ROUND ELIMINATED: –

LEADING LEAGUE APPEARANCES (MAX: 42): 42 – J. Cannon, V. Hilaire, P. Hinshelwood, 40 – W. Gilbert

LEADING LEAGUE GOALSCORERS: 7 – D. Swindlehurst, 6 – I. Walsh

1980/81

PALACE LEAVE THE ELITE IN SOME IGNOMINY

August 1980 saw one of the most sensational transfers in the history of Crystal Palace FC, for Kenny Sansom joined Arsenal in a £1 million exchange deal that brought former Queens Park Rangers striker Clive Allen to Selhurst Park after spending only two months at Highbury, along with goalkeeper Paul Barron for a further investment of £400,000. The loss of Sansom was to prove significant, for Palace's defence suffered badly in 1980/81, whereas Allen never justified his massive fee while with the Eagles, scoring 9 times for us from 25 games this season before moving back to QPR the following June for a greatly reduced sum.

For everyone connected with our Club, 1980/81 was simply dreadful. Palace began with a 0-3 reverse at Liverpool and lost 9 of the first 10 games up to mid-October, although we had miserable misfortune at Coventry on 6 September, when none of the officials saw a smashing Clive Allen shot rebound from the stanchion inside the net and the 'goal' being disallowed. At the same time, with the Eagles firmly rooted to the foot of the table, there were stories of disagreement between manager Terry Venables and the Palace board and, sure enough, to the dismay of many, Venables left Palace on 14 October to take charge of QPR. Terry was to have a highly successful subsequent managerial career and of course he had lifted Palace from the anonymity of the Third Division to the top flight but, when he left us, we were in a perilous condition and it had become evident that he was either unable or unwilling to remedy the problems.

Palace gave the manager's job to long-serving Ernie Walley – only to replace him with Malcolm Allison from 1 December, but by now it had become obvious that a take-over of the Club was imminent, and by mid-January the forthright Ron Noades, then the chairman of Wimbledon, together with a small, enterprising consortium had emerged as the most favoured contender and completion took place on 26 January 1981.

Malcolm Allison was dismissed as manager on the morning of the transfer of ownership and replaced by Dario Gradi, the former Wimbledon boss and England amateur international who thus became Palace's sixteenth post-war manager and our fourth in three turbulent months at Selhurst Park. Palace's first result after the change of ownership was a 0-2 defeat at Middlesbrough on 31 January where Jim Cannon and Tony Sealy were both sent off and Clive Allen missed a penalty, and this was soon followed by the departure of Gerry Francis to QPR in February for a paltry £150,000.

Here's the 'goal' that Palace scored at Coventry on 6 September 1980, but which was not seen by any of the officials.

Palace actually lost the first seven matches under the new administration, but before this were already a Club and a team indisputably heading for relegation and completely lacking in morale. New young players were drafted in to replace the departing stars who were heading for Loftus Road seemingly in droves, and we were hit by injuries and suspensions, but the manager did not help matters by declaring that it was not part of his responsibility to keep Palace in the top flight, although he later explained that in saying that he was merely seeking to alleviate the pressure felt by some members of his team.

On the transfer deadline day in early March there were further hectic dealings as part of the early attempts by Mr Noades to bring financial sanity to the Club's overstretched resources. Great favourite Peter Nicholas moved to Arsenal for £500,000, with experienced Caterham-born David Price joining us from the Gunners for £80,000. Brian Bason came from Plymouth for a similar sum, and Tommy Langley from QPR for £120,000, with Tony Sealy joining the Palace exiles at Loftus Road for £80,000. All three new men appeared in the home fixture against Sunderland on 14 March, but Palace still lost to a goal conceded just before the half hour, though a David Price equaliser earned the new manager his first point when we travelled to Leicester a week later.

Two further defeats, at home to Leeds and at Manchester United, were sufficient to make survival statistically impossible a full month before the end of the season, but frankly this was almost a relief to the long-suffering supporters. When the season ended with a thirteen-point gap between us and the twenty-first-placed club, no-one at Selhurst Park was in the least sorry.

SEASON: 1980/81

GROUND: Selhurst Park

MANAGER: Terry Venables until 14 October 1980, then Ernie Walley until 1 December, then Malcolm Allison until 26 January 1981, then Dario Gradi

LEAGUE/DIVISION: Football League First Division

FINAL POSITION: 22nd

BIGGEST VICTORY: 5-2 *v.* Middlesbrough, 23 August 1980

HEAVIEST DEFEAT: 0-5 *v.* Everton, 20 September 1980

FA CUP – ROUND ELIMINATED: 3rd

LEAGUE CUP – ROUND ELIMINATED: 3rd

FULL MEMBERS CUP – ROUND ELIMINATED: –

LEADING LEAGUE APPEARANCES (MAX: 42): 38+1 – W. Gilbert, 38 – P. Hinshelwood, 33 – P. Barron, J. Cannon

LEADING LEAGUE GOALSCORERS: 9 – C. Allen, 5 – I. Walsh, T. Sealy

1981/82

PALACE MAKE ANOTHER MANAGERIAL CHANGE

As the first executive boxes at Selhurst Park were being built during the summer of 1981, Clive Allen left the Eagles during June, inevitably, for Queens Park Rangers, in a deal that brought 6ft 3in centre half Steve Wicks to the Palace but cost the club an additional £200,000. Steve was troubled initially by injury and then Palace had to sell him (back to Rangers) for little more than half his value of £675,000 in March in order to raise much-needed money.

The first match of 1981/82 was at home to Cambridge United and Paul Hinshelwood (Palace's Player of the Year in both our top-flight seasons from 1979 to 1981) was twice on target in little more than half an hour from penalties. The first, after only 55 seconds, is surely the fastest penalty awarded at our ground. The game was unusual because Cambridge also replied from the spot after the interval. Meanwhile, at Loftus Road, Palace's reserves were engaged in the first competitive match to be played on an artificial surface, as Rangers pioneered the fad of plastic pitches that plagued the Football League for a decade or more.

It was not until our fourth match that Palace scored a goal from open play. Ian Walsh was twice on target either side of the break to beat Charlton while Steve Wicks excelled in defence, so that it was soon evident that we needed greater striking power if we were to make an impact upon the division. Shrewsbury began their lengthy hoodoo over Palace at the end of September, winning 1-0 at Selhurst Park and leaving the Palace in the bottom third of the table with manager Dario Gradi complaining about our 'woeful finishing'.

Teenager Shaun Brooks, captain of the England Youth team at the time, came into our side and scored in the next home match, a welcome 3-1 success over Rotherham, and Palace won the next match as well, 1-0 at Wrexham, thanks to full-back Steve Lovell, to secure our first away win in 32 attempts over 19 months!

An exciting new arrival at the end of October was Bristol City striker Kevin Mabbutt, secured from Ashton Gate for £200,000, but we lost on his debut at Luton and it was only when that intelligent and articulate young man scored his first Palace goal on 24 November against Norwich City (2-1) that Palace won another League match, and by then we were under new management.

Steve Kember's first spell as Palace boss was for most of 1981/82.

Dario Gradi had not been the most fortunate of Palace managers but, on Tuesday 10 November 1981, with Palace fifteenth in the Second Division, he was dismissed and replaced by the ever-popular Steve Kember, who was our Youth team coach at the time. Dario has subsequently proved his managerial qualities and few at the Palace blamed him for our predicament, but the Club of November 1981 undoubtedly needed a lift and it was inevitable that he should go.

Steve Kember immediately provided the lift. He led Palace to an unexpected victory at the tough venue of Roker Park, where a Jim Cannon goal just before the hour beat top-flight Sunderland in a third round League Cup tie, and Palace made a good start in the League under our new boss, drawing at Oldham then beating Norwich and Bolton at Selhurst Park to move into the top half of the table.

However, it would not be accurate to suggest that overall results under Steve Kember were any improvement upon those secured under his predecessor. Apart from a 4-0 beating of high-ranking Oldham in mid-April they were not, and we finished 1981/82 in fifteenth position, which was precisely where we had been when Steve had taken over in November. In fact the highlight of the second half of the term was an FA Cup run to the quarter-finals, where victories over Enfield (3-2), Bolton (1-0) and Orient (1-0 after a scoreless first match at Selhurst Park) took us into the last eight and a tie against the eventual finalists, Queens Park Rangers. Playing before easily the biggest crowd to watch us all season, 24,653, we lost a match that was strangely lacking in passion, on the artificial pitch, to a goal scored by Clive Allen just three minutes before the end.

SEASON: 1981/82

GROUND: Selhurst Park

MANAGER: Dario Gradi to 10 December 1981, then Steve Kember

LEAGUE/DIVISION: Football League Second Division

FINAL POSITION: 15th

BIGGEST VICTORY: 4-0 *v.* Oldham Athletic, 17 April 1982

HEAVIEST DEFEAT: 1-4 *v.* Derby County, 13 March 1982

FA CUP – ROUND ELIMINATED: 6th

LEAGUE CUP – ROUND ELIMINATED: 4th

FULL MEMBERS CUP – ROUND ELIMINATED: –

LEADING LEAGUE APPEARANCES (MAX: 42): 42 – J. Cannon, 41 – N. Smillie

LEADING LEAGUE GOALSCORERS: 8 – K. Mabbutt, 5 – V. Hilaire

1982/83

ALAN MULLERY'S FIRST SEASON AT SELHURST PARK

Crystal Palace FC announced the appointment of Alan Mullery as our new manager early in the summer recess of 1982 but, although Mullery was a big name in football in the early 1980s, the appointment did not meet with the approval of Palace fans. Alan had had a distinguished playing career with Fulham, Spurs and England, been awarded the MBE, then gained substantial success in management at Brighton. But his two years at the Palace were bitterly disappointing ones to the club, the fans and, no doubt, to him. Palace concluded this 1982/83 season in fifteenth place (again!) and dropped to eighteenth in 1983/84. Alan's formerly proven ploy of securing experienced men nearing the end of their careers for modest fees or even on free transfers failed to produce any cohesion or the beginnings of a settled, effective side. There was little if any money available to strengthen the team by major transfer action because, while the commercial aspects of the club had been greatly and successfully expanded under Ron Noades, the income from our gates had fallen alarmingly to their lowest post-war average level in 1981/82 and, of course, the continued lack of success meant that they dropped even further under Alan's management.

On the strength of two draws then two victories at the start of 1982/83, Palace were a top-six side for the first five weeks of the season but, by the end of October, we had slipped into the bottom half of the table and, by the time we approached the last match of the term, there was still a chance that we might be relegated. Our Selhurst Park opponents, by a black coincidence, were Burnley. Only four years previously we had beaten them to gain the Second Division championship, but this evening we had to salvage at least a point to retain our Second Division status!

A crowd of nearly 23,000 loyal Palace fans – almost three times the average gate – came to help their favourites survive and saw Ian Edwards, Mullery's first signing for our club, from Wrexham back in June, steer the ball home just after the hour from a Henry Hughton cross. The relief was evident and huge as the fans swarmed across the pitch and the champagne flowed in the dressing room at the close of the game.

Other incoming transfers during the season were strikers Chris Jones from Manchester City, on a free in November, who scored after only four minutes on his debut (but Palace still lost at home to Wolves 3-4) and Ally Brown from West Bromwich Albion in March. But perhaps

Left: Gavin Nebbeling became a regular member of Palace's defence this season.

Mullery's best signing for Palace that season was full-back Gary Locke, who came to us from Chelsea, initially on loan in January, and stayed to play 101 matches for Palace over the ensuing years.

Another player to make a major contribution that season was Gavin Nebbeling, who teamed up with Jim Cannon at the centre of our defence when Billy Gilbert was having to fill in at full-back, then had a spell at number three himself. Gavin was still learning the game at this stage but was to play a most useful role in Palace's recovery under Steve Coppell later in the 1980s.

Palace had an FA Cup tie against top-flight opponents in 1982/83 and beat Birmingham 1-0 in the fourth round at Selhurst Park, thanks to an Ian Edwards goal, before going out in a replay at Burnley in round five on the last day of February, where the Clarets won with a twice-taken penalty. The match programme is one of the most sought-after modern issues for Palace collectors because of the small number that Burnley had been able to have printed.

SEASON: 1982/83

GROUND: Selhurst Park

MANAGER: Alan Mullery

LEAGUE/DIVISION: Football League Second Division

FINAL POSITION: 15th

BIGGEST VICTORY: 4-1 *v.* Derby County, 7 May 1983

HEAVIEST DEFEAT: 1-4 *v.* Carlisle United, 18 September 1982, 1-4 *v.* Grimsby Town, 4 December 1982

FA CUP – ROUND ELIMINATED: 5th

LEAGUE CUP – ROUND ELIMINATED: 3rd

FULL MEMBERS CUP – ROUND ELIMINATED: –

LEADING LEAGUE APPEARANCES (MAX: 42): 42 – V. Hilaire, 41 – J. Cannon

LEADING LEAGUE GOALSCORERS: 10 – K. Mabbutt, 7 – P. Hinshelwood

1983/84

MULLERY'S PALACE IN FURTHER DECLINE

Season 1982/83 had been disappointing enough for Crystal Palace and its fans, but 1983/84 was worse. Not once were we so much as near the top third of the table; in fact we were never in the upper half!

During the summer months of 1983 Paul Hinshelwood left us to join rising Oxford United after playing a total of 319 first-class games for us. Arriving were big Andy McCulloch from Sheffield Wednesday, who cost us £20,000, Les Strong from Fulham, Sunderland's Stan Cummins and tall centre half John Lacy from Spurs, while George Wood, the former Arsenal and Scotland goalkeeper, was certainly one of Mullery's better acquisitions from among his many experienced signings. Best of all was to be young Phil Barber, signed from Aylesbury Town in February 1984, who was to assist the club to promotion, then in the top flight and also in the 1990 FA Cup finals.

Bleak news however, even before the new season started, was that leading scorer Kevin Mabbutt, who had missed four months of the previous term with a pelvic injury had gone down within minutes of a friendly against Southampton with a complicated knee injury. In fact, Kevin's career was blighted from that moment, even if he did play a few games for us later in this term and during 1984/85. In fairness to the manager his loss was a severe handicap. Mullery's reaction was to sign unsettled striker Tony Evans from Birmingham.

The immediate impact of the new arrivals was minimal. Palace went until 27 September before winning a League game, and by then we were in the relegation places and had been dismissed from the League Cup. Peterborough from the Fourth Division had reversed a 3-0 defeat from the Selhurst Park first leg in the second encounter at London Road and then, to our distress, dismay and huge embarrassment knocked us out in the ensuing penalty competition.

Peter Nicholas returned from Arsenal in an unusual transfer whereby he was still registered at Highbury and Palace did not have to find the £150,000 fee until the close season. There was a brief improvement in our fortunes during November, when a late header by substitute Jerry Murphy despatched Cardiff in midweek, Andy McCulloch and Murphy again put paid to Oldham the following Saturday, Tony Evans was on target at Chelsea where the feature of the match was an early scorching drive by Gary Locke against his former employers, and then a David Giles effort beat Sheffield Wednesday, who were resurgent under Howard Wilkinson and previously undefeated all season.

Jim Cannon (left) and Andy McCulloch put pressure on Chelsea's defence in a Second Division match in April 1984 (0-0).

But it was all too short-lived. We lost six of the next seven League games and in the end it took until our penultimate home match, against Swansea on 5 May, before our Second Division survival was assured. Two first-class set pieces doomed already-relegated Swansea (who included former Palace striker Ian Walsh), with Jim Cannon on target after twenty-four minutes and Kevin Mabbutt seconds before half-time, so that the only happy Welshman at Selhurst Park that afternoon was Peter Nicholas, who was making his 150th appearance for the Eagles.

Palace won again at Carlisle on the May Bank Holiday, where the feature of the game was a glorious Phil Barber goal that climaxed a run from within the Palace half but, with several senior players absent, Palace lost their last game of the season, at home to Blackburn, and two days later manager Mullery found that he had lost his job too, dismissed for the first time in his career.

There followed the brief, extraordinary three-day flirtation between the Club and Dave Bassett before, on 4 June 1984, Steve Coppell and Ian Evans took over at the Palace helm.

SEASON: 1983/84

GROUND: Selhurst Park

MANAGER: Alan Mullery

LEAGUE/DIVISION: Football League Second Division

FINAL POSITION: 18th

BIGGEST VICTORY: 3-1 *v.* Middlesbrough, 1 October 1983, 3-1 *v.* Cambridge United, 8 October 1983, 3-1 *v.* Newcastle United, 21 January 1984

HEAVIEST DEFEAT: 1-3 *v.* Newcastle United, 17 September 1983, 1-3 *v.* Manchester City, 14 January 1984, 1-3 *v.* Brighton & Hove Albion, 21 April 1984

FA CUP – ROUND ELIMINATED: 4th

LEAGUE CUP – ROUND ELIMINATED: 1st

FULL MEMBERS CUP – ROUND ELIMINATED: –

LEADING LEAGUE APPEARANCES (MAX: 42): 42 – G. Wood, 40 – V. Hilaire

LEADING LEAGUE GOALSCORERS: 7 – T. Evans, 5 – D. Giles

1984/85

STEVE COPPELL AND IAN EVANS BEGIN TO RESTORE PALACE'S DIGNITY

Steve Coppell had been a brilliant penetrative outside right for Manchester United and England before his playing career was ultimately terminated by an agonising knee injury, initially incurred while playing for England against Hungary at Wembley in November 1981. It eventually became necessary for him to retire in 1983 and, some twelve months later, following a meeting with Palace chairman Ron Noades, he was appointed manager at Crystal Palace FC. It was at Mr Noades' suggestion that Steve invited Palace star Ian Evans to assist him and there was no little irony that the duo, who were to do so much to rebuild the playing fortunes of our club, should both have had their own careers cut short by disgraceful tackles.

The immediate prospects of changing Palace from a struggling team into possible promotion contenders were hampered when Billy Gilbert and Vince Hilaire both moved on to other clubs, but Steve Coppell made his first signing for the Eagles by securing big Trevor Aylott from Luton Town as part of the deal that took Vince Hilaire to Kenilworth Road. Another valuable signing was that of perky left-back Brian Sparrow from Arsenal, but Steve's most effective early signing was that of £30,000 Alan Irvine from Everton. Alan, a winger with pace and guile, was intelligent and articulate, and for obvious reasons his manager appreciated all these qualities.

Blackburn Rovers provided the opposition at Selhurst Park for manager Coppell's first senior match in charge of Crystal Palace on 25 August 1984 but Palace, missing skipper Jim Cannon, who had fractured a jaw in a pre-season game, could only scratch out a 1-1 draw. Following this we took heavy damage in a 1-4 defeat at Shrewsbury, then lost 0-2 to powerful Birmingham. A defeat at Brighton left Palace at the bottom of the Second Division – but it was from such depths that Palace were to rise, phoenix-like under Steve and Ian, to restored status and dignity.

Palace were still limping along near the foot of the table when Steve signed two strikers, Steve Galloway from Sutton United and Andy Gray from Dulwich Hamlet. The latter acquisition was to be the first indication of a supreme talent of manager Steve Coppell that was to be deployed greatly to Palace's benefit in the coming years. Steve was able to discern true footballing potential even when it was in a raw state, and his successful recruitment of men from the lower

Early in 1984/85 Jim Cannon eclipsed Terry Long's 480 Palace appearances. Terry is seen here presenting Jim with a silver salver to mark the achievement.

divisions, reserve-team football or non-League sides, then the refinement of them into quality players, was a feature of his managerial tenure at Crystal Palace. Two more quickly followed: tall, academic defender Ken O'Doherty from University College Dublin and creative, versatile Tony Finnigan.

Steve also signed two proven players to remedy Palace's lowly position as the season advanced. Midfield dynamo Kevin Taylor joined us from Derby with veteran giant centre half Micky Droy coming across from Chelsea.

Two matches within three days at the end of April 1985 held the key to Palace's eventual Second Division survival; a visit from promotion-hunting Portsmouth, who were complete with Billy Gilbert and Vince Hilaire, then a daunting, re-arranged trip to promotion favourites Blackburn. Palace beat Pompey in front of our best crowd of the season at Selhurst Park, with Micky Droy spearheading our 2-1 success with an early opener and a back-header that enabled Andy Gray to deliver the seventy-sixth-minute winner. At Blackburn, Micky was again involved in the decisive strike, flicking on a rare Palace corner just before the hour, for Alan Irvine to rise unchallenged at the far post and head home. Those victories secured our status and Micky quickly became a great favourite with our fans, but Jim Cannon was unquestionably the only choice for Player of the Year, while the future for Palace now looked brighter. Steve Coppell had offloaded several of the fading but highly paid men recruited by his predecessor, even if many fans were saddened by Jerry Murphy's determination to leave us for Chelsea.

SEASON: 1984/85

GROUND: Selhurst Park

MANAGER: Steve Coppell

LEAGUE/DIVISION: Football League Second Division

FINAL POSITION: 15th

BIGGEST VICTORY: 3-0 *v.* Oldham Athletic, 25 November 1984

HEAVIEST DEFEAT: 0-5 *v.* Oxford United 29 December 1984

FA CUP – ROUND ELIMINATED: 3rd

LEAGUE CUP – ROUND ELIMINATED: 2nd

FULL MEMBERS CUP – ROUND ELIMINATED: –

LEADING LEAGUE APPEARANCES (MAX: 42): 42 – G. Wood, 40 – J. Cannon

LEADING LEAGUE GOALSCORERS: 8 – T. Aylott, 5 – A. Gray, A. Irvine

1985/86

'GOOD, BUT NOT GOOD ENOUGH'

Micky Droy's willingness to re-sign for Palace for 1985/86 was great news for our club and all our fans, as was the addition to our playing ranks of tall, angular Steve Ketteridge from Wimbledon for £15,000 to add midfield steel, but it was also during the summer of 1985 that manager Coppell acquired a player from the non-league ranks who was to become a household name across the nation and assist Palace to glory – twenty-one-year-old Ian Wright from Greenwich Borough. Maybe later in his managerial reign at the Palace Steve's sure touch in the transfer market deserted him to our cost, but it should never be forgotten just how brilliantly he served Palace in these matters through the mid and late 1980s.

It was in the wind and rain at Shrewsbury that Palace's 1985/86 League season began. The Gay Meadow has not often been a happy venue for Crystal Palace but here on Sunday 18 August we recorded our first opening day success for four years (2-0) and our fans were heard to sing Steve Coppell's name as we controlled the second half. Fancied Sunderland were beaten by a Micky Droy header twenty minutes from time the following Saturday at Selhurst Park, but this momentum faltered, possibly because many of our number were distracted upon learning that we were to face Manchester United in a two-legged League Cup second round tie.

Palace unquestionably surprised United with our confident, attacking style, but after a scoreless first half at the Palace in the first leg, United goalkeeper Gary Bailey (whose father Roy Bailey had graced the Palace goalmouth 119 times some thirty years earlier) denied Phil Barber with a magnificent save. Moments later Peter Barnes beat George Wood at the near post and in those seconds the match was won and lost. Norman Whiteside increased United's advantage just twenty-one seconds into the second leg at Old Trafford and Steve Coppell quipped afterwards: 'The form United are in, I'm surprised we were able to hold out for so long!' 'But', Steve added, 'we responded wonderfully well and goalkeeper George Wood did us proud.' In fact George had perhaps his best game for us, making three outstanding saves reminiscent of his Scottish international days.

Palace continued to flounder along in the Second Division. We lost 1-3 at Charlton in a game of four penalties – but the news of lasting significance from The Valley that afternoon was that Charlton would be leaving their headquarters and moving into Selhurst Park as Palace's tenants, in a unique ground-sharing arrangement.

It was on Saturday 12 October, when Palace were at home to promotion candidates Oldham Athletic, that most Eagles fans saw the enormous potential value of Ian Wright. With four minutes remaining Palace's injury-depleted side was trailing by the odd goal in three. In a desperate late

Left: By the beginning of 1985 Andy Gray was a first-team member of the Palace squad.

rally Kevin Taylor equalised for us and then substitute Wright headed in a cross from Alan Irvine to produce an unexpected result and an early demonstration of his match-winning prowess.

Ian made astonishing progress in this 1985/86 season, going on to finish as our joint-second-top scorer with 9 goals, and Steve Coppell was happy to call the former plasterer's labourer his 'super-sub', so that with Ian's burgeoning talent and the further stiffening of our defence with the arrival of West Ham full-back Paul Brush, we slowly became a side that looked as if it might challenge for the promotion places, although overall we lacked the consistency to do that. Even in early April we were still able to harbour serious hopes that we might snatch the third promotion place, but matters went awfully wrong when we travelled to Grimsby on Saturday 12 April. By the middle of the first half we were in arrears and had had Kevin Taylor sent off. Grimsby scored again and the referee awarded them a ninetieth-minute penalty for good measure.

In the last analysis Palace finished fifth and manager Coppell aptly summed up the season by saying that this placing was 'probably a true reflection of our ability over the season – good, but not good enough'.

SEASON: 1985/86

GROUND: Selhurst Park

MANAGER: Steve Coppell

LEAGUE/DIVISION: Football League Second Division

FINAL POSITION: 5th

BIGGEST VICTORY: 3-0 *v.* Leeds United, 19 April 1986

HEAVIEST DEFEAT: 1-3 *v.* Charlton Athletic, 7 September 1985, 1-3 *v.* Wimbledon, 26 December 1985

FA CUP – ROUND ELIMINATED: 3rd

LEAGUE CUP – ROUND ELIMINATED: 2nd

FULL MEMBERS CUP – ROUND ELIMINATED: 1st

LEADING LEAGUE APPEARANCES (MAX: 42): 42 – J. Cannon, 41 – A. Irvine

LEADING LEAGUE GOALSCORERS: 10 – A. Gray, 9 – P. Barber, I. Wright

1986/87

PALACE FORFEIT POSSIBLE PLAY-OFF PLACE IN FINAL MATCH

Palace opened the 1986/87 League season, augmented by Anton Otulakowski, a much-travelled winger from Millwall, with a 3-2 win at Barnsley. They did so with a makeshift team in which versatile Gary Stebbing featured at left-back and thereby completed the unusual record of appearing in every number of the eleven outfield shirts!

Stoke were beaten 1-0 at Selhurst Park and then a third victory was gained at Odsal over Bradford City (2-1), but Palace were brought crashing back to earth by a single penalty-goal defeat at resurgent Derby, though Micky Droy secured our own narrow win over Huddersfield back at the Palace.

We had a chance to go top of the Second Division for the first time since our championship of May 1979 when Sheffield United came to town on 13 September, but the talented Blades were rather too sharp for us and cut us down with a 1-2 scoreline. However, three weeks later we did claim the top spot after beating Millwall 2-1, coming from behind in a real thriller, with second-half goals from Anton Otulakowski and Tony Finnigan.

But, regrettably, from there on matters went largely downhill for the Eagles and, after a sequence of four consecutive defeats, Steve Coppell found it necessary to dispense with Micky Droy. Our fans realised that this tough decision was the right one and Gavin Nebbeling took over the vacated berth at the heart of our defence and performed as well as anyone in the remainder of the season as Palace chased a place in the newly introduced Football League play-offs.

Two new men assisted in this cause. Twenty-four-year-old Mark Bright joined Palace from Leicester City for £75,000 and scored on the stroke of half-time in his Palace debut, during a thrilling 3-3 draw with Ipswich at Selhurst Park. His partnership with Ian Wright blossomed into the most prolific in the club's history – a brilliant signing by manager Coppell.

Later in the season we were joined by former Spurs and Brighton centre half Gary O'Reilly. Gary seldom had a prolonged run in our senior side due to injuries, but he was to prove a key member of our side in several vital games, as we shall see.

Palace's best spell of the whole season was in midwinter and climaxed with what was probably our best win of the entire term, given the pedigree of our opponents, because the Eagles beat top-flight Nottingham Forest in a third round FA Cup tie on a frozen Selhurst Park pitch, with a spectacular strike from Alan Irvine after twenty-four minutes separating the sides.

Alan Irvine netted a spectacular goal to defeat top-flight Nottingham Forest in a third round FA Cup tie at Selhurst Park on 11 January 1987.

But then, just when it mattered most, Palace's impressive form wavered. Tottenham beat us in the FA Cup fourth round at White Hart Lane, then we found ourselves back in eleventh place in the Second Division after losing at Reading on 21 February. A better showing, including a 6-0 drubbing of Birmingham City at Selhurst Park, took us to the fringes of the play-off positions, but following a disappointing 1-1 draw with West Bromwich Albion on Easter Saturday we put on our worst show of the entire season at Brighton on Easter Monday and lost 0-2.

Palace recovered their dignity somewhat by beating Oldham and promotion-bound Portsmouth at Selhurst Park, so that we retained a slim hope of a play-off place right up to the final game of the season, which took us to Hull. A victory there, allied to a defeat for Ipswich, would enable us to snatch fifth place in the table and take part in the knock-out competition for promotion... or so we dreamed! Inside ninety seconds Alex Dyer (who was to sign for the Eagles some eighteen months later) had us in arrears and he scored again early in the second half to dash our hopes completely.

Scotsmen Jim Cannon and George Wood were the winner and runner-up respectively in the supporters' Player of the Year award. Both had appeared in every match and thoroughly deserved the honours but, with Selhurst Park rivals and tenants Charlton successfully defending their top-flight status in the play-offs (which had a slightly different format to today), there was undoubtedly a sense of anti-climax at the end of 1986/87.

SEASON: 1986/87

GROUND: Selhurst Park

MANAGER: Steve Coppell

LEAGUE/DIVISION: Football League Second Division

FINAL POSITION: 6th

BIGGEST VICTORY: 6-0 *v.* Birmingham City, 14 March 1987

HEAVIEST DEFEAT: 1-4 *v.* Birmingham City, 18 October 1986

FA CUP – ROUND ELIMINATED: 4th

LEAGUE CUP – ROUND ELIMINATED: 3rd

FULL MEMBERS CUP – ROUND ELIMINATED: 1st

LEADING LEAGUE APPEARANCES (MAX: 42): 42 – G. Wood, J. Cannon, 41 – K. Taylor, 36+5 – T. Finnigan

LEADING LEAGUE GOALSCORERS: 8 – M. Bright, K. Taylor, I. Wright, 6 – T. Finnigan, A. Gray

1987/88

PLAY-OFF PLACE DENIED AGAIN

Personnel changes at the Palace were few in the summer of 1987. Steve Ketteridge went to Leyton Orient and Alan Irvine to Dundee United, then Kevin Taylor joined Scunthorpe in September. Meanwhile Palace secured midfielder Geoff Thomas, the former captain of Crewe, and Neil Redfearn, a strong-running winger from Doncaster. Also to fill an increasingly significant role was defender Alan Pardew, who had joined us in March 1987 from Yeovil for a bargain £7,000.

A very evident change at the Palace for this season was in our colours. For only the second time in twelve years we dispensed with the all-white strip with the distinctive red-and-blue sash, in favour of regular red-and-blue stripes, while the Football League would now allow the use of two substitutes.

Palace's programme began on Saturday 15 August at Huddersfield where, alongside Thomas and Redfearn, John Salako was making his first full appearance for our club. Palace were two ahead with a Mark Bright brace early in the second half, but the Terriers managed to level matters before the end. Such profligacy would cost us dear at the season's close.

Palace's inconsistency upon their travels allied to occasional lapses at home made it impossible for us to get nearer than close to the top of the Second Division table but, to assist in this cause, we recruited left-back David Burke from Huddersfield, for whom he had played against us in the first game of the season. He had an impressive debut for us when we beat Millwall on 10 October and was ever-present in the remainder of the season.

Two impressive wins on opponents' grounds now helped the cause enormously. At Bournemouth all the scoring took place before the break. Palace were two goals in arrears after just twelve minutes yet won 3-2, while at Manchester City the home goalkeeper was sent off and Palace scored three times in a quarter of an hour amid great controversy. Unfortunately, at this stage of the season, Palace's prospects were damaged by a row that erupted between manager Steve Coppell and the volatile Andy Gray, which eventually led to Andy's departure to Aston Villa amid great acrimony. Palace replaced Gray with former Southend skipper Glenn Pennyfather, and the little fellow scored for us in an important match at Leicester early in January, which was to prove the end of a Palace era, for we let slip a 4-2 lead following a rare blunder by goalkeeper George Wood. George had become a great favourite and had missed just three League matches in four-and-a-half years, but he was no longer quite equal to the demands of the top end of the Second Division. He was given a free transfer and he moved to Cardiff

Right: Geoff Thomas joined the Eagles for 1987/88. (Illustration by Phil Neill Caricatures)

City, while Palace signed England Youth and Under-21 star Perry Suckling from Manchester City for £100,000.

Palace made a first-ever Wembley appearance in the Football League Centenary tournament but it became increasingly clear that the challenge for the play-off places was going to be an extremely close-run thing. In the end, everything hinged upon the last game of the season and Palace required a favour elsewhere. Our last game was at home to Manchester City. We had to win and rely on champions Millwall conceding no more than a point to Blackburn at The Den.

A season's best crowd of 17,555 watched Palace score twice early in the final quarter of the dour clash, so now matters at Millwall were of supreme importance. A BBC report gave the latest score at The Den as 3-3! Enough to put Palace fifth. But other stations provided different information and the reality was that Blackburn had scored an emphatic 4-1 win, so that they and not the Palace had taken the fifth place. There was bitter disappointment everywhere at Selhurst Park and no little anger about the spurious information, but there was nothing anyone could do. Palace had finished sixth in the Second Division for the second season running and, under the arrangements at the time, been denied a play-off place again.

SEASON: 1987/88

GROUND: Selhurst Park

MANAGER: Steve Coppell

LEAGUE/DIVISION: Football League Second Division

FINAL POSITION: 6th

BIGGEST VICTORY: 6-0 *v.* Birmingham City, 5 September 1987

HEAVIEST DEFEAT: 1-4 *v.* Aston Villa, 21 October 1987

FA CUP – ROUND ELIMINATED: 3rd

LEAGUE CUP – ROUND ELIMINATED: 3rd

FULL MEMBERS CUP – ROUND ELIMINATED: 1st

LEADING LEAGUE APPEARANCES (MAX: 44): 42 – N. Redfearn, 41 – G. Thomas

LEADING LEAGUE GOALSCORERS: 24 – M. Bright, 20 – I. Wright

1988/89

TOP-FLIGHT STATUS REGAINED VIA THE PLAY-OFFS

It was inevitable after the brilliant goalscoring efforts of Mark Bright and Ian Wright the previous term that Palace would base their playing policy for 1988/89 on an attacking strategy, but Steve Coppell wisely augmented his defence. Welsh international centre half Jeff Hopkins arrived from Fulham for a tribunal-set fee of £240,000 while John Pemberton had joined us from Crewe in a £60,000 deal towards the end of 1987/88. Midfielder Dave Madden came from Reading and was to prove a cool head when Palace were awarded several penalties in crucial or even decisive games late in the season.

But although its finale was glorious, Palace's 1988/89 season was at best stuttering to begin with. We sat out the opening day because Swindon's ground-improvement work had not been completed, then drew and lost at home to Chelsea and Watford respectively. Four more draws left us still without a win and in twelfth place at the end of September but, with Bright and Wright now finding the target regularly and the defence becoming more settled after enforced absences, Palace reached the top half of the table by the end of October. We were engaged in an astonishing match earlier that month at Blackburn. Although we had fallen behind we had forged in front soon after half-time and Mark Bright extended our lead so that with twenty minutes remaining Blackburn were looking a beaten side. However, the referee awarded them what appeared to be a gratuitous penalty and at 2-3 Rovers took new heart. Simon Garner netted twice for them in as many minutes only for Gary O'Reilly to nod a late Palace equaliser, but in the dying seconds Rovers scored a devastating fifth goal to deny us any reward.

Palace got back to winning ways at Bradford City a week later and arriving around this time was forward Alex Dyer from Hull, although his major impact with us was in the Full Members Cup.

Mark Bright notched a hat-trick in our 4-0 win over Walsall on 2 January but we then lost skipper Geoff Thomas to an injury that proved difficult to diagnose. In fact Geoff was unable to play again for Palace's senior team for the rest of the season, but Steve Coppell made a last attempt to build a promotion side for 1988/89 by signing outside right Eddie McGoldrick from Northampton Town for £200,000.

By mid-February most Eagles' eyes were fixed upon a prestigious Full Members Cup semi-final, at Nottingham Forest. Over 3,000 Palace fans were at the City Ground to see Ian Wright

Right: Steve Coppell took Palace back to the top division via the play-offs in 1988/89. (Illustration by Phil Neill Caricatures)

nullify Forest's early opener, and then Palace threatened to create a major upset... but with Forest rocking and just six minutes left, a bizarre refereeing decision saw acting captain David Burke sent off after he and Franz Carr had jostled one another some forty yards from goal. This handicap was inevitably too great against a side of Forest's pedigree and their England men Stuart Pearce and Neil Webb both netted in the last three minutes.

There followed Palace's first change in our managerial team in more than four-and-a-half years, for Ian Evans left us to take charge at Swansea City. Steve Coppell's choice of replacement was the perky, knowledgeable Geordie Stan Ternent, who had formerly managed Blackpool and been deputy at Bradford City.

A series of eight victories (interspersed with one poor display at Shrewbury) from the middle of March lifted Palace from mid-table into serious promotion challengers. Among these was an amazing Easter Monday match against Brighton that made footballing history. Ian Wright opened the scoring midway through the first half with a brilliantly taken goal from an almost impossible angle out on the left-side edge of the penalty area, adjacent to the byline, to provide the 100th strike of the Wright/Bright partnership. Five minutes later the referee dismissed Brighton's Mike Trusson for a foul on Eddie McGoldrick and, amid great crowd atmosphere, Palace appeared to be heading for a substantial victory when Mark Bright blasted a thirty-eighth minute penalty into the net following a foul upon himself.

Palace were then awarded two more penalties before the interval and missed them both. John Keely saved well from Mark Bright, then Ian Wright's effort hit a post and the crowd were in a ferment of emotions: excitement, tension, anger, disbelief and frustration. More was to follow! Five minutes into the second half Brighton were awarded a penalty and Alan Curbishley reduced their arrears, but then, after sixty-five minutes, Palace gained their fourth penalty, for handball, only for John Pemberton to blast the ball high over the bar. Palace were now completely unnerved and we had to hold on grimly to retain our lead, but even so it took a save of breathtaking ability by Perry Suckling to deny Curbishley an equaliser near the end.

Our match at Plymouth on 22 April kicked off at 3.06 p.m. after a minute's silence in memory of those who had died in the Hillsborough disaster at Sheffield the previous Saturday. Mark Bright's shot after twelve minutes gave us the lead, which he doubled nine minutes into the second half and, despite John Pemberton being dismissed with a quarter of an hour to go, the game finished with cries of 'Eagles, Eagles' ringing around Home Park.

Ian Wright stabs the ball past Blackburn's Terry Gennoe for Palace's first goal of the play-off second leg at Selhurst Park on 3 June 1989.

The match at Swindon, postponed from the opening day of the season, was finally played on Tuesday 25 April – surely Palace's longest-ever postponement. Lou Macari's side, with justifiable aspirations of their own, administered our only defeat of the last eleven Second Division matches through a typical thirty-sixth-minute effort from Steve White, who had made us suffer in his Bristol Rovers days ten seasons previously. Swindon could have won by a greater margin but Perry Suckling saved a ferocious penalty on the hour from Ross McLaren.

That setback left Palace in fourth place but we still had a chance of clinching outright promotion, and victory over visiting West Bromwich Albion by the narrowest of margins certainly helped our cause. The goal, by Ian Wright after sixty-four minutes was a superbly struck effort from the edge of the penalty area and represented the fiftieth strike of the season by the Wright/Bright pairing.

That took us to a Maine Road May Day showdown with Manchester City two days later. Ian Wright equalised early in the second half, but Palace could not snatch a win even though City were forced to deploy a deputy goalkeeper, Nigel Gleghorn, for an hour. Another draw followed at Leicester on 6 May when two Dave Madden penalties put us on terms, then gave us the lead, but a rare blunder by Perry Suckling near the end allowed Leicester an equaliser and we surrendered two crucial points.

This left the Palace with two more home games to complete the Second Division programme, a rearranged midweek date with Stoke City and the last game against relegated Birmingham City. Stoke put up dour opposition but had no answer after Dave Madden slotted home his fourth penalty for us ten minutes before the interval.

Still with a chance of outright promotion, Palace had to beat Birmingham by a convincing margin and hope that Manchester City would lose to Bradford City. A carnival crowd of 17,581 gave Palace huge backing and it was not long before Ian Wright gave us the lead following a right-side corner but, almost as if that had been their cue, Birmingham supporters flooded onto the pitch in their hundreds in the corner by their compound in a seemingly planned invasion and attacked the Palace fans nearby. As our supporters and stewards scuffled with the aggressors it seemed a long time before about a dozen mounted police entered the fray from the opposite corner and herded the troublemakers back into their places. The game was delayed for almost half an hour but upon its resumption Palace cut loose. Ian Wright completed an impressive hat-trick and Palace were four up with barely half an hour played. Birmingham rallied somewhat but with still a quarter of our match to be played we learnt that Manchester City had gained a draw at Valley Parade so that it all became rather sterile and pointless at Selhurst Park.

Having finished third, Palace were embroiled in the play-offs for the first time in our existence, and our semi-final opponents were Swindon. In sizzling heat and enormous tension, Swindon gained a narrow advantage by winning 1-0 through an own goal off poor Jeff Hopkins, but any hopes the Robins had of progressing were quickly extinguished by a seventh-minute aggregate equaliser by Mark Bright and an Ian Wright volley half an hour later, and from there on there would be no way back for the Wiltshire men.

Our opponents for the play-off final were Blackburn Rovers, but at that time the final was a two-legged, home and away affair, with Palace at Ewood Park for the first match. We were not anywhere near our best in this game and our defensive frailties were all too clearly exposed. Howard Gayle scored twice for Rovers midway through the first half but then spurned the chance of a hat-trick by firing a penalty wide. Four minutes from time Eddie McGoldrick netted his first Palace goal, only for Simon Garner to restore Rovers' two-goal advantage after more careless Palace defending.

And so to Selhurst Park for the showdown on Saturday 3 June in front of a capacity 30,000 crowd. Palace needed a quick goal and they got it after sixteen minutes when David Burke and Phil Barber combined on the left to set Alan Pardew free. His precise cross was perfectly weighted for Ian Wright to force the ball past Terry Gennoe at the second attempt for his 32nd goal of the season.

Now the tension lifted! With the big crowd giving thunderous support, Palace had Blackburn on the rack, but the visitors defended well and managed to retain their precious lead to the interval – though for no more than two minutes after it!

Mark Atkins' clumsy challenge on Eddie McGoldrick was deemed to be a foul by referee George Courteney, and Dave Madden stepped up to despatch the penalty low to Gennoe's left, with commendable aplomb. Euphoria filled the ground, except for the disconsolate visitors' corner, for the 2-0 scoreline would give Palace the promotion for which we all longed. But we were unable to finish the matter off, and Rovers sought a response of their own. With the aggregate scores locked at 3-3, extra time became necessary. Still neither side could produce the decisive thrust until the 118th minute when Eddie McGoldrick battled his way to the byline and sent over a cross with Rovers' tiring defence nowhere. Ian Wright rose, unchallenged, to head past the exposed 'keeper and the ground erupted in delight and relief.

When Steve Coppell paid tribute to the achievement a little later in the afternoon, he claimed that this was his 'best moment in football', and to be honest, at that time it was the same for every Palace fan.

SEASON: 1988/89

GROUND: Selhurst Park

MANAGER: Steve Coppell

LEAGUE/DIVISION: Football League Second Division

FINAL POSITION: 3rd

BIGGEST VICTORY: 4-0 *v.* Walsall, 2 January 1989

HEAVIEST DEFEAT: 3-5 *v.* West Bromwich Albion, 26 November 1988

FA CUP – ROUND ELIMINATED: 3rd

LEAGUE CUP – ROUND ELIMINATED: 3rd

FULL MEMBERS CUP – ROUND ELIMINATED: Area Semi-final

LEADING LEAGUE APPEARANCES (MAX: 50 including play-offs): 50 – Mark Bright, 48+2 – P. Barber, 47+2 – A. Pardew

LEADING LEAGUE GOALSCORERS: 27 – I. Wright, 21 – M. Bright

1989/90

EAGLES ARE WEMBLEY CUP-FINALISTS

The audacious summer 1989 signing of Andy Gray brought the Palace prodigal back to Selhurst Park from Queens Park Rangers for £500,000 to stiffen our midfield for top-flight duty. Andy's arrival proved to be another successful move by Steve Coppell because Andy added power and strength to our cause while also improving sufficiently himself to earn a full England cap in November 1991.

Intriguingly, Palace's First Division return began over at Andy's former club, but we were beaten by a Rangers side that had considerable experience at this level and who scored twice after the break.

The first home game three days later was a terrific opener – Manchester United! Palace lit up our new electronic scoreboard at the Whitehorse Lane end before the match, only for United to dampen the exuberant atmosphere by taking the lead after seventeen minutes through England captain Bryan Robson. Palace responded positively enough, but it looked as if we were heading for another defeat until, with barely ninety seconds remaining, a lightning strike by Ian Wright from Alex Dyer's deft touch brought delight as well as relief. Dour, defensive Coventry stole the points with a deflected free-kick on the second Saturday of the season but a rather spiritless Wimbledon were defeated with a goal in each half from Geoff Thomas and Ian Wright – and then came our infamous trip to Liverpool.

Palace had the temerity to attack Liverpool, and we were punished severely. Certainly the 0-9 defeat highlighted the paucity of top-flight talent in our defence but, as we shall see, the tactic was proved to be correct, with changed personnel, in wonderfully exciting fashion later in this season. The Eagles then emphasised the fact that we were no worse than many First Division sides by gaining a creditable draw at Southampton four days later, courtesy of Jeff Hopkins' headed equaliser, but, in the wake of the Anfield defeat, manager Steve Coppell secured the country's first £1 million goalkeeper in Nigel Martyn from Bristol Rovers and then signed former Wimbledon centre half Andy Thorn, from Newcastle for £650,000. Andy's debut was at Manchester United on 9 December, where Palace won 2-1 with a brace from Mark Bright to gain our first away win of the season in the League, then Andy himself put us on the way to another 2-1 success in our 'away' match against Charlton at Selhurst Park.

Coinciding with the arrival of the two new players had been another change at assistant manager level. Stan Ternent left to take over at Hull City and Palace wisely promoted long-serving reserve and youth team boss Alan Smith, who had been with the Club since 1983 and helped to develop such stars as Richard Shaw and John Salako.

The famous Alan Pardew goal that beat Liverpool in the 1990 FA Cup semi-final at Villa Park.

The strengthened Palace side climbed slowly to First Division security, even in the absence of Ian Wright with a broken leg sustained on 20 January in a home defeat by Liverpool, and broken again against Derby (1-1) precisely two months later, but manager Coppell signed experienced striker Garry Thompson from Watford towards the end of March and an early, conclusive goal on his debut against Aston Villa provided an immediate dividend.

But of course 1989/90 will always be remembered by Palace fans as the season when the Eagles went to Wembley to contest the FA Cup final. That possibility looked remote in early January when Portsmouth, our third round visitors, were leading and comfortably holding us at bay in the chill drizzle – but substitute Geoff Thomas equalised and then Palace were awarded a penalty in the last minute that was rapped home by Andy Gray. Huddersfield (4-0) posed few problems but victory over Rochdale in round five was hard won, earned by a close-range strike from Phil Barber just after the hour and a brilliant Nigel Martyn save in the last minute, then a scrappy quarter-final at Cambridge was settled by a scuffed Geoff Thomas goal fourteen minutes from time.

Palace's semi-final opponents were Liverpool at Villa Park, and the sheer size of our task here was enormous. Liverpool were the Cup holders and the clear leaders at the top of the First Division table, where they looked every inch the champions. They had already beaten the Palace 9-0 and 2-0, while Palace were missing Ian Wright and Eddie McGoldrick, as well as proven defenders Jeff Hopkins and David Burke, so it is not hard to see why the pundits and even many Palace fans feared that our exit from the competition was at hand. However, Steve Coppell and his men refused to go along with such gloomy prognostications. 'One-off matches are great occasions for the underdogs,' averred the Palace manager. Palace fans certainly knew that Liverpool would be surprised by the Eagles' determination and staying power. Indeed, in the end, while no-one was in the least surprised that Liverpool scored three more goals against us to take their season's tally against the Palace to an amazing fourteen, almost everybody was completely astounded when we notched up four goals of our own! That was what completely upset the script and totally confounded the apparently all-knowing media gurus.

Not, it must be admitted, that there was really any suggestion in the somewhat dour first half that the huge and boisterous following of Palace fans at Villa Park would be present to witness such a glorious occasion for, although we settled down quickly and showed little sign of nerves, Palace's difficult task was made much harder when, after only fourteen minutes, our offside trap failed, allowing Ian Rush to take a superb pass from Steve McMahon and beat Nigel Martyn for his twenty-third goal of the season. It may have been significant too that, in this first period, Rush had to leave the field after twenty-nine minutes with a bruised rib and Palace spent the rest of the half ensuring that no further damage was sustained to their cause.

However, Palace's performance in the second half and in extra time surpassed anything that the Club had ever previously produced to destroy Liverpool. Within sixteen seconds of the restart Palace were level. John Pemberton strode away down the right flank on a sixty-yard run, then put over a cross that created sheer panic in Liverpool's defence. Phil Barber's effort was thwarted, then John Salako's shot was blocked by substitute Steve Staunton, but the ball flew to Mark Bright on the volley and Palace's great goalscorer hit a shot that rocketed into the top corner of Grobbelaar's net, right in front of the jubilant Palace fans who now, like the players, sensed that the day and the match could be theirs.

Liverpool simply could not cope with the sustained aerial assault and Palace, having exposed their weakness, exploited it regularly. At every opportunity they launched high balls into the danger zone and began to take control of the game. Come the sixty-ninth minute and Liverpool were facing possible defeat when an Andy Gray free-kick was headed down by Phil Barber, and Gary O'Reilly thumped the ball emphatically into the net from ten yards' range. But, for all Palace's efforts, Liverpool still possessed talent of the topmost quality and they responded in the eighty-first minute with a two-goal salvo in ninety seconds to retrieve the lead, McMahon netting with a scorching drive from the edge of the penalty area and John Barnes from the penalty spot after John Pemberton was somewhat harshly adjudged to have fouled Staunton.

That double blow would have ended the challenge of most clubs but Palace set out to discover another chink in the Liverpool armour and, with just two minutes of ordinary time remaining they found it. Again, Liverpool had no answer to a lofted free-kick from John Pemberton and in the ensuing mêlée Andy Gray headed Palace's equaliser.

Palace might have won it there and then had an Andy Thorn header gone in instead of rocking the crossbar, but Liverpool could not take advantage of that reprieve and, in the compelling extra-time period, Palace produced the final twist to a magical afternoon. Liverpool were once more in complete disarray following a Palace set piece early in the second period when an Andy Gray corner on the left was flicked on by Andy Thorn at the edge of the six-yard area for Alan Pardew to head the decisive fourth goal into the net, behind which were ranked our now-ecstatic fans.

Two issues exercised the minds of Palace folk as the 1990 FA Cup final approached. The first concerned Ian Wright's recovery from the twice-broken leg that had kept him out of the semi-final, while the second was the pressing matter of securing a ticket from the Eagles' modest allocation of little more than 14,000. But, if the Palace fans at Wembley were fewer in number than the followers of Manchester United, they certainly gave the team a huge boost during the preliminaries with the spectacular release of thousands of red-and-blue helium balloons just as the players entered the arena.

And Alan celebrating it!

Heartened by this display, Palace started the game well and after little more than a quarter of an hour they were awarded a free-kick out on the right. Andy Gray feinted a right-footed cross but Phil Barber delivered a left-footed curler that Gary O'Reilly reached before anyone else and his header looped off Pallister, over Leighton and into the net in front of the phalanx of Palace fans. United replied ten minutes before half-time with a goal from Bryan Robson, which took a wicked deflection off John Pemberton's shin.

The second half and extra time provided glorious entertainment and will rank among Palace's best ever performances for a long, long time. Mark Hughes put United ahead soon after the hour, but then Steve Coppell made his perfectly judged substitution, bringing on Ian Wright to replace Phil Barber after sixty-nine minutes. Within three minutes Palace were level with a goal to match the finest the old stadium had ever seen. The lissom, eager Palace striker skipped clear of the lunging Mike Phelan, turned inside Pallister – the defender who alone at £2.5 million had cost more than our entire team – then shot low past Leighton for 2-2. The initiative now lay with Palace and they might have won the Cup there and then. United were uncertain, but while Palace found the goal we wanted we could not do so until two minutes into extra time. It was another strike of the highest quality. Young John Salako put over a testing cross from the left. Wright saw it first and early and volleyed the ball into the net while flying some five feet above the turf! What a Cup winner it would have been, but United still had sufficient time to regroup and show one more moment of high-class finishing, Hughes making it 3-3 and forcing a replay the following Thursday.

Little comment on that game is required. It was tense, dour and closely contested – and won by United on the hour, although the proceedings and outcome turned on the referee's decision

The two captains prior to the 1990 FA Cup final: Geoff Thomas (left) and Bryan Robson.

to award a Palace free-kick outside the penalty area (by some distance!) when the marks of the incident on the turf clearly showed that the foul on Geoff Thomas had occurred inside it.

One day, hopefully before too long, Palace will have another opportunity to contest the final for the famous trophy and this time return to Selhurst Park with it in triumph.

SEASON: 1989/90

GROUND: Selhurst Park

MANAGER: Steve Coppell

LEAGUE/DIVISION: Football League First Division

FINAL POSITION: 15th

BIGGEST VICTORY: 3-1 *v.* Southampton, 10 February 1990

HEAVIEST DEFEAT: 0-9 *v.* Liverpool, 12 September 1989

FA CUP – ROUND ELIMINATED: Final

LEAGUE CUP – ROUND ELIMINATED: 3rd

FULL MEMBERS CUP – ROUND ELIMINATED: Area Final

LEADING LEAGUE APPEARANCES (MAX: 38): 36 – M. Bright, 34+2 – A. Pardew, 35 – A. Gray, 33+2 – G. Thomas

LEADING LEAGUE GOALSCORERS: 12 – M. Bright, 8 – I. Wright

1990/91

PALACE'S BEST YET – THIRD IN THE LEAGUE AND WEMBLEY WINNERS!

Arriving early in the 1990 close season to augment Palace's defence was John Humphrey, the former Charlton skipper, for £450,000, although unsettled John Pemberton chose to move to Sheffield United in July for £300,000. Palace's other major summer acquisition was giant Welsh international centre half Eric Young from Wimbledon for £850,000. Quibbles about the size of the fee for the thirty-year-old evaporated as the season progressed and Eric was soon dubbed 'Ninja' by the fans on account of his headband, which resembled those worn by the cartoon turtles of the time, while dominating opposing strikers in awesome fashion at the heart of Palace's best defence for years.

Meanwhile there was major restructuring at Selhurst Park where 5,000 seats were installed to make the Arthur Wait Stand an all-seater, with new dressing rooms and a reception area being built into the much-older main stand.

The 1990/91 playing season began at Luton, on the Hatters' plastic pitch. Eric Young immediately endeared himself to those Eagles fans who had infiltrated the Kenilworth Road members-only security system by heading us in front after a quarter of an hour, although Luton managed an equaliser on the stroke of half-time. The opening home game the following Tuesday was the all-London clash against Chelsea. Andy Gray thumped a fifth-minute penalty but departed soon afterwards when he and Dennis Wise were sent off following a brawl, and there was no way back for the Blues after Ian Wright lofted a fine effort over Dave Beasant from twenty yards. A fierce Garry Thompson header disposed of visiting Sheffield United, then Palace routed Norwich 3-0 at Carrow Road to go second in the table. Indeed, throughout 1990 we were never out of the top five all season and consistently held third place for the entire second half of it.

Highlights of this excellent record were the single-goal victory over Liverpool in a televised match on the Sunday after Christmas when, if the Reds found us at our peak, they simply had no answer to our challenge and it was probably on the strength of his electric performance in this game that Ian Wright was shortly afterwards awarded his first full England cap. Ian created the goal that won the match three minutes before half-time. He left Gary Gillespie floundering near the right corner flag, sped goalwards along the byline, then flashed across a low centre that Mark Bright turned past Grobbelaar with aplomb – all in far less time than it takes to read it!

Of course there were times when Palace betrayed their inexperience, but other top clubs fell to our striking power. We won at Nottingham Forest on 2 February with a late Eric Young header to avenge an FA Cup defeat five days earlier and infuriate the Forest chairman, then at Leeds on 23 March when John Salako tapped home a late winner. Tottenham were beaten at the Palace in mid-April with another Eric Young goal, early this time, in only the sixth minute. Ian Wright scored a virtuoso hat-trick at Wimbledon in the penultimate game and Manchester United retired from Selhurst Park at the end of the season with a three-goal beating, but it was the victory at Plough Lane in our last visit there (indeed, it was Wimbledon's final senior game at their tight little headquarters, from where they had progressed so marvellously from obscurity to top-flight status) that sticks in the memory.

Admittedly the first half was dreadful – stunningly, numbingly, boringly dreadful – but the second will never be forgotten by any Palace fan fortunate enough to have secured a ticket to see the game. Ian Wright was quite unplayable for a quarter of an hour and he won the match for us with flair and brilliance.

Garry Thompson headed on a long Andy Thorn free-kick for Terry Phelan to nod away as far as Ian, who was steaming into the penalty area to support the attack. Without breaking stride he struck the ball low, hard and just inside the post for his 22nd goal of the season in the fifty-fourth minute. The second goal, six minutes later, was unforgettable. Steve Coppell described it as 'one of the finest pieces of individual skill I have ever seen'. The Palace striker collected Nigel Martyn's clearance just inside the Wimbledon half. He took the ball on his instep and lifted it over Dean Blackwell on the volley, then, spotting that Hans Segers was off his line, struck an audacious lob from some forty yards over the stranded, embarrassed 'keeper, and it flew into the net off the inside of the post. Some Palace folk regard it as the best goal Ian scored for our Club; some say it is the best goal they have ever seen. It was certainly in a class that Palace strikers have seldom emulated.

In comparison the third goal was mundane, but it was still a quality strike. John Humphrey overlapped to take a pass from John Salako and his diagonal cross was turned in at the far post by Ian Wright from a tight and ever-diminishing angle to establish a series of club records. It was, among other things, Palace's first hat-trick on an opponents' ground since 1963, and easily our fastest at top level.

However, in retrospect most Palace fans of the period would recall 1990 as the season in which we won a Wembley cup final. Fittingly it was the Full Members Cup, the competition that had been the brainchild of Palace chairman Ron Noades. Played on a single match, knock-out basis, it had provided the smaller clubs with useful revenue and the prize of a Wembley final was its great lure. Palace had defeated Bristol Rovers, Brighton, Luton and Norwich: now our Wembley opponents on Sunday 7 April were Everton. No one pretended that there was a parity between this competition and the FA Cup in which we had been narrowly beaten at the national stadium eleven months before, but the victory did bring huge satisfaction to the Palace club and its followers.

After the teams had received a tumultuous reception in terms of colour and noise, the first half was an interesting exercise in the contrast of styles. Everton were always neat, sometimes even pretty yet, even with a fairly attacking line-up, they showed little menace. There was always an air of tension about and perhaps it was as well that the half ended in a downpour of rain to help keep the participants' tempers off the boil, as Palace played to their proven strengths of physical fitness, direct attack, an emphasis on set pieces and of course, top-quality finishing.

Ian Wright shields the ball from a Bristol Rovers defender in Palace's second round 2-1 win at Selhurst Park in the Zenith Data Systems Cup. Ian did not score in this game, but he was twice on target in the Wembley final.

It was precisely midway through the second half that Palace forged ahead. A John Salako corner on the left was headed on by Eric Young and Geoff Thomas cleaved his way through the Toffees' static defence to net with a brave diving header. Geoff was at his peak at this stage of his career and there was no question that his inspirational leadership fully deserved the Man of the Match award for this game.

Everton responded almost immediately, Robert Warzycha flicking the ball past Nigel Martyn from close range. The pace of the encounter became quite tremendous and as it progressed towards the end of normal time either side might have won it, but it was during the extra thirty minutes that Palace claimed, gained and retained the ascendancy.

With four minutes to go until the extra-time interval, Palace turned the match, Ian Wright taking the pace off a huge clearance from Nigel Martyn with the sole of his boot, then turning away from a marker before beating Neville Southall with his right foot. *Glad All Over* boomed out across the stadium from the Palace fans for it seemed unlikely that weary Everton would be able to get back on terms again now. Indeed, in the last quarter of an hour, Palace scored twice more. First a cross by Eddie McGoldrick was touched on intelligently by Mark Bright and John Salako placed a diving header beyond the exposed Southall and just under the crossbar. Only two minutes later, Ian Wright capitalised again upon Mark Bright's selfless hard work, his pace taking him onto a header from his colleague and then sliding the ball past the now-demoralised goalkeeper to secure his own second Wembley 'double'.

Now Palace fans simply made Wembley into the Selhurst Park of north London. They sang, cheered, shouted, waved, applauded – and some normally quite reserved folk even danced! –

with delight and abandon. Their joy knew no bounds and certainly the sight of Geoff Thomas receiving the trophy will remain forever with those present. Regrettably, there was one sour note at the end when Neville Southall boycotted the presentation of medals as a one-man protest that was no credit to a fine goalkeeper or to his club, but there was no doubt from Everton's attitude when they visited Selhurst Park for a League match a fortnight later that they deeply resented Palace's Wembley victory.

Emerging towards stardom in this 1990 season had been the two youngest members of the Palace side, winger John Salako and defender Richard Shaw. The former scored a remarkable fifty-yard goal during an FA Cup replay at Nottingham Forest while Richard Shaw had netted early in the League game against Brian Clough's men in September. Salako had seized his opportunity with some style, become the regional Barclays Young Eagle of the Month twice in four months and was about to become the great success of England's Australasian tour. Versatile Richard Shaw had been with Palace since his schooldays. He missed only two matches in this campaign but few would argue that his best performance had been in the League game at Forest when he completely shackled the enigmatic but sometimes brilliant Nigel Clough.

Other products of the Palace youth scheme, Simon Osborn and Gareth Southgate, made debuts towards the end of the season, as did rangy striker Stan Collymore, signed from Stafford Rangers for £100,000. Just before the finale Palace revealed a new lucrative sponsorship deal with Tulip Computers and then it was announced that, with Charlton on their way back to The Valley, we would be sharing Selhurst Park with Wimbledon from July.

SEASON: 1990/91

GROUND: Selhurst Park

MANAGER: Steve Coppell

LEAGUE/DIVISION: Football League First Division

FINAL POSITION: 3rd

BIGGEST VICTORY: 3-0 *v.* Wimbledon, 4 May 1991, 3-0 *v.* Manchester United, 11 May 1991

HEAVIEST DEFEAT: 0-4 *v.* Arsenal, 23 February 1991

FA CUP – ROUND ELIMINATED: 3rd

LEAGUE CUP – ROUND ELIMINATED: 4th

FULL MEMBERS CUP: Winners

LEADING LEAGUE APPEARANCES (MAX: 38): 38 – J. Humphrey, N. Martyn, G. Thomas, I. Wright, 36 – R. Shaw

LEADING LEAGUE GOALSCORERS: 15 – I. Wright, 9 – M. Bright

1991/92

CHANGING TIMES FOR CRYSTAL PALACE FC

The summer of 1991 saw the departure from the Palace of Phil Barber, who moved to Millwall for £100,000 after making 288 appearances for the Eagles, while cup final goalscorer Gary O'Reilly rejoined Brighton and Garry Thompson went to Queens Park Rangers. Joining us were centre half Lee Sinnott from Bradford City, who cost £350,000 and, more significantly, Welsh Under-21 defender Chris Coleman from Swansea for £275,000.

By the start of the new season Steve Coppell had become Palace's longest-serving post-war manager, but 1991/92 was to prove controversial for Crystal Palace and Steve's popularity began to wane as he faced criticism about his judgement in the transfer market. To begin with, to the disappointment of our fans, Palace were unable to play their opening-day home fixture against Leeds because the £2 million ground improvements were not completed in time. Then, little more than three weeks into the season, Palace's relationship with the media, susceptible since the 1990 FA Cup final replay, soured again after a stormy match at Everton. But, in an historical context, the major event of 1991/92 and the beginning of the end of a Palace era was the departure of Ian Wright. His last match for us before his £2.5 million move to Arsenal was on the bright and breezy afternoon of 21 September 1991 at Oldham.

John Salako had put us ahead with a spectacular header just before the quarter-hour mark but Oldham levelled virtually on the stroke of half-time. But Palace were quickly back in front after the restart with a fabulous, albeit final, Ian Wright goal. He ran with the ball from inside the Palace half of the centre circle for some fifty yards to the edge of the Oldham penalty area, outpacing every attempt to catch him, then finished powerfully and clinically, left-footed and low past the goalkeeper's right hand. It was his 117th goal in his 277th appearance for Crystal Palace and a marvellous valedictory. Again Oldham responded, with the aid of a deflection, but with some two minutes remaining Mark Bright settled the affair with an emphatic volley from close range. The startling news of Wright's transfer began to unravel over the weekend and the deal was completed and announced formally on the Monday, forty-eight hours after the Boundary Park victory. To a man Palace fans were sad to see Ian leave, but he had made clear his desire to play for a club involved in European competition and, in spite of inducements to stay, he chose to move away.

Palace's replacement for Wright was Marco Gabbiadini, who joined us from Sunderland for £1.8 million but, while Marco scored some valuable goals for us – his first helped us to victory at Coventry, his second, as we shall see, to our biggest prize of the season, at Anfield – the move never really appeared satisfactory. Palace seldom played to Gabbiadini's strengths, while his fitness looked questionable. Thus, when Derby County offered £1.2 million at the end of January, Palace accepted the bid – and this came only a short while after we had taken another substantial loss on a transfer that had failed to work out. Paul Bodin, recruited from Swindon the previous spring for £550,000, returned to Wiltshire for less than half that sum.

In the wake of the departures and a spate of injuries, young players now came to the fore. David Whyte made a promising full debut, Simon Rodger and Simon Osborn were becoming first-team regulars and so was Gareth Southgate, but then came further controversy when disgruntled Andy Gray left again, initially on loan to Tottenham, so that by the time of the last game of the season at Queens Park Rangers, Palace fielded no fewer than eight new faces from the line-up that had appeared in the first match.

Out on the pitch it was an eventful season too. Palace gained a remarkable 3-2 victory over tenants Wimbledon in our first home match in which three men were sent off including our goalkeeper Nigel Martyn, whose splendid deputy for almost an hour was John Salako. The rearranged match against Leeds on 1 October brought another stirring victory, secured by a late Bright header on Marco Gabbiadini's debut, but that evening will forever remain etched in Palace memories for the sight of John Salako lying crumpled by the Holmesdale Road goal, having fallen badly after putting in a testing tenth-minute header. An exploratory operation the following day revealed the severance of both cruciate ligaments behind his left knee, one of the worst injuries a footballer can sustain and one that denied his presence in the Palace cause for many months to come.

Chris Coleman outstrips Steve Staunton during Palace's 0-0 draw with Aston Villa at Selhurst Park on 21 March 1992.

But the best and happiest memories of 1991/92 concern our victories over Liverpool, for Palace did the 'double' over the Reds. Ever since our 0-9 humbling at Anfield, the Eagles and their followers have taken special relish in beating Liverpool. The semi-final victory over them was simply the first instalment in paying back the Merseysiders and this 2 November 1991 win at their headquarters was another huge contribution towards restoring parity between the clubs in the minds of Palace supporters. It was also a fabulous demonstration of something we had sensed at the semi-final, then experienced at Selhurst Park the previous December: Liverpool's much-vaunted supporters are not nearly so noisy or vocal as the northern media would have everyone suppose. Not for the first time they were found wanting by comparison with the massed ranks of 3,000 Palace fans in the Anfield Road stand, who were in great voice before, during and after the match and, even when our side was in arrears, continued to provide lusty encouragement, so that it represented the highlight of the entire 1991/92 season.

The teams entered Liverpool's famous arena to a barrage of noise, a balloon welcome from the Palace fans and in pouring rain, but with Eddie McGoldrick sweeping immaculately behind a defence that was tight and controlled, it was apparent from the early exchanges that either side might win. In fact, from about the half-hour mark, Palace began to assert themselves and to impose our authority on Liverpool as our confidence grew, but just before half-time burly Swedish international Glenn Hysen headed his side in front following a left-side corner

Palace may have lacked a little ambition earlier in the game, but we scarcely deserved to be in arrears and the interval discussion in the dressing room inspired a new sense of purpose and direction so that, playing towards the Kop, Palace took the second half to their hosts with a display of passion, character and no little skill. The Liverpool defence, which had been uneasy under pressure all afternoon, soon paid the price. Six minutes into the second period Marco Gabbiadini scythed the ball past Bruce Grobbelaar from close range to restore the status quo following a first-class move down our right flank that involved four other players and culminated in a low cross from near the corner flag from overlapping full-back Gareth Southgate.

From then on the destiny of the points was never really in doubt as Palace, providing compelling entertainment and in spite of losing experienced men to injuries, continued to attack the bewildered Reds, whose fans were quite unable to raise their team's wilting performance. To the mounting enthusiasm, anticipation and realisation among Palace's packed supporters, the Eagles reshuffled — and dominated the home side so thoroughly that, when they scored again in the seventy-second minute when our right-side corner was flicked on by central defender Eric Young then headed into the net by Geoff Thomas, it was long overdue!

Liverpool naturally roused themselves, but to a crescendo of deafening sound from the splendid Palace support, the Palace men held off the Reds' rally with tenacity and even aplomb. The Palace programme team dubbed the Liverpool conquerors 'The Anfield Avengers' and there was no doubt that this success was one of the greatest Palace victories of all time. And for those who had been present at the 0-9 defeat of two seasons before, it was a marvellous, unforgettable and ecstatic occasion.

When Liverpool came to a blustery, cool Selhurst Park for the return fixture in mid-March Eric Young himself was their nemesis. Five minutes before the interval an Andy Thorn free-kick created mayhem in the visitors' penalty area. Mark Bright soared above his marker to flick the ball on and it ran towards the corner of the goal-area near the byline in front of the Holmsedale Road terrace (as it still was). Bruce Grobbelaar and Eric challenged for the ball but, as the

Mark Bright scored 22 Palace goals this term.

extrovert goalkeeper sought to smother it, the Eagles' giant pivot stuck out a lanky leg and stroked the ball back from Bruce's attempted grasp before regaining his own balance and driving it into the far inside netting of the goal from an acute angle. That was sufficient to provide Palace with their fourth win over Liverpool in five matches and a superb first-ever 'double'.

Eddie McGoldrick, one of the Palace heroes in that Anfield triumph, won the Player of the Year award and certainly the Republic of Ireland international's creative versatility was invaluable to the Club in 1991/92, but Mark Bright, in his last full season with the Eagles, played in every League and Cup match of the entire campaign, and notched 17 top-flight goals. Many Palace fans of the period actually regard season 1991/92 as Mark's best one of all in our colours. Not only did he captain the Palace team for a few games in early winter, but he was our only player to play every game this term and his tally of League goals remains the highest ever scored by a Palace striker at the highest domestic level.

Further encouraging evidence of the advances made by Crystal Palace this season materialised as the Palace Youth team surged into the FA Youth Cup semi-final for only the fourth time in the Club's history, and then overcame Wimbledon with a 2-1 victory in the first leg and a fabulous, titanic 3-3 draw in the second. By the time of the final our Juniors were already champions of their division of the South East Counties League but, pitted against an outstanding team from Manchester United we lost 1-3 at Selhurst Park and 2-3 at Old Trafford.

SEASON: 1991/92

GROUND: Selhurst Park

MANAGER: Steve Coppell

LEAGUE/DIVISION: Football League First Division

FINAL POSITION: 10th

BIGGEST VICTORY: 2-0 *v.* Everton, 4 April 1992, 2-0 *v.* West Ham United, 20 April 1992

HEAVIEST DEFEAT: 1-5 *v.* Nottingham Forest, 23 November 1991

FA CUP – ROUND ELIMINATED: 3rd

LEAGUE CUP – ROUND ELIMINATED: 5th

FULL MEMBERS CUP – ROUND ELIMINATED: 4th

LEADING LEAGUE APPEARANCES (MAX: 42): 42 – M. Bright, 38 – N. Martyn

LEADING LEAGUE GOALSCORERS: 17 – M. Bright, 6 – G. Thomas

1992/93

PALACE ARE RELEGATED IN CONTROVERSIAL CIRCUMSTANCES

The FA generated huge publicity about the formation of its new Premier League in the summer of 1992 but regrettably the Eagles' initial participation in it was to be minimal, for although our 1992/93 season began in fine style when we opened our account with a pulsating 3-3 draw at sunny Selhurst Park against money-laden Blackburn Rovers, this term was ultimately to prove a bitterly disappointing one for everyone at Crystal Palace FC.

Palace's opening game in the new League requires some comment for, although a posse of photographers from the national daily and Sunday papers thronged the Whitehorse Lane end in anticipation of Alan Shearer's exploits for the visitors, Palace's ace goalscorer Mark Bright notched the ground's and the club's first-ever Premier League strike before our admiring Holmesdale Road supporters after little more than half an hour. His crisp, downward header from Richard Shaw's searching left-side cross bounced into the net beyond the reach of Rovers' goalkeeper Bobby Mimms. Just before the interval Stuart Ripley equalised for the visitors, but showing tremendous character against expensively assembled stars, Palace forged ahead again before the hour when Gareth Southgate crashed a right-footed, twenty-yard volley into the roof of Rovers' net. Alan Shearer then justified his enormous £3.6 million transfer fee and beat Nigel Martyn with two spectacular drives, but Palace refused to submit and replied with another fine goal deep into injury time. Our youthful pair of substitutes, Simon Rodger and Simon Osborn contrived it: the former's flighted free-kick was headed home precisely by the latter.

The draw with Blackburn was followed by three more: at Oldham (1-1) in some adversity; at Tottenham (2-2) where Andy Thorn and Neil Ruddock were dismissed after skirmishing together, and at home to Sheffield Wednesday (1-1). Three defeats followed and then Mark Bright was transferred to Sheffield Wednesday with Palace receiving the talented if diminutive midfielder-cum-striker Paul Williams and £350,000 in return. Bright had craved a move for some time, but Palace fans regretted his departure because he was a proven goalscorer. Only Ian Wright among our post-war marksmen could match Mark's Palace record of 92 Football/Premier League goals in our colours, but Williams' skill-factor clearly influenced Steve Coppell in this deal because Palace had come under a lot of media criticism (not always well-informed, but strident nevertheless) about our direct style of play and this was now being echoed by some of our fans.

Palace knocked Liverpool out of the League Cup in a Selhurst Park replay in mid-December 1992. Andy Thorn is seen heading home our extra-time winner.

A new arrival at Selhurst Park early this season was £1 million striker Chris Armstrong from Millwall. Manager Coppell was convinced that Chris had the predatory instinct and positional sense of a top-class striker and in this signing revealed again all his ability to recognise raw talent. Although this was to prove Steve's last successful import it was highly effective, for Chris quickly responded with important goals for Palace and his 15 strikes from 35 League outings represented a haul of the highest pedigree from a man who had not performed at this level before. His first goals, a stunning right-footed volley and a spectacular header, within a minute of each other just after the hour upon his debut, secured a point against visiting Oldham, and the following Saturday he netted another brace to provide Palace with our first victory in the Premier League, against Everton at Goodison Park. This time they both came early: a clever, diving, glancing header after eight minutes and a supreme effort when Chris rounded Welsh international goalkeeper Neville Southall ten minutes later. It was largely those pairs of goals that brought Chris his first 'Barclays Young Eagle of the Month' award with Palace in September 1992, but the emerging skills of midfielder Gareth Southgate brought him a similar award, and the two Palace tyros received their silverware together before our home match against Manchester City on 17 October.

However, in spite of Armstrong's commendable early return, it became apparent as the autumn progressed that Premier League survival would be the limit of our ambitions this term. We were not scoring enough goals, failing even from the penalty spot on three occasions. We were conceding them to the opposition with disturbing largesse and, with Andy Gray never replaced after his £1 million move to Spurs and Geoff Thomas looking a spent force even before he was sidelined by injury, we lacked sufficient authority in midfield. Seasoned supporters recognised these signs for they were evidence of a side that was in real danger.

By the end of November Palace were next to bottom after a 0-5 thrashing at Liverpool but, immediately and delightfully, surprised the Anfield men by holding them to a 1-1 draw in front of their own fans in the League Cup with a makeshift side. Liverpool manager Graeme Souness responded with one of his ill-tempered and unsporting outbursts but only provided Palace with just the stimulus we needed to overcome his expensively assembled outfit in the replay at Selhurst Park in the week before Christmas.

In fact the League Cup was to provide the only real pleasure for Palace and their fans this season because we proceeded from beating Liverpool to dismiss our powerful London neighbours Chelsea in the quarter-finals in the first week of January. The Selhurst Park pitch was sodden and the match was played throughout in a continuous downpour – and these conditions had an effect upon the outcome with only five minutes gone. Eddie McGoldrick completed some skilful defending near the touchline then sent a long, raking pass upfield. It reached the Blues' danger zone where Frank Sinclair ill-advisedly attempted to play the ball back to his goalkeeper, only to watch in horror as it stuck, as if in glue, in a pool of water in the 'D' on the edge of the penalty area, in front of the packed Holmesdale terrace. Chris Coleman showed great awareness and was able to reach the ball first by slithering through the mire, and his left-footed shot passed the exposed goalkeeper, then ran on towards the goal slowly, agonisingly and itself held back by the sodden turf, but in a bizarre piece of apparent slow motion, it retained just sufficient pace to creep across the goal-line, although it stopped just a foot inside the net and certainly never reached the netting. It was certainly one of the strangest goals ever witnessed.

Nigel Martyn made the first of many splendid saves that evening to deny Chelsea a quick response, but he had no chance with the fine shot delivered by Andy Townsend after eighteen minutes, although Townsend's contribution to the evening was largely overshadowed by the Eagles' own midfield supremo Geoff Thomas, who was now beginning to resemble the player who had won 9 full England caps in the previous two years.

However, a little after half an hour Palace were in front again. Eric Young flicked on an Eddie McGoldrick free-kick and the ball was retrieved at full stretch by Andy Thorn. Andy prevented Kevin Hitchcock from holding onto it and it skidded through to George Ndah who was able to prod it over the line from three or four yards for his first senior goal for our club.

Fellow teenager Grant Watts made another telling input to Palace's League Cup progress just three minutes after the interval. Simon Rodger lofted a centre into the goalmouth that Grant raced onto. He leant back and, while falling, lashed a left-footed killer blow into the bottom corner of the Chelsea net as Hitchcock dived the other way.

The match progressed to its end amid wonderful crowd backing from our supporters. Many were drenched to the skin but all were delighted to have witnessed Palace's success that had at last ended the long, long wait to reach the last four in this competition. However, Arsenal beat us in both legs of the semi-final and we were never able to use our victories in this cup as stepping stones towards redeeming our ailing Premier League season.

Thus, after a Good Friday afternoon trouncing (0-4) by Wimbledon we were in acute danger. Storming successes over Middlesbrough (4-1) on Easter Monday and over Ipswich (3-1) on May Day appeared to have remedied the situation, but the last relegation place was still unfilled and any one out of ourselves, Sheffield United or Oldham could take it. Oldham won well at Aston Villa twenty-four hours later and the Blades secured a second away victory in four days to ensure their survival on the Tuesday.

On Wednesday 5 May Palace gained a 0-0 draw at Manchester City with a praiseworthy battling performance, but at the same time Oldham won again, beating a Liverpool side whose collective performance was woeful and their goalkeeper's nothing short of pathetic, so that now everything hinged on the final Saturday of the season. If Palace could avoid defeat at Arsenal we would be safe. Failure to do so would mean that an Oldham victory, however narrow, over Southampton at Boundary Park would doom us to relegation.

Palace's demanding task was made formidable when Ian Wright despatched an early chance and Eddie McGoldrick spurned the opportunity of an immediate riposte, so that once we were aware that Oldham had gone ahead, the prospects were ominous. Despite creating several openings we could find no way through. Then when we pushed up in a desperate search for the goal that might yet save us, Arsenal scored again, ten minutes from time and right at the end. Some of our team left the pitch in tears as Steve Coppell stepped onto the arena to offer each player a consoling gesture.

This was to be Steve's last public act as our manager for, after a brief holiday, he announced his resignation. In fairness to him it should be stated that under the old system of two points for a win Palace would have survived and that only once before under the current system had a club been relegated from the top flight with 49 points.

SEASON: 1992/93

GROUND: Selhurst Park

MANAGER: Steve Coppell

LEAGUE/DIVISION: FA Premier League

FINAL POSITION: 20th

BIGGEST VICTORY: 4-1 *v.* Middlesbrough, 12 April 1993

HEAVIEST DEFEAT: 0-5 *v.* Liverpool, 28 November 1992

FA CUP – ROUND ELIMINATED: 3rd

LEAGUE CUP – ROUND ELIMINATED: Semi-final

FULL MEMBERS CUP – ROUND ELIMINATED: –

LEADING LEAGUE APPEARANCES (MAX: 42): 42 – N. Martyn, E. McGoldrick, 38 – E. Young, 31+7 – C. Coleman

LEADING LEAGUE GOALSCORERS: 15 – C. Armstrong, 8 – E. McGoldrick

1993/94

PALACE RETURN TO THE TOP FLIGHT AS CHAMPIONS

Alan Smith, tall, stylish and urbane, a splendid communicator and motivator and a football man through and through, was the obvious choice to succeed Steve Coppell as Palace's manager in the summer of 1993. He had been at Selhurst Park for almost ten years and proved a thoroughly capable assistant to Steve since 1989. It had been under his guidance that Gareth Southgate then more latterly 'The Bisto Kids', Simon Osborn and Simon Rodger, were nurtured into first-team players alongside their predecessors Richard Shaw and John Salako. However, Alan's first task upon taking full charge at Crystal Palace was a hugely demanding one, for the Club and many of its followers were greatly depressed by the experience of relegation. Yet, with a combination of energy, enthusiasm, commitment and flair, Alan and his coaching team of Steve Harrison, former Eagles striker David Kemp and the hugely popular Steve Kember restored morale and set the Club's sights firmly upon the swiftest possible return to the top flight.

This goal was achieved, ultimately in an imperious manner, but initially Alan lost two of his troupe of international stars when Geoff Thomas and Eddie McGoldrick moved to Wolves and Arsenal respectively for big fees. These departures disappointed many fans although it was largely recognised that, if the players' loyalties could not be guaranteed, then it was better that they left us, but manager Smith had already generated a new optimism at the Club while our supporters were much encouraged by the new manager's announcement that Palace would be adopting a more sophisticated mode of play in our quest for an immediate return to the Premier League. 'I've decided that we will use a "pass-and-move" style this season,' said Alan. 'I think this will prove acceptable to everybody. People don't want to see the ball being constantly pumped through the middle.' To be sure, the new-look Eagles were frequently much more refined than we had been for many years.

However, the early optimism surrounding our prospects for 1993/94 was somewhat muted by the two opening results, for Palace could only draw at home 0-0 with Tranmere on the first Saturday of the season, then went down 0-2 at Bristol City a week later. These setbacks had the effect of putting the Palace establishment firmly on its mettle and thus there followed an emphatic riposte to the cynics and doubters that, over a period of eight days, certainly established the Eagles among the favourites for promotion. Nottingham Forest, who had invested heavily in their attempt to regain Premier status, were dismissed from Selhurst Park in a superb evening game, when Eric Young's header opened our season's account and Dean Gordon rifled the second. Playing at left-back, Gordon was to become a vital and attractive member of the Palace side this season, progressing rapidly to the England Under-21 side and contributing some fine goals in our cause. Then Portsmouth, another likely contender for honours, were routed 5-1 after scoring first and three days later Birmingham were beaten 4-2 at St Andrews, where our football was neat, sharp and highly incisive, clever Paul Williams setting us on our way with his first Palace goal.

With Palace flying high and looking increasingly serious promotion contenders there occurred on Saturday 2 October 1993 one of those footballing occasions that might have come straight out of *Boy's Own*. John Salako, sidelined by a second cruciate ligament operation since the previous November and precisely two years and one day after the dreadful initial injury, returned to Palace's starting line-up for the first time for the visit of Stoke City to score a devastating and spectacular hat-trick that absolutely delighted our fans on that rain-soaked afternoon and took Palace to the top of the table.

It would be a mistake to pretend that Palace's progress to the First Division championship in 1993/94 was completely straightforward. It was not, because we had an achilles heel in the matter of our away form and this fragility on our travels might have cost us dear. Autumn defeats at Derby and Notts County (the latter after we had secured a 2-0 lead), then on a snow-flecked pitch at freezing Bolton in midweek, undid our hold on top place, then depressing midwinter ones at Millwall and Wolves implied that we might lack the ability to sustain our promotion challenge. It was at this point that manager Alan Smith demonstrated his acumen by securing Liverpool's England international striker or midfielder Paul Stewart on loan. The signing was inspired, brilliantly effective and the catalyst that provoked Palace to an emotional and completely successful conclusion to the season. Stewart was majestic, out of his class at Division One level and a controlling influence both on particular matches and upon his teammates. With Stewart playing up front alongside the prolific Chris Armstrong, the Eagles rapidly matured into the strongest side in the section by a considerable distance and demonstrated an attractive brand of resilience, sophistication and fortitude, while Stewart himself quickly became a huge favourite with the Palace fans. A widening gap of several points was built between ourselves at the top of the table and our challengers.

The matter of away performances was confidently settled. Palace actually secured a total of eleven away League victories in this season – a tally only ever improved upon at our Club by Arthur Rowe's promotion-winning side of 1960 – and, allied to this, Palace's defence tightened over the last third of the term into one of the best in the Club's history. It was in fact the meanest in the division over the season but it conceded just 9 goals during the last 14 matches and during that period recorded no fewer than seven clean sheets. Those statistics are impressive, but they become more so when it is pointed out that Palace had lost their experienced skipper and central defender Andy Thorn with cartilage and hamstring problems back in November. Such an absence could have been crucial, but Chris Coleman moved to partner Eric Young at the heart of the back four, while Dean Gordon filled the vacated left-back berth with astonishing yet increasing maturity to great effect. These three men, along with experienced and proven Nigel Martyn in goal and John Humphrey at right-back gelled to provide a thoroughly redoubtable rearguard.

Paul Stewart, Palace's loan signing, was brilliantly effective for the Eagles through the second half of 1993/94.

Assuming responsibility as captain was cultured, adaptable Gareth Southgate, who was now performing in midfield. Articulate and a splendid Club ambassador, Gareth quickly became an influential and respected skipper, as well as the youngest in the history of the Club, over a prolonged period, at the age of twenty-three years. Meanwhile, in a season that contained a whole catalogue of spectacular Eagles goals, Gareth himself netted some terrific efforts among his total of 9 League strikes, although perhaps the most memorable goal of all was the astonishing one despatched by Chris Armstrong at Barnsley in November after just ten seconds' play!

The arrival of Damian Matthew, a £150,000 recruit from Chelsea in February and Alan Smith's first full signing for the Club, added a refined option to Palace's midfield, then, as the promotion run-in gathered momentum, Palace invested £1.1 million to bring talented Watford winger Bruce Dyer to Selhurst Park. Now, with a squad of seventeen or eighteen men from whom to select, and unhampered by serious injuries (apart of course from the continuing absence of Andy Thorn) Palace really began to look the part of champions-elect.

A performance of fluency and panache at breezy Portsmouth on 5 March 1994 was crowned with a headed goal from Eric Young just after the hour, and a trio of narrow but significant victories over Oxford and Millwall at Selhurst Park and at a cramped and crowded Southend took the Eagles to the brink of promotion. Then a single-goal win at Luton, gained with a Chris Coleman volley following a first-minute corner, followed twenty-four hours later by a 2-2 draw between our closest challengers Millwall and Nottingham Forest at The New Den, were sufficient to ensure the season's success.

Captain Gareth Southgate holds the First Division championship trophy aloft.

Palace's objective now was the title itself and that quest continued with another one-goal success over dour visitors Barnsley in our penultimate home match on St George's Day (although our goalscorer, following a Simon Rodger corner, was Welsh international, Eric Young) and thus the stage was set for us to clinch the championship when we faced Middlesbrough at Ayresome Park on Sunday 1 May before a national television audience. Although Boro scored first, top-quality headed goals from Gareth Southgate and David Whyte before the interval and an immaculate third just before the hour from Chris Armstrong ensured the prize was ours.

The season finished for Palace on Sunday 8 May with a home game against Watford. Inevitably, with the championship trophy to be awarded, there was a packed crowd, a season's best in fact at our capacity of 28,749, but this was also an emotional and historic afternoon for another reason because the Holmesdale Road terrace was to be closed after the match for redevelopment to meet the requirements of the all-seater stadia demanded by the Taylor Report. Thousands of fans wanted to be present for 'The Last Stand' on the Holmesdale (even if we could not all get onto it at once) and the occasion was turned into a pageant of massive proportions.

The celebrations were impressive: the imposing 106-year-old trophy and the players' medals were presented by Football League president Mr Gordon McKeag, and Alan Smith received a second Manager of the Month award for the post-war record of six consecutive League victories Palace had achieved in April. The most spectacular welcome ever accorded to a Palace team greeted the players as they entered the arena, with thousands of balloons and a crescendo of noise being released to the strains of *Glad All Over*, so that the atmosphere was festive in the extreme.

But, with shades of thirty years previously, Palace could not quite deliver the finale we all desired. Watford played bravely, sensibly and well. They survived intense periods of pressure in both halves and, like Oldham in 1964, scored the goals in the second period that won the game for them. Nevertheless, Palace's stars brought the championship trophy back onto the pitch after the final whistle and paraded it for our fans to see in a rousing lap of honour.

Alan Smith's achievement in winning the title and taking Palace back to the Premier League in his first season in full charge at Selhurst Park was nothing short of outstanding, but further dignity was conferred upon the club later in the week of the celebrations when Nigel Martyn and Chris Armstrong both appeared as substitutes in an England 'B' international side that beat Northern Ireland 4-2 at Hillsborough.

SEASON: 1993/94

GROUND: Selhurst Park

MANAGER: Alan Smith

LEAGUE/DIVISION: Football League Division One

FINAL POSITION: 1st

BIGGEST VICTORY: 5-1 *v.* Portsmouth, 28 August 1993

HEAVIEST DEFEAT: 0-3 *v.* Millwall, 1 January 1994

FA CUP – ROUND ELIMINATED: 3rd

LEAGUE CUP – ROUND ELIMINATED: 3rd

FULL MEMBERS CUP – ROUND ELIMINATED: –

LEADING LEAGUE APPEARANCES (MAX: 46): 46 – C. Coleman, N. Martyn, G. Southgate, E. Young, 39+6 – D. Gordon

LEADING LEAGUE GOALSCORERS: 23 – C. Armstrong, 9 – G. Southgate

1994/95

A GLORIOUS VICTORY AT HIGHBURY AND TWO FINE CUP RUNS… BUT RELEGATION AGAIN

Having won promotion in such fine style and as emphatic champions in 1993/94, the Eagles and their supporters viewed Palace's return to the top flight with confidence, boosted by the arrival of three signings in the summer of 1994. Vastly experienced former England skipper Ray Wilkins arrived from Queens Park Rangers; tough, resilient defender Darren Pitcher came from Charlton while former Stockport striker Andy Preece cost £350,000.

The opening-day fixture for the Palace was at home to Liverpool, but with the Holmesdale Road end now undergoing redevelopment the fans were confined to the three other sides of Selhurst Park – and most of us found it a chastening afternoon, for Liverpool meted out a 1-6 beating, among the heaviest we have ever suffered on any of our home grounds.

Nevertheless, tense and faced with several controversies as the season ultimately became, it was certainly not without its thoroughly praiseworthy performances and exciting victories, even if, in retrospect, all Palace fans will agree that the regrettable and peculiar feature of 1994/95 was that too many of these triumphs were recorded in cup ties and we would willingly have forfeited them all if it had meant that we would have secured our Premiership survival. As it was, Palace became the only club in the country to appear in the last four of both the major Cup competitions, and lost the two-legged League Cup semi-final against Liverpool by the narrowest of margins.

Looking back on 1994/95, while the cup successes were thoroughly impressive, probably the best and most satisfying performance of the entire season came early in the campaign on 1 October when, in wonderful style, the Eagles travelled over to Highbury and recorded our first-ever League victory there in glorious and emphatic manner. Palace's chief executioner on this dull and drizzly Saturday afternoon was John Salako who, playing as a striker, scored both Palace goals precisely upon the third anniversary of the terrible cruciate ligament injury he had sustained in a top-flight match at Selhurst Park against Leeds. How the enclave of Eagles fans cheered their favourites and derided their Arsenal counterparts as the home side struggled, then failed, to match our verve, enthusiasm and skill.

Salako was playing alongside Chris Armstrong and the lithe, twinkling duo made Arsenal's big defenders, Tony Adams and Andy Linighan, appear statuesque, and both our goals were delightful affairs. Midfielder Bobby Bowry set up the first after nineteen minutes with a ball-winning tackle that allowed Armstrong a clear run at goal. The pacy striker brushed past Linighan before shooting against the far post in front of the north stand, leaving John Salako a simple tap-in task. Shortly before half-time a superb pass from skipper Gareth Southgate found Armstrong in acres of space on the right flank and his low, scudding cross was swept home gratefully and gracefully by Salako.

Ian Wright was able to head a consolation goal for his new employers, but the day was eventually Palace's amid a tension that was palpable, while the occasion was particularly sweet for those Palace fans who over the years had witnessed many severe maulings for our team at the imposing north London ground.

In the final analysis the 1994/95 season hung upon the events of its last five weeks. Although Ray Wilkins' contribution to the Club had proved minimal due to injury, even before he departed in December to manage QPR, Palace had been boosted by the £700,000 additions of Northern Ireland striker Iain Dowie in January and Eire midfielder Ray Houghton in March. We lined up for the FA Cup semi-final against Manchester United at Villa Park on Sunday 9 April with a quiet confidence despite our lowly position in the table, and produced a superb display that ranked alongside the 1990 performance against Liverpool at the same venue even if it did not quite achieve the same outcome. A pulsating, enthralling encounter of great skill and commitment ensued and for Palace fans the only disappointment was that our reward was merely a replay. Palace had much the better of the first half. Peter Schmeichel was certainly the busier 'keeper but even his telescopic arms could not reach the ball in the thirty-second minute

Palace boss Alan Smith with Manchester United manager Alex Ferguson at the FA Cup semi-final replay.

when John Salako leapt high at the far post to head back a right-side cross from Chris Armstrong, and Iain Dowie was able to nod into the net from close range. United's first equaliser took a deflection from a free kick and the tie was into extra time before Chris Armstrong lobbed over Schmeichel from some fifteen yards. But United replied promptly and with neither side able to find a killer strike a replay became necessary the following Thursday.

However, it only became apparent on the morning after the game that Nigel Martyn had sustained a broken index finger of his left hand in a clash with United's David Beckham in only the second minute and, having played through in considerable pain, would now miss not just the replay but also several games of the crucial run-in to the end of the Premiership season, upon which so much depended.

Palace looked to Rhys Wilmot to deputise. Rhys had joined us at the start of the season from Grimsby in an £80,000 deal to provide cover for Martyn, but had played only three minutes of top-flight football for us since the move. It was also necessary for Dean Gordon to replace Chris Coleman in Palace's starting line-up but as in the 1990 FA Cup finals between the clubs, the second game was an anti-climax. We conceded two set-piece goals in the last quarter of an hour of the first half, were unable to reply and the whole occasion was marred by the sending off of United's shamed Roy Keane for stamping on Gareth Southgate, and of Darren Patterson for retaliation.

Meanwhile, in the Premier League Palace retained an even if awkward chance of earning survival: eight matches remained but only three of them were at home and the first of these was on the sunny afternoon of Good Friday, 14 April, against Tottenham. Curiously both the goals of a 1-1 draw were scored from long range against the run of play. As half-time approached Chris Armstrong ripped a low drive into the bottom left-hand corner from twenty-five yards, while Spurs' equaliser was an eighty-eighth minute spectacular, if controversially awarded, Jurgen Klinsmann free-kick.

On the cool, blustery Easter Monday every game bar one in the Premier League fixture list had a bearing on matters near the foot of the table, but a thoroughly commendable single-goal victory, gained with a crashing Iain Dowie header from Ricky Newman's left-side corner as the hour approached in the passionate clash at Queens Park Rangers, provided hope for the Eagles even if we were still in the bottom four. Perhaps it was predictable that Palace then lost 1-2 to the powerful champions-elect, Blackburn, at Ewood Park in a rare Thursday fixture, but the Lancashire fans were mighty relieved to hear the final whistle for a Palace rally, sparked by Ray Houghton's first goal for us, came within the width of a post of bringing us a point.

So to the run-in of five games in fifteen days upon which the Club's future stature would depend, but 1994/95 was the season in which the Premier League was to be reduced to twenty clubs and so would consign a total of four sides – the largest number ever to have been relegated from the top flight – to the Football League. Palace went down by the odd goal in three to well-placed Nottingham Forest in our penultimate home game on 29 April, so the rearranged fixtures of the evening of Wednesday 3 May were inevitably going to be vital ones for the clubs still realistically involved in the relegation fracas, but Palace were the only one to be playing away and lost 1-3 at Southampton.

The final home match, against West Ham on the baking hot afternoon of Saturday 6 May was Gareth Southgate's 150th League game for the Palace, but it was his fellow midfielder Ray Houghton who was Palace's inspiration and the veteran star set up the goal that provided the

Iain Dowie netted Palace's opener in the 2-2 draw in the initial semi-final tie.

Eagles with their first home victory over the Hammers in ten attempts, and a slender Premiership lifeline in front of a packed, anxious but enthusiastic crowd. Palace dominated these proceedings throughout, but the crucial moments came five minutes into the second half when a Houghton shot struck the hands of Julian Dicks, but cannoned back to him. His second effort rebounded from Ludek Miklosko to Chris Armstrong who responded to his critics by lashing the ball past the giant Czech keeper into the Whitehorse Lane net from six yards.

Palace's season now finished with two demanding and distant away games, at Leeds on Tuesday 9 May then at Newcastle the following Sunday and victory at one or the other was essential to our quest. Regrettably both tasks proved beyond us. Our 1-3 defeat at Leeds, compounded by the other midweek results, left us a remote possibility of survival but, even if almost a thousand of our fans travelled to Tyneside, it was soon evident that there was to be no miraculous escape. Palace conceded the earliest goal of the Premiership proceedings that day, courtesy of a deflection, and the match was all too soon beyond our reach, despite a defiant second-half rally in pouring rain, which brought goals from Chris Armstrong and Ray Houghton and at least ensured dignity to our departure from the top flight.

Relegation was a bitter pill for Palace to swallow and it led, inevitably, to the departure by mutual consent of manager Alan Smith. Alan had been at loggerheads with chairman Ron Noades for several months, but discerning fans will recognise that the perverse fact is that his efforts for the Eagles and our ninetieth anniversary had only been shorn of at least some measure of glory by the closest of margins in two cup semi-finals and by the arbitrary and contentious ruling that relegated more clubs from the top division than ever before in the history of the game.

SEASON: 1994/95

GROUND: Selhurst Park

MANAGER: Alan Smith

LEAGUE/DIVISION: FA Premiership

FINAL POSITION: 19th

BIGGEST VICTORY: 4-1 *v.* Coventry City, 2 November 1994

HEAVIEST DEFEAT: 1-6 *v.* Liverpool, 20 August 1994

FA CUP – ROUND ELIMINATED: Semi-final

LEAGUE CUP – ROUND ELIMINATED: Semi-final

FULL MEMBERS CUP – ROUND ELIMINATED: –

LEADING LEAGUE APPEARANCES (MAX: 42): 42 – G. Southgate, 41 – R. Shaw, 38+3 – D. Gordon

LEADING LEAGUE GOALSCORERS: 8 – C. Armstrong, 4 – I. Dowie, A. Preece, J. Salako

1995/96

BRILLIANT REVIVAL TAKES PALACE TO WEMBLEY

Despite relegation, Palace immediately began preparation for the forthcoming season when it was hoped that a strong and disciplined attempt would be made to restore the Club to the top flight. The first step was the early signing of Plymouth Argyle's Marc Edworthy at a fee of £350,000 with a view to him taking over the right-back position.

Then a changed managerial structure was announced. Ray Lewington, considerably experienced in management with Fulham, had been a member of our 1994/95 coaching staff, and would take charge of the playing side for us with Peter Nicholas, a firm Palace favourite from his two playing spells with the Eagles and a highly successful Youth team manager. Then in early June it was announced that the strategic post of technical director at our Club would be filled by our former manager Steve Coppell. Steve's first task was to try to stem the outflow of talented players in the wake of Alan Smith's departure.

First to go was Chris Armstrong, who joined Tottenham for £4.5 million, then Gareth Southgate moved to Aston Villa for £2.5 million. Another major fee was received from Coventry when John Salako joined the Sky Blues for £1.5 million. Andy Preece joined Blackpool for £200,000, Bobby Bowry took the short trip to Millwall for £220,000 and just after the start of the new season Darren Patterson left us for Luton Town for £150,000.

However, during the summer Palace secured fiery Welsh Under-21 defender Gareth Davies from his local club, Hereford United, for £120,000 and Millwall's midfield skipper Andy Roberts for a club-record fee of £2.5 million with Ricky Newman moving to The New Den as part of the move. Within twenty-four hours, Scottish Under-21 midfielder David Hopkin arrived from Chelsea for a £750,000 fee and popular former Palace full-back Brian Sparrow rejoined us to be our Youth team coach.

If the team was in the process of being restructured during the summer of 1995 then so too was the Palace stadium, for the new Holmesdale Road all-seater stand was nearing completion. Double tiered and with a capacity of 8,500, it cost the Club nearly £6 million, but was financed by long-term season ticket sales plus grants and loans from banks and the Football Trust. It was opened for the use of supporters for our second home match of 1995/96 on Saturday 26 August when Charlton Athletic were our visitors and was officially opened before the game by Ron Noades and Steve Coppell in a traditional ribbon-cutting ceremony.

Above: Carl Veart stoops to head Palace's second goal at The Valley in the 1995/96 play-off semi-final first leg against Charlton.

Left: Carl Veart celebrates after scoring Palace's second goal in the play-off semi-final first leg.

Nevertheless, the turnover of playing staff continued. Popular Iain Dowie and Player of the Year Richard Shaw left for West Ham in September and Coventry in November respectively, with strikers Dougie Freedman from Barnet and Gareth Taylor from Bristol Rovers coming in. Several former members of the Youth team made League debuts and seventeen-year-old Leon McKenzie became the first Palace teenager for over twenty years to score on his senior debut when he ensured a second round second leg League Cup victory over Southend.

Not surprisingly, only occasionally did the constantly changing side play with conviction, and to good effect. It became a rarity for us to keep a clean sheet, despite the deployment of Andy Roberts as a sweeper, although young left-back Dean Gordon became Palace's most capped Under-21 player when he made his twelfth appearance for England in a European Championship qualifier against Portugal in September.

Chris Coleman moved to ailing champions Blackburn in mid-December for a major £2.8 million fee, but a brace of away wins on the two Saturdays before Christmas looked to be a turning point for this 1995/96 season. A 2-1 success was secured at in-form Stoke, then on 23 December Dean Gordon completed a twenty-five-minute first-half hat-trick at West Bromwich Albion with two penalties and a close-range header to enable us to cruise to a 3-2 win while establishing himself as the only Palace defender besides Ian Evans ever to net three times in a fully competitive match and to join the select band of Palace men to have done so away from home.

Palace's advance was then confirmed by another away win on New Year's Day, this time at Portsmouth (3-2) where David Hopkin notched two well-struck goals. But our dismissal from the FA Cup by Port Vale in a mist-shrouded Vale Park replay, after a sterile 0-0 draw at Selhurst Park and a 1-1 home draw against Ipswich led to a further change in the managerial structure for, following two more draws, former Wimbledon, Watford and Sheffield United manager Dave Bassett was installed. Dave's intention was to provide 'winning and eye-catching' football.

If Dave Bassett's impact was not quite immediate, it was still quickly and highly effective. Palace became a team transformed under him so that, within a month, we had soared up the table, established ourselves firmly among the leading clubs and become almost awesome at Selhurst Park. But a sequence of home victories was eventually stifled by Portsmouth, managed by former defender Terry Fenwick, in a tedious 0-0 draw where Andy Roberts struck what many thought was the winner after prolonged added time only for everyone to discover that the referee had blown his whistle a split-second earlier and that the goal would not count.

Palace made swift amends by crushing Millwall 4-1 at The New Den the following week, when Nigel Martyn saved a first-half penalty and all the goals, including one on his debut by on-loan full-back Kenny Brown and a late brace inside two minutes from the now-sparkling George Ndah, came in the second period. Meanwhile a further and considerable boost to Palace's morale and prestige was provided by the Youth team under Brian Sparrow, which had won their divisional title of the South East Counties League for the third season in succession and reached the semi-final of the FA Youth Cup, bowing out only in extra time at the end of two legs to a physically much stronger Liverpool side. Saturday 20 April 1996 saw Palace at Wolves in front of a 25,000 crowd of Black Country partisans – our biggest audience of the season (bar Wembley) by far – but, showing greater application than our hosts, David Hopkin had us ahead after thirty-one minutes and Bruce Dyer settled the outcome ten minutes after half-time. That left Derby County a single point ahead of us with two games each to play – with the next one a Derby-Palace clash at the Baseball Ground! The opening was electric:

Derby were ahead within two-and-a-half minutes, but Palace were level barely two minutes later. The initiative then ebbed and flowed and the encounter began 'to have 1-1 written all over it' to quote Dave Bassett, as the hour mark passed but Derby netted with a header at our unguarded far post from a corner midway through the second half to which we could not reply to consign us to the play-offs.

Palace's opponents in the end of season showdown were Charlton. Inevitably, the games were played in a supercharged atmosphere before packed crowds, although the weather was much cooler than it had been at this stage for the 1989 matches. At The Valley in the first leg, Charlton led after just fifty-five seconds and had chances to extend that advantage before the break, but Palace surged forward after the interval and goals from a Kenny Brown volley and Carl Veart's stooping, close-range header emphasised our superiority in the second period. The Addicks' grip on matters was made even more tenuous when Palace skipper and undoubted Man of the Match, Ray Houghton, struck a glorious fourth-minute effort into the top corner of the Holmesdale Road goal in the second leg, and there was no way back for Charlton after that.

The Wembley final on Bank Holiday Monday, 27 May 1996, was against Leicester City, as by this stage, the single promotion place was determined in a one-off contest at the national stadium. Nothing could be gleaned as to the possible outcome from the results between the sides in the two League matches, for both had won on their opponents' grounds, and both by an odd goal at that! Equally, both outfits had changed their managers during the season and become much more effective sides thereby.

Both clubs also had major representations among the 73,573 Wembley attendance and it was reckoned that the Palace had some 34,000 fans present for this occasion while, for the third time in our four visits to the Twin Towers in six years, the game went into extra time.

Palace seized an early lead in the thirteenth minute when Andy Roberts stayed upfield after initiating an attack and, following a clever exchange of passes with Ray Houghton, delivered a low, right-footed thunderbolt into the bottom-left corner of the Leicester net. Palace might have added to their lead before and after the break, when Kevin Poole saved absolutely brilliantly from first George Ndah and then Dougie Freedman, but Nigel Martyn was called into important action after the hour, as Leicester applied increasingly fearsome pressure, tipping an Emile Heskey effort over the bar in immaculate fashion, though Palace's custodian had no chance of saving Garry Parker's seventy-sixth-minute penalty, awarded for a foul on Muzzy Izzet, despite diving the correct way.

Now Leicester were the dominant side but Palace took them into extra time and clawed our way back to a moral parity, so that a penalty shoot-out appeared to be inevitable. That certainly was the opinion of Leicester manager Martin O'Neill, for in the final minute he brought on his giant Australian goalkeeper, the 6ft 7in Zeljko Kalac. But 'Spider's' involvement was unnecessary because, in the 120th minute (the excellent referee later revealed that there were just two seconds of play left on his watch at the moment of the goal) Leicester's former Palace reserve striker Steve Claridge volleyed past an exposed Nigel Martyn off his shin and with a hint of a deflection to leave the Eagles and their supporters nothing tangible to show for a quite remarkable season, other than the memories of a most-praiseworthy revival coupled with the bonus of another trip to Wembley.

SEASON: 1995/96

GROUND: Selhurst Park

MANAGER: Steve Coppell (as technical director) to February 1996, then Dave Bassett

LEAGUE/DIVISION: Football League Division One

FINAL POSITION: 3rd

BIGGEST VICTORY: 5-0 *v.* Grimsby Town, 5 March 1996

HEAVIEST DEFEAT: 0-3 *v.* Huddersfield Town, 24 February 1996

FA CUP – ROUND ELIMINATED: 3rd

LEAGUE CUP – ROUND ELIMINATED: 3rd

FULL MEMBERS CUP – ROUND ELIMINATED: –

LEADING LEAGUE APPEARANCES (MAX: 49 including play-offs): 49 – N. Martyn, 47 – M. Edworthy

LEADING LEAGUE GOALSCORERS (including play-offs): 20 – D. Freedman, 13 – B. Dyer

1996/97

PALACE ARE WEMBLEY WINNERS ONCE MORE

Palace's cruel manner of defeat at Wembley left Eagles fans totally drained as well as completely frustrated, while it also appeared to have affected the Club itself, for close-season matters were extremely slow-moving and then thoroughly curious at Selhurst Park. Our failure to regain Premier status cost Youth team manager Brian Sparrow his job as Peter Nicholas returned to coach the Eagles' successful Junior side, leaving Dave Bassett and Ray Lewington to assume control of the First Division squad. England international goalkeeper Nigel Martyn left us for Leeds for £2.5 million having played 349 senior games for the Palace, and the deal made him Britain's most costly goalkeeper for the second time.

But that, by the end of the first week of August, was that as far as the senior playing personnel were concerned. It was the quietest close-season we have known at the Palace for many years – but then the Club did move into serious transfer action, only to secure yet another goalkeeper to add to the three young custodians we had signed during the summer break. The most interesting of the latter was 6ft 5in, twenty-one-year-old Carlo Nash from Clitheroe for £35,000 but on 7 August 1996 Palace signed Chris Day from Spurs for £200,000. Day, thrice capped by England Under-21s, arrived with high commendations but lacking any League experience, though he performed well enough for the Palace in the first six months of the season. The only other acquisition was made just two days before the season got underway when Australian Olympic Games skipper Kevin Muscat arrived from South Melbourne.

Palace's opening match of the 1996/97 season was at Birmingham. It was deferred by twenty-two hours for live Sunday coverage at 1 p.m. Fans adjusted to this previously curious kick-off time and it certainly seemed strange on that boiling afternoon at St Andrews where temperatures soared to ninety-two degrees, but Palace themselves seemed less affected than Birmingham and we were most unfortunate to go down to a single goal conceded midway through the first half.

Six days later, at home to Oldham, Palace unveiled their new-look home strip of narrower red and blue stripes than used in any modern season. Palace overran the Latics in the first half with David Hopkin's display characterising his whole splendid season, and he netted our first goal of a 3-0 win in only the tenth minute. But we could not continue in such irresistible fashion and could only manage a goal-less draw at home to West Bromwich Albion, then a 1-1 result at Huddersfield where Darren Pitcher was stretchered off with badly damaged cruciate ligaments in his right knee.

In the second half of September, Palace had a superb run that quickened the interest of every Eagles fan. First we overwhelmed visiting Manchester City, the pundits' favourites for promotion, 3-1 on 14 September, with David Hopkin quite outstanding. Then, despite the truth of the rumours circulating Elm Park that Carlo Nash would have to deputise for Chris Day, our very own 'Clitheroe Kid' had a fine debut! He made an important early save, was largely untroubled as Palace romped to a 5-0 lead within an hour and saw matters through to an ultimate 6-1 triumph.

Palace continued in rampant form. Bury were despatched 4-0 in the ensuing midweek League Cup action and another 6-1 goal glut followed in front of our own supporters when Southend were our visitors on the last Saturday in September. That bonanza of 16 goals in 3 games within eight days was easily Palace's best within modern times, and only Johnny Byrne and company had bettered it since the Second World War.

Palace continued to perform well enough to reach third place in the First Division table by the end of October and second a month later. It was evident that, augmented now by powerful Southampton striker Neil Shipperley at a cost of £1.2 million and the return of Dean Gordon after a long achilles tendon injury, we were among the more consistent of the promotion hopefuls. However, Palace's grip on the top positions slackened in midwinter. At the end of January we had slipped to tenth but, with the defence much strengthened by the £100,000 arrival from Arsenal of Andy Linighan we were firmly back in contention by February and had looked particularly impressive in a 3-0 victory at Wolves.

But now Palace and their fans were astonished to learn that manager Dave Bassett was leaving us to become general manager at Nottingham Forest. Understandably, Ron Noades expressed himself as 'left reeling' by this departure and some fans were openly angry, but the Club moved swiftly to redress the situation and the next morning, Friday 28 February 1997, announced that our former boss, Steve Coppell, would return to the Palace helm. There were 14 League matches and ten weeks of the regular season remaining in which Steve would determine Palace's immediate future.

At Oxford United the following afternoon the portents appeared pretty good, for Palace routed 4-1 a club with one of the best home records in the country. Wing-back Dean Gordon put us on the way to victory with a headed goal some ten minutes before half-time.

Admittedly, Palace's form over the last quarter of the season was mixed, although a run of five undefeated games was sufficient to ensure a play-off place, but not enough to claim the second outright promotion position. That possibility had disappeared when Barnsley, lying second and our visitors on 19 April, held us 1-1, equalising a soaring Neil Shipperley header on the half hour with a penalty almost immediately after half-time.

Palace then powered to only our second post-war double over Reading with a 3-2 victory in a rearranged game to re-enter the play-off places, but we still needed to win at Swindon on Saturday 26 April in our penultimate fixture to ensure that we took the last remaining play-off place. Palace were emphatically the better side and won with goals in the last minute of each half from Neil Shipperley.

Although they could still finish as high as fourth Palace, like every other member of the division's top six clubs, were unable to claim a victory in our last match, against Port Vale, and it was quickly established that our 1-1 result against the Burslem side meant that we were pitted against Wolves in the play-offs.

Meanwhile, Palace's magnificent run of recent successes at Youth level had continued and the young Eagles were now finalists in both the Southern Junior Floodlit Cup and the prestigious

Dougie Freedman receives congratulations after scoring his first goal in the play-off semi-final against Wolves.

FA Youth Cup itself. In praiseworthy performances, our lads beat Arsenal in both legs of the former competition, but lost the latter 1-3 on aggregate to richly talented Leeds United.

The first half of Palace's home leg of the play-off semi-final against Wolves was largely played in rain, heavy at times, and there was nothing to choose between the two sides. It was just after the hour, in the strengthening sunshine that Palace, now attacking our favoured Holmesdale Road end, achieved the breakthrough when Simon Rodger's inswinging corner was planted firmly into the net by a downward Neil Shipperley header and, with only two minutes left, that was the extent of the scoring. There then exploded one of the most gripping and astonishing culminations to a game that Palace fans have ever witnessed.

Dougie Freedman brought Palace fans to their feet with a dipping volley only for Wolves to respond within a minute but, with the game into injury time, Palace netted again in a glorious finale. A long free-kick found Andy Linighan, who headed the ball down for Dougie Freedman to flick a devastating lob over the exposed goalkeeper from twelve yards. Despite the unbridled hostility we encountered at Molineux in the second leg, Palace coped well with the intense demands of the evening, though we conceded a Mark Atkins goal just after half an hour. The night swung our way in the sixty-sixth minute when recently crowned Player of the Year David Hopkin showed all the pace, power and eye for goals that had drawn such attention from the Premiership's big clubs. David beat two defenders and then the goalkeeper from the edge of the penalty area to tilt the affair our way again. Wolves now needed two goals to take the game into extra time and scored one with just six minutes left but, even with generous added-on time, could not repeat the effort and Palace had secured a second Wembley visit in successive years. Watching the wild, jubilant carousal among the Eagles' fans at Molineux, it was impossible to think of any other Palace occasion when our supporters have celebrated in such fashion after seeing our team beaten! Once more Palace took over 30,000 fans to Wembley for the 1997 play-off final, when we contested the right to a Premiership place with Sheffield United, who had beaten us home and away in the ordinary Division One fixtures between the clubs earlier in the season. This time Palace certainly had the better of the first half but matters were more even after the break as the temperature rose towards the nineties. Chances, however, were few, with both sides at their most dangerous from set pieces. But then, with the game into its penultimate minute, there came the decisive moment.

Playing towards the mass of their own fans, Palace gained a corner on the right. Andy Roberts played the ball short for Simon Rodger to put over an inswinger with his trusty left boot. The Blades' Carl Tiler headed it away from above the penalty spot, but it fell to David Hopkin, standing unmarked some twenty-two yards out from goal to the left of the 'D'. David had time to control the ball on his left foot, transfer it to his favoured right, look up, adjust his balance, take aim and then, leaning back, unleash a stunning spectacular strike that was fitting to settle any showpiece at the national stadium. The ball curled round and over the United rearguard then dipped into the right-hand corner, leaving the goalkeeper merely a spectator and bringing an eruption of sound from our supporters as every Palace person in the arena leapt from their seats punching the air in joy and relief.

Neil Shipperley puts Palace ahead against Wolves.

Of course Palace had won promotion to the top flight before but never in such dramatic fashion. The celebrations on and off the Wembley pitch, from participants, management and fans alike, were truly fitting for the events, as *Glad All Over* boomed out over the loudspeakers to echo the sentiments in the hearts of every Palace person present.

SEASON: 1996/97

GROUND: Selhurst Park

MANAGER: Dave Bassett to 28 February 1997, then Steve Coppell

LEAGUE/DIVISION: Football League Division One

FINAL POSITION: 6th

BIGGEST VICTORY: 6-1 *v.* Reading, 21 September 1996, 6-1 *v.* Southend United, 28 September 1996

HEAVIEST DEFEAT: 0-3 *v.* Sheffield United, 12 April 1997

FA CUP – ROUND ELIMINATED: 3rd

LEAGUE CUP – ROUND ELIMINATED: 3rd

FULL MEMBERS CUP – ROUND ELIMINATED: –

LEADING LEAGUE APPEARANCES (MAX: 49 including play-offs): 48 – A. Roberts, 45+3 – M. Edworthy, 44+2 – K. Muscat, 42+4 – B. Dyer

LEADING LEAGUE GOALSCORERS (including play-offs): 17 – B. Dyer, 15 – D. Hopkin

1997/98

PALACE ENDURE TRAUMATIC TIMES IN THE TOP FLIGHT

The summer of 1997 should have been a wonderful few weeks for Crystal Palace fans following the Club's magnificent, dramatic, hugely exciting victory at Wembley to secure a return to the Premiership. However, not only was the close season extremely slow-moving but the rumours of David Hopkin's desire to leave Selhurst Park simply would not go away and, eventually, to the dismay of us all at that time, 'Hoppy' departed for Leeds at a fee of £3.5 million.

But, if the summer had been largely low-key to this point, it now accelerated at great pace! The Hopkin departure provided Palace with sufficient funds to move audaciously for the Juventus winger and Italian international, thirty-one-year-old Attilio Lombardo. The former Sampdoria star had become familiar to British football fans by way of the coverage of the Italian League, Serie A, on Channel 4 television where the wily, balding luminary had displayed dazzling skills, and the prospect of him appearing for the Palace was absolutely mouth-watering. Despite appearing initially to have foundered, the deal resurfaced at the end of July and on 1 August 1997 Palace concluded the most spectacular signing in their history at a fee announced at some £1.58 million. Of course it fell considerably short of being a club record in purely monetary terms, but in those of flair, talent, ambition and value for money it was certainly the most exciting transfer anyone at the Palace had ever known. The interest of the local public was captured by the move: the number of fans at the 1997 Open Day on the following Sunday was greater than at any previous one, and the Club's Mitcham Training Ground was besieged by media men two days later to meet the new star. Another surely related addition to Palace's staff at that time was that of much-respected Ray Wilkins, who returned to Selhurst Park ostensibly to assist with the coaching, but one of Ray's many talents was that he could speak fluent Italian!

More prosaic summer signings included goalkeeper Kevin Miller, formerly of Exeter and Birmingham, from Watford for £1.25 million and that of Icelandic international centre half Herman Hreidarsson. Miller later earned the opprobrium of our fans, but he played every Premiership game for us in 1997/98 while our previously unheard of centre half developed into a powerful and effective defender upon whom manager Steve Coppell came to rely, and in so doing became a considerable favourite with our fans.

Attilio Lombardo.

Palace's first fixture back in the top flight was at Everton. We chose to field just three men (Dean Gordon, Simon Rodger and Bruce Dyer) who had previously appeared for our Club in the Premiership in our starting line-up on an afternoon that was not only extremely hot but also with a debilitating high humidity level. The emotional temperature had also been jacked up by the local Merseyside media, who recklessly chose to cast slurs at Attilio Lombardo with jibes about him only coming to Palace to improve his pension for which, being prematurely bald, he appeared to be on the point of qualifying!

But Attilio had the last laugh. He netted Palace's opening goal in the thirty-fourth minute (a rare top-flight debut goal at our Club and our first such in the Premier League), then earned the penalty from which Bruce Dyer increased our advantage thirteen minutes from time. A few minutes later Attilio was substituted, leaving the field to the acclaim of Palace's travelling fans whose vociferous rendition of 'Just one Lombardo' to *O Sole Mio* was another contribution to a memorable afternoon.

Palace were inevitably unable to build upon their opening-day success. We were beaten by a Neil Redfearn goal for visiting Barnsley the following Tuesday evening, to provide an early example of the poor form we would display at Selhurst Park virtually throughout the season and that would, ultimately, cost us our Premiership status.

It was just now that Eagles fans learned of the arrival of a new director who was eager to inject additional funds for the purchase of top-quality players, and towards the development of Selhurst Park into a super-stadium for the approaching millennium. His name? Mark Goldberg – and much more will be heard of him, though not for the reasons we (or he) would have wished!

Palace recovered their Premiership momentum by securing a fully merited 2-0 victory at Leeds. This was a really pleasing Palace success because the Peacocks' connections with us at this time were considerable. They were managed by our former midfield star of the 1976/77 promotion side, George Graham, and, as well as David Hopkin they possessed England international goalkeeper Nigel Martyn. The second goal, scored by Attilio Lombardo six minutes into the second half, was such a sublime exhibition of skill that when Attilio left the pitch half an hour later after picking up a knock, the formerly partisan Leeds crowd joined the Palace fans in a standing ovation in recognition of a performance from a dimension not often witnessed in British football.

The Eagles' Premiership momentum now slowed, although we won again 'at' Wimbledon thanks to Lombardo's third goal for the club, but it was in mid and late September that Palace and their fans received a nasty shock that was to prove an unhappy omen for the season's ultimate destiny. We were engaged in League Cup second round action against Hull City, who were placed ninety-first in the Football League. A 0-1 first round defeat at Boothferry Park was embarrassing enough but worse followed at Selhurst Park when we permitted the Tigers to extend their lead after half an hour, then found ourselves unable to do better than level the aggregate, even with the aid of extra time, and so departed from the competition.

Despite that reverse there were several most creditable Premiership performances that gained victories away from home, while at Selhurst Park a 0-0 draw against Arsenal was regarded by Palace fans as our best showing of the term to this date (18 October) given the quality of the Gunners' side, perhaps best exemplified by their strike force, which comprised Ian Wright and Dennis Bergkamp.

Palace's progress through the rest of 1997/98 was often lacklustre. After our excellent 1-0 win over Tottenham at White Hart Lane on 24 November, gained by a Neil Shipperley strike, we deteriorated virtually out of all recognition. It was four months before the Eagles managed to win another League game and by that time we had slumped to bottom place in the table, with the Club in chaos and supporters bewildered. All the time there were hints emanating from the boardroom that Mark Goldberg was intent on mounting a full-scale takeover bid for Crystal Palace.

After Andy Roberts had joined Wimbledon for £1.8 million, and Palace had taken a 2-6 beating at Chelsea, Steve Coppell stood down as our manager. He was succeeded by Attilio Lombardo in a bizarre appointment, but Palace won at a somewhat distracted Newcastle on 18 March although we were still locked in bottom place. Three more defeats, two of them at Selhurst Park, left us adrift of the other strugglers and obviously consigned to the drop.

But now, at the sixteenth attempt, Palace secured a home win in the Premiership! Derby County were overconfident and unfocussed and paid heavily for their arrogance. Palace won 3-1, all the goals coming late in the contest.

Statistically Palace were relegated when Manchester United won a televised match on 27 April, after which chairman Ron Noades, assisted by Ray Lewington and Brian Sparrow, took over the managerial role, but it was at the final home game on Sunday 10 May that Palace fans were at last able to gain some hope for the future when late substitute Clinton Morrison netted with his first touch on his debut to defeat Sheffield Wednesday and provide Palace with 'a double' for good measure to bring the season's curtain down.

Reflecting upon that season any Palace fan is still humiliated by the appalling home form our Club displayed and suffers a measure of embarrassment at the huge number of players we deployed through the term – 36 of them in all for 38 Premiership matches, including no fewer than eleven foreign men, only two of whom, Attilio Lombardo and Herman Hreidarsson, played in even half the matches.

The ill-conducted takeover of the Club cannot have aided our cause at all. For fully six months of 1997/98 the ultimate ownership and control of Crystal Palace was unclear, leaving fans, management and players completely bemused. The arrival of Mark Goldberg as Palace's

new owner and chairman in early June was welcomed by many Palace fans at the time, but the highly public disagreements between him and the outgoing chairman had left Steve Coppell lacking authority. It created the need for new leadership that was then vested in a reluctant successor and certainly created further confusion, not to say a stiff measure of ridicule from sections of the media.

Mark Goldberg assumed control of Crystal Palace on 5 June 1998 at a cost of some £22.8 million. Outgoing chairman Ron Noades had led the Club since January 1981 and had transformed the ailing outfit into one that competed with dignity at the highest level. He remains the second-longest-serving chairman at Crystal Palace FC behind only the original holder of the office, Mr Sydney Bourne, and soon bought a controlling interest at Brentford.

SEASON: 1997/98

GROUND: Selhurst Park

MANAGER: Steve Coppell to 11 March 1998, then Attilio Lombardo to 27 April 1998, then Ron Noades

LEAGUE/DIVISION: FA Premiership

FINAL POSITION: 20th

BIGGEST VICTORY: 3-1 *v.* Sheffield Wednesday, 25 October 1997

HEAVIEST DEFEAT: 2-5 *v.* Bolton Wanderers, 2 May 1998

FA CUP – ROUND ELIMINATED: 5th

LEAGUE CUP – ROUND ELIMINATED: 2nd

FULL MEMBERS CUP – ROUND ELIMINATED: –

LEADING LEAGUE APPEARANCES (MAX: 38): 38 – K. Miller, 37+1 – D. Gordon

LEADING LEAGUE GOALSCORERS: 7 – N. Shipperley, 5 – M. Bent, A. Lombardo

Opposite: Player of the Year for 1997/98 Marc Edworthy.

1998/99

PALACE ARE FORCED INTO ADMINISTRATION

New chairman Mark Goldberg moved quickly in the 1998 close season to restore vision and credibility to Crystal Palace FC by appointing the former England, Australia, Tottenham and Crystal Palace manager Terry Venables as our head coach, with a back-up staff that included Dave Butler, who had been our physiotherapist under Terry twenty years earlier and former Palace and England defender Terry Fenwick, although by no means all Palace fans welcomed the appointments or considered them to be wise ones.

Two interesting transfers soon followed involving defenders. Dean Austin arrived at Selhurst Park from Spurs, for whom Terry Venables had first recruited him from Southend in 1992, then England Under-21 star Dean Gordon, our longest-serving player at that time, left for Middlesbrough for £900,000 having made 241 appearances for the Eagles over seven seasons.

A unique piece of Palace history was made in late July 1998 when we were engaged in a European tie. The lure of the Intertoto Cup was that sufficient progress in it allowed entry into the prestigious UEFA Cup, but Palace lost both legs of our tie against Samsunspor of Turkey 0-2.

In the week before the new season began it was announced that Palace were in negotiations for the purchase of the captain of the Chinese national side, twenty-nine-year-old defender or midfielder Fan Zhiyi, and that Fan's younger international teammate Sun Jihai was also arriving for a trial. No Chinese had ever played professionally in England before and the media interest in the two men was intense.

Palace paraded a new virtually all-red strip for our opening day home game against Bolton. Terry Venables received a rapturous reception upon his return to management at Selhurst Park and he gave club debuts to Dean Austin and the splendidly emerging Hayden Mullins but, with Palace seemingly having secured a 2-1 victory, we conceded an equaliser in the dying moments, right in front of the disbelieving Holmesdale Road stand.

The season became an extraordinary roller-coaster one. Results varied enormously and players signed or left at bewildering pace. The two Chinese made their British debuts in a League Cup second round first leg game at Bury, but Palace lost 0-3. Craig Foster, the midfield captain of Australia joined us, but striker Neil Shipperley moved to Nottingham Forest for £1.2 million and Herman Hreidarsson rejoined Ron Noades over at Brentford for £750,000.

An attendance landmark of sorts was reached when the television audience for Palace's Division One clash with Sheffield United was said to be over a billion because the match was beamed live to China and the Far East where huge interest had been generated in Eagles' two oriental stars and Fan Zhiyi enhanced his popularity in both South-East Asia and south-east London by having a fine match and a key involvement in Palace's goal.

But now, though nearly October, the first storm clouds began to appear over the financial horizon at Selhurst Park. Rumours were circulating that Palace were prepared to sell at least three of their leading players. Fact-based or not, these stories were unsettling for Palace fans and players alike, and indeed the Club's record signing Valerian Ismael did move to Lens within the month, Michele Padovano joined Metz (with the Eagles making substantial losses on both men) and the enigmatic Bruce Dyer left for Barnsley for £700,000. A fee of double that sum was paid to Manchester City for Lee Bradbury and then Yugoslavian international centre half Gordan Petric arrived from Glasgow Rangers for £300,000.

Palace won a match packed with incident and talking points against Portsmouth 4-1 on 7 November, but the hearsay and gossip throughout the winter continued to focus upon our clearly escalating financial predicament. It was understood that chairman Mark Goldberg was unable to sustain Palace's soaring overheads and that even the sales of players had proved insufficient. Following a bad defeat at Bolton on 10 January 1999 there occurred enormous changes. The Eagles were obviously not promotion-bound and current outgoings could not be allowed to continue. A cull was essential. Terry Venables (seriously disaffected by the absence of promised funds for further purchases) became a part-time consultant to the Club (a euphemism for his departure) and his extensive entourage left with him.

Steve Coppell took over (again) as our manager, but Matt Jansen was transferred to Blackburn for £4.1 million, Attilio Lombardo departed for Lazio for £500,000 and Palace folk simply squirmed with embarrassment and worse as our club was subjected to tirades of jibes, criticism and ridicule from a media made angry at being kept outside and uninformed while important meetings spanning twelve hours about the Club's finances and their implications took place at Selhurst Park throughout Thursday 14 January 1999.

A dismal sequence of results made it all too clear by mid-February that what remained of 1998/99 was likely to be a grim struggle against relegation and the correspondence columns of the *Croydon Advertiser* were packed with letters from angry, disillusioned fans, but relief was provided by a narrow Selhurst Park victory over Barnsley at the end the month to secure a first win there in three-and-a-half months. Then came perhaps Palace's best result of the entire term in a midweek match against promotion hopefuls Ipswich Town. Trailing to an early goal, Palace turned the contest on its head either side of half-time. Hayden Mullins (already easily and obviously Palace's Player of the Year) rose to head a spectacular equaliser, then Clinton Morrison put us in front. Ipswich levelled just after the hour but Palace gained a thrilling and deserved success with some twenty minutes left, Clinton pouncing upon a loose ball and firing into the far corner.

Later in March, though, the inevitable happened – Palace were placed legally into administration with debts of some £22 million. But this was only the beginning of the trauma – several more players left, others went out on loan to other clubs to reduce the wage bill while the rest were told of swingeing pay cuts. Forty-six members of the office and backroom staff were made redundant, causing enormous anguish since some of them were loyal supporters who had been in employment at the Club for many years.

Amid all the acrimony and high emotion there were, mercifully, two sources of relief. Not only did Palace's depleted squad provide several quite excellent results, which kept the Club well clear of relegation (in fact we finished the season in the top half of the table!), but the

Above left: Fan Zhiyi. (Illustration by Phil Neill Caricatures)

Above right: Terry Venables returned as Palace manager for 1998/99.

Football League assured the Eagles that there was no substance to press rumours that, unless we could give the League searching financial assurances, we would lose our membership during the coming close season.

Actually the six weeks from the end of February to mid-April, which were the ones that saw the survival of our Club hang by the slenderest of threads, were the ones in which Palace secured their best run of results all term. But surely the most memorable one among them all, surpassing even a victory over promotion-bound Bradford City and an Easter Monday draw with champions-elect Sunderland, was the Easter Saturday visit to Norwich.

This trip to Carrow Road fell just a few days after Palace had entered the shadowlands existence of 'Administration' and was seized upon by our supporters as an opportunity to express their allegiance to the Club, along with their disgust towards those whom they conceived to be mainly responsible for the Club's astonishing plight. The support offered to the makeshift team was almost beyond belief in the circumstances, both in the numbers (well over 2,000 fans made the trek to Norfolk) and in the noise generated. The team responded wonderfully to this magnificent display of loyalty: the single, winning goal came early, secured by Dean Austin in only the thirteenth minute, with a firm, downward, unmarked header. Norwich never looked like responding and, while Palace had four youthful debutants and seven teenagers involved, a 3-0 scoreline would certainly not have flattered us, after Clinton Morrison and Andrew Martin both hit the City woodwork. Manager Steve Coppell rightly called the team's display 'magnificent' but it was due (and the players acknowledged the fact) in no small degree to the inspiration our side was able to draw from the equally superb support provided by our fans. The scenes at the final whistle almost defy words. Having bayed for the end for several minutes, the Palace section of the crowd erupted into unrestrained delight when it came. Players and fans saluted each other – at one in adversity and with a battle deservedly won – together.

By the time of the last home match, a 2-2 draw with Huddersfield, Palace were using seven teenagers in the side on a regular basis, with the central defensive pairing of Hayden Mullins (now twenty years old) and David Woozley (who was still nineteen) our youngest ever in those positions. But perhaps the most fitting finale for 1998/99 came at the last match of the entire term at Queens Park Rangers, where Palace provided fifteen of the players taking part, because Andy Linighan was on loan with the Hoops and featured in their defence! Andy even came across to Palace's travelling contingent at the end to show his appreciation of them and to demonstrate his own continuing commitment to the Palace Club.

SEASON: 1998/99

GROUND: Selhurst Park

MANAGER: Terry Venables to January 1999, then Steve Coppell

LEAGUE/DIVISION: Football League Division One

FINAL POSITION: 14th

BIGGEST VICTORY: 5-1 *v.* Norwich City, 17 October 1998

HEAVIEST DEFEAT: 0-6 *v.* QPR, 9 May 1999

FA CUP – ROUND ELIMINATED: 3rd

LEAGUE CUP – ROUND ELIMINATED: 2nd

FULL MEMBERS CUP – ROUND ELIMINATED: –

LEADING LEAGUE APPEARANCES (MAX: 46): 38+2 – H. Mullins, 27+10 – C. Morrison

LEADING LEAGUE GOALSCORERS: 12 – C. Morrison, 8 – M. Jansen

1999/2000

DIGNITY SALVAGED AT LAST

While there were hopes that Palace might be in the hands of a new owner by the opening day of the 1999/2000 season, the harsh realities of the summer months were actually only overcome by the Administrators borrowing £750,000 to meet the Club's outgoings and by deferring some of the (already reduced) wages and signing-on fees of the senior players.

Early in the summer Simon Paterson, the officer fronting the administration for Moore Stephens, declared that he would find a suitable purchaser for Crystal Palace by the end of July and, after some twelve weeks in administration, a pair of local businessmen showed interest in doing so. However, when they refused to reveal their identities speculation mounted that Mark Goldberg was involved in some way with this bid. To Palace fans such a thing was unacceptable. Mr Goldberg's dealings had been at least partially responsible for the parlous state in which the Club now found itself and his further involvement was not to be tolerated. At this stage, in June 1999, he was still the chairman, although no longer the owner, of the Club. So much for the early settlement then – but what no-one realised at that time of course was that the dreadful administration saga was going to run throughout this entire 1999/00 season!

Simon Paterson's primary function as the Administrator was to ensure the survival of Crystal Palace FC. Unquestionably he behaved with complete integrity, yet Palace fans and some employees and Club officials found his actions and statements difficult to approve while, in common with so many modern-day business leaders, he often came across in the media as somewhat patronising and arrogant. Given Simon's remit he was, ultimately, successful, but it is entirely legitimate to question whether, had it not been for the most welcome but eleventh hour intervention of Simon Jordan, he would have been able to fulfil that charge. Indeed, in March 2000 he did express the view that there was 'no point in carrying on if no exit from administration has been agreed by the transfer deadline' though, perhaps, that statement might simply have reflected his frustration with the whole protracted saga. Thus, while Simon Paterson's judgement at times appeared to demonstrate at least a measure of partiality, it must be accepted that it is doubtful if any other appointment could have done the job any better, or more quickly. What is certainly true is that when he was able to hand the Club over to its new owner in July 2000 every Palace fan was extremely relieved to see him depart.

A rare pre-season friendly was staged at Selhurst Park against our former play-off adversaries Leicester City (1-1), but this occasion was noteworthy as the last one at which our fans could watch the Eagles line up in the traditional numbered shirts in the one to eleven sequence at our ground before the introduction of squad numbering was adopted across the Football League.

Chairman Mark Goldberg resigned during the first week of the season and was replaced by long-time supporter, director and company secretary Peter Morley, but the Club's financial crisis really dominated everything. Palace secured £250,000 from Barnsley for goalkeeper Kevin Miller, who had been unwilling to play for us after his wages had been delayed during the summer. Palace fans excoriated Kevin both for his attitude and his behaviour and invariably derided him mercilessly whenever he reappeared at Selhurst Park, but it should not be forgotten that he played all 38 Premier League matches for the Eagles in 1997/98.

A poor opening to the season saw us at the bottom of Division One after a 1-2 defeat at Manchester City on 11 September – our lowest ranking for precisely fifteen years and a damning indictment of the damage that had been done to the Club in its recent past. The fact that Palace immediately retrieved that embarrassing situation by beating Grimsby 3-0 at Selhurst Park, and usually remained clear of the relegation places after that, was an outstanding tribute to manager Steve Coppell. A shrewd manipulator of the loan-transfer market and a brilliant motivator of his players, Steve maintained both the morale of the whole Club and a League position that would ultimately retain our Division One status.

Steve lost the services of his leading goalscorer, Swedish international Matt Svensson, at the end of January when the striker was sold to Charlton for £600,000 to help to meet the recurring costs necessary for Palace's continued existence even in the indistinct, unreal world of administration. Fortunately though, Clinton Morrison returned after a long lay-off due to a dislocated shoulder and, beginning with a brace in a televised 4-2 win at Swindon, scored regularly throughout the remainder of the season to finish as our top scorer of 1999/00 with 15 League and Cup goals. An experienced defender who spent the winter months with Palace was ex-Wimbledon star Terry Phelan, who was on Everton's books at the time. Terry finished the term at Fulham and lined up for them against us when we met them at Craven Cottage in April.

Two other loan players who became great favourites with our fans and were important members of the team that clawed its way to lowly midtable security were youthful defender Ashley Cole from Arsenal and Finnish striker Mikael Forssell from Chelsea. Cole's name is a household one among England's football fans but, although he had played a single game for Arsenal previously, it was with Crystal Palace that he first came to any degree of prominence. He was with us for the final three months of this 1999/00 season and made 14 appearances for us. He netted one wonderful goal for us too... read on for details! Mikael was only eighteen when he first joined us in February 2000 and played 13 times that spring, scoring 3 goals to assist the struggle for survival, then to everyone's delight returned to us for 2000/01.

But without in the least minimizing the value of these temporary acquisitions, Palace's survival actually depended upon three members of our own playing staff: the two experienced defenders, Dean Austin, who became our captain in mid-March after Simon Rodger's season was ended by injury, and Player of the Year Andy Linighan. Both missed just one League fixture all season, and the emerging, talented and versatile Hayden Mullins usually looked a class above most of his Division One opponents at this stage of his career. Among his invaluable 10 League goals was a most glorious strike at Walsall, secured with a magnificent volley that many fans would rate as our best goal of the whole season.

The contributions of Palace's young tyros should not be undervalued either. Palace's teams were containing at least five men under the age of twenty-one, and in demanding

Above left: Clinton Morrison was Palace's top scorer in 1999/00 with 15 League and Cup goals.

Above right: New owner and chairman of Crystal Palace FC Mr Simon Jordan.

circumstances too, so that it is a tribute to them as well as to the manager and coaches that they coped so well. In fact they did even more than that: lads like central defender David Woozley, midfielder Wayne Carlisle and striker Andrew Martin in particular advanced their careers with dignity and some flair.

As the spring of 2000 advanced there occurred a magnificent attempt by a group of Palace fans to rally their contemporaries and to raise substantial funds so that at least there was some reserve that could be put towards the multi-millions that were required to bring the Eagles out of administration. Calling themselves 'The Crystal Palace Supporters' Trust', Richard House, Paul Newman, Jim Piddock and Ray Bateup set up the trust as an Industrial and Provident Society. It was officially launched on the day of Palace's home match against Manchester City, Saturday 4 March 2000. Steve Coppell placed himself firmly at the head of the initiative and an initial target of £10 million was set to be raise by donations and loans.

Palace eventually ensured their Division One survival in our last home game, which took place on a warm, sunlit, late April afternoon. Our visitors were Blackburn Rovers, managed by a former adversary of ours, Graeme Souness, and featuring our erstwhile star Matt Jansen in their expensively assembled line-up. Indeed, Matt elegantly put his side ahead midway through the first half but, for all their wealth of talent Rovers were never entirely at ease with Palace's forcing style and, especially in the second half, there were times when the visitors were in disarray. Ashley Cole hit a spectacular and deserved equaliser on the hour, high into the top corner of the Whitehorse Lane netting from the edge of the penalty area, Rovers' Lee Carsley was dismissed and Clinton Morrison flashed home a close-range header to win the game for the Eagles.

Division One status was now assured, but as the Club moved into its fifteenth month in administration there emerged the fact that there had been contact with Charlton and Gillingham over the possibility of us playing our home games on one of their grounds!

But now, astutely judging the timing of his entry, a further bidder for the Club emerged in the person of Palace fan and former schoolboy player Simon Jordan, the Pocket Phone Shop tycoon, who had been born and brought up in Whitehorse Lane. Although seemingly discouraged by the Administrator, Simon appeared to Palace fans to have only the Club's best interests at heart. At last the end came. Late in the afternoon of Wednesday 5 July 2000 there arrived the news that every Palace fan had longed to hear. The Club had been taken over by a new company called 'Crystal Palace 2000' under the chairmanship of Simon Jordan, at a cost thought to have been in the region of some £10.5 million and by that single act Mr Jordan immediately became one of the most important men in the entire ninety-five-year history of Crystal Palace FC.

SEASON: 1999/00

GROUND: Selhurst Park

MANAGER: Steve Coppell

LEAGUE/DIVISION: Football League Division One

FINAL POSITION: 15th

BIGGEST VICTORY: 4-0 *v.* Portsmouth, 2 October 1999

HEAVIEST DEFEAT: 1-7 *v.* Huddersfield Town, 28 August 1999

FA CUP – ROUND ELIMINATED: 3rd

LEAGUE CUP – ROUND ELIMINATED: 2nd

FULL MEMBERS CUP – ROUND ELIMINATED: –

LEADING LEAGUE APPEARANCES (MAX: 46): 45 – D. Austin, H. Mullins, 44+1 – A. Linighan

LEADING LEAGUE GOALSCORERS: 13 – C. Morrison, 10 – H. Mullins

2000/01

SURVIVAL AT STOCKPORT

Within a week of his takeover Mr Jordan effected two incoming transfers of young players from Arsenal who swiftly became considerable favourites with our fans, Tommy Black and Julian Gray, for an aggregate fee of £1 million, but the Eagles then suffered two embarrassing pre-season defeats in friendlies at Crawley (1-5) and behind closed doors to Reading (0-4). Perhaps partly in response to these losses manager Steve Coppell secured the much-travelled, hugely experienced thirty-two-year-old central defender Neil Ruddock from West Ham for an undisclosed fee and, to the genuine pleasure of all Palace fans, the season-long return on loan of Chelsea's young Finnish international striker Mikael Forssell. Ruddock's contribution to the Palace left his reputation in tatters but nineteen-year-old Forssell was a wonderful signing for, playing alongside twenty-year-old Clinton Morrison, he became a valuable goalscorer and the youthful pair notched a total of 34 League and Cup goals throughout the season.

However, with just eleven days to go before the opening of the 2000/01 League season, there occurred an event at the Palace that Eagles fans have rued ever since. In circumstances that remain unclear, Steve Coppell relinquished his managerial position here (for the fourth time) and was again, as in 1993, replaced by his former assistant manager and successor, Alan Smith. Alan had spent the previous three years in charge of Fulham's youth academy and brought with him from Craven Cottage Glenn Cockerill and former Palace skipper Ray Houghton to begin their senior coaching careers.

Alan swiftly augmented his playing pool by signing Middlesbrough's left-back Craig Harrison and £750,000 Manchester City midfielder Jamie Pollock, along with young Arsenal goalkeeper Stuart Taylor on loan. All three made their Palace debuts on the first day of the new season, as did Neil Ruddock, while Julian Gray and Tommy Black came on as late substitutes, so that we actually fielded no fewer than six debutants on that hot afternoon at the home of ultimate Division One runners-up Blackburn Rovers, a figure that reflected the ferment at our club at that time. Palace lost a tough opening fixture, conceding twice in the five minutes before half-time and being unable to reply.

The first home game, delayed to Sunday 20 August for live television coverage, against Queens Park Rangers, ended 1-1 and it has to be admitted that much of the first half of 2000/01 was a disappointment for everyone at Crystal Palace. Our hopes and expectations for the season had been buoyed by the takeover and the positive attitudes struck by the chairman and new manager, but results were largely poor and we were even among the relegation places in late October. The season then appeared to have turned when, in early November, the Eagles gained (statistically) our best League win of the term, beating visiting Sheffield Wednesday 4-1, then triumphed 3-1 at Wolves. Scoring in both those games was the re-signed Dougie Freedman, who returned to Selhurst Park from Nottingham Forest for a £600,000 fee on 23 October 2000. There was no doubt whatsoever as the season progressed that it was rescued from disaster by his return. He had scored twice in only his second game, at Bolton, when he was our hero in a brave 3-3 draw, while his season's tally of 11 League strikes included three more absolutely vital ones as we shall later see.

Astonishingly though, because Dougie was not eligible to represent us in the League Cup competition, it was here that Palace secured some outstanding victories over Premiership opposition. We beat patently overconfident Leicester 3-0 at Filbert Street in round three, although the national sporting media all but ignored the fact, with Latvian international midfielder Andrejs Rubins netting the conclusive third strike with a thunderous thirty-yard drive shortly after half-time. It took a dramatic penalty shoot-out that finished 6-5 in Palace's favour to dispose of visiting Tranmere in round four and Palace then dumped Sunderland out of the competition by winning 2-1 to ensure a third appearance for the club in the semi-finals. Mikael Forssell and Clinton Morrison were the Palace scorers who despatched the Wearsiders, who were a top-six Premiership side at the time but were never given the opportunity to demonstrate the fact. Thus, as in 1994/95, Alan Smith had led Palace to the last four under these auspices

Dougie Freedman, whose late goal at Stockport in the final match of the season secured Palace's Division One survival.

Latvian international goalkeeper Alex Kolinko made several excellent saves to help Palace to a League Cup victory over Liverpool.

despite the club's precarious and deteriorating League standing, and it is this run, along with the first leg of the semi-final against Liverpool at Selhurst Park, which our fans will long recall as the highlight of Alan's second tenure as our manager.

This fixture was Palace's first home game of 2001 and drew a capacity crowd to Selhurst Park, but the Reds, five times winners of the competition and favourites to do so again, were made to pay a heavy price for profligate finishing, so that most of the big attendance went home delighted by an inspiring Eagles victory. The evening was raw and blustery and Palace were perhaps a little surprised by the manner in which Liverpool matched our early pace as the visitors set up golden chances for Michael Owen and Emile Heskey in the first quarter of the game that both England aces spurned. From that point the contest turned in Palace's favour – Westerveld doing brilliantly to parry a Clinton Morrison drive when the Palace striker took a pass from Mikael Forssell. It demonstrated that the Division One outfit were by no means overawed and had the potential as well as the confidence to surprise the Premiership sophisticates.

After the break the Eagles owed a considerable debt to Latvian international goalkeeper Alex Kolinko, who made several excellent saves, but the Reds simply had no answer to Palace's passion or our two magnificent goals. Eleven minutes after the restart Andrejs Rubins drove a searing left-footed shot from the edge of the penalty area high into the net leaving Westerveld helpless and bringing the entire Holmesdale Road stand to its feet as one man. Then, some twenty minutes later, after an intense spell of Palace pressure, Mikael Forssell controlled a left-side cross from Craig Harrison for Clinton Morrison to hammer a right-footed rising drive into the top corner of the netting. Liverpool showed their calibre with a speedy reply, but could not break through again and left Selhurst in an angry and frustrated humour.

However, historical perspective asserts quite clearly that this success over Liverpool was the high spot not merely of 2000/01 but also of Alan Smith's second managerial tenure at Selhurst Park. In reality the season tapered away quickly – we lost at home to Sunderland in an FA Cup replay after Clinton Morrison had given us the lead and Steve Thomson forced extra time with an eighty-ninth minute equaliser, then were annihilated at Anfield in the second leg of the League Cup semi-final. Our League position, never a healthy one, deteriorated further, even with the £1.5 million return of David Hopkin to our ranks, so that for some four weeks before the end of the season the Eagles were placed twenty-second in the table, appearing to be consigned and almost, it seemed, resigned to relegation.

Then, following a dreadful showing in the last home game of the term, against Wolves (0-2), chairman Simon Jordan dismissed Alan Smith and Ray Houghton and gave long-standing Palace favourite Steve Kember the responsibility for securing Palace's safety from the two remaining games. Both were difficult, against similarly threatened sides, and both were away matches.

The situation was dire: the possibility of avoiding relegation no longer lay in Palace's own hands. It was necessary for the Eagles to gain a victory at Portsmouth to give themselves a lifeline, then to win again at Stockport in the final match and trust that Grimsby, Huddersfield or Portsmouth failed to secure any reward. The first task was accomplished in brilliant style at Portsmouth, as Steve Kember's remodelled side produced Palace's best first half for a long, long time to assume control. Dougie Freedman's double, just before half-time, to restore our two-goal margin straight from the kick-off after Pompey had reduced their deficit, then another goal quickly after the break provided us with a 4-1 victory; sufficient to put us ahead of Portsmouth and out of the three relegation places at their expense on the narrowest possible margin of goal difference.

Now, suddenly, it seemed as if the Eagles could survive. Everything would depend upon the results of the last games, due to be played on Sunday 6 May. With those matches remaining, this is how the foot of Division One stood:

		P	W	D	L	GD	Pts
19	Grimsby Town	45	13	10	22	-20	49
20	Huddersfield Town	45	11	15	19	-8	48
21	CRYSTAL PALACE	45	11	13	21	-14	46
22	Portsmouth	45	9	19	17	-15	46
23	Queens Park Rangers	45	7	18	20	-30	39
24	Tranmere Rovers	45	9	10	26	-31	37

At Stockport the Eagles left matters extremely late. Portsmouth had powered their way to a commanding lead so were clearly safe, Grimsby were ahead and although Huddersfield were losing to Birmingham, Palace needed to score.

So to the climax. Stockport hit the near post then the referee ignored what appeared to be the most obvious handball by David Hopkin, before our saviour became Dougie Freedman. He received possession some fifteen yards inside the Stockport half, drove forward with his usual neat, darting control, then on into the penalty area where he cut inside a defender before thrashing home a rising drive from some ten yards. There was a tense finale in front of our goal to be endured but ultimately this narrow win ensured our survival because Huddersfield lost and took the third relegation place.

Fan Zhiyi won the Player of the Year award despite appearing in fewer than two-thirds of the games, but he was the obvious, correct and comprehensive victor. However, like his immediate predecessor Andy Linighan, Fan's Palace career was abruptly terminated early in the following season and Palace fans lamented the loss of a man who had won their hearts.

SEASON: 2000/01

GROUND: Selhurst Park

MANAGER: Alan Smith to April 2001, then Steve Kember

LEAGUE/DIVISION: Football League Division One

FINAL POSITION: 21st

BIGGEST VICTORY: 4-1 *v.* Sheffield Wednesday, 4 November 2000

HEAVIEST DEFEAT: 1-4 *v.* Gillingham, 26 December 2000, 1-4 *v.* Sheffield Wednesday, 14 April 2001

FA CUP – ROUND ELIMINATED: 3rd

LEAGUE CUP – ROUND ELIMINATED: Semi-final

FULL MEMBERS CUP – ROUND ELIMINATED: –

LEADING LEAGUE APPEARANCES (MAX: 46): 41+4 – C. Morrison, 40+1 – H. Mullins

LEADING LEAGUE GOALSCORERS: 14 – C. Morrison, 13 – M. Forssell

2001/02

MANAGERIAL MAYHEM

Probably, most Palace fans would have welcomed the appointment of Steve Kember as the Club manager after the manner in which he had contrived the Eagles' Division One survival against all the odds – but on the last day of May 2001 chairman Simon Jordan installed the former Norwich City and Manchester United captain and centre half Steve Bruce. As a player at club level Steve's career had been a distinguished one, but as a manager at Sheffield United and Huddersfield success had eluded him and his loyalty had been debatable.

Palace's pre-season form had been unconvincing in friendlies against lowly opposition but, after surprising Premiership new boys Fulham before going down to a Saha strike, we started the new term in tremendous fashion, coming back from 0-2 down to win 3-2 at promoted Rotherham. Clinton Morrison made a goalscoring debut for Eire as a substitute when the Republic held Croatia 2-2 in Dublin on 15 August 2001 and three days later he scored twice in the Eagles' 4-1 victory over Stockport. His second goal, in the last minute, took his Palace tally to 50 in all competitions.

In early September Steve Bruce made his first major signing for Palace when he paid Bradford City £1.3 million for goalkeeper Matt Clarke. Matt made his debut for us in our Selhurst Park match against Millwall on 8 September, the first serious meeting of the local rivals for five seasons, but the game was decided by two second-half goals from our previous player and former play-off executioner, Steve Claridge.

Dougie Freedman reached his 50th Palace goal to earn the Eagles a 1-1 draw at Everton in a League Cup tie and we kept our nerve better in the ensuing penalty shoot-out to claim another top-flight scalp in this competition. Equally, Palace's home form in Division One was excellent during the weeks of early autumn and our fans came to relish the prospect and reality of seeing a rampant side winning matches, usually by comprehensive margins, at Selhurst Park. Between mid-September and late-October the Eagles dismissed Grimsby 5-0, when central defender Tony Popovic netted glorious headers either side of the interval, and Barnsley 1-0 with a last-minute goal – again a header — from Finnish international star Aki Riihilahti. Sheffield Wednesday retired with a 4-1 beating, which Palace gained by an early brace from Dougie Freedman, then another pair from Clinton Morrison. This took Palace to fifth in the table, our best placing since our return to Division One three years before.

A fortnight later tenants Wimbledon were trounced 4-0. On a sticky, humid afternoon Palace wrested the initiative as the half hour approached. The opening goal split Wimbledon wide

New Palace manager Steve Bruce.

open as a diagonal pass from Jovan Kirovski enabled Morrison to fire left-footed across Kelvin Davis and into the inside of the netting at the right-hand post at the Holmesdale Road end of the ground. Nine minutes later Dougie Freedman sent over a cross from the byline and Kirovski swept the ball into the net after a near-post dummy by Clinton Morrison had confounded the visitors' defence. The heat took its toll on the pace of the game after the break but Palace fans could sense that there was more to come. Sure enough, with eleven minutes remaining Aki Riihilahti drove a thirty-yard strike into the top corner and the Dons' misery was complete when poor Wayne Brown unaccountably headed a cross from Palace's right into his own net with five minutes to go.

A two-goal success over Bradford City gained by Clinton Morrison strikes early and late had the Eagles up to second place, then a 1-0 win at Wolves put us top! Norwich were beaten 3-2 in a televised match... but from that point our season began to disintegrate. Palace's progress was halted at the end of October by a home defeat from ultimate runners-up West Bromwich Albion, although this match saw the eighty-eighth minute debut of sixteen-year-old Wayne Routledge, who thus became the third-youngest player ever to appear for Crystal Palace in senior competitive games, behind only Phil Hoadley and Kenny Sansom.

Earlier in October a Palace rarity had occurred in the international matches played on the sixth of the month because Palace men were in goalscoring opposition at Hampden Park, where Dougie Freedman netted on his Scotland debut and Andrejs Rubins replied for Latvia in the Scots' 2-1 win. Alex Kolinko was also playing in goal for Latvia.

However, in the first few days of November 2001 there followed a bout of managerial mayhem in one of the least edifying sagas in Palace's history when Steve Bruce sought to resign his charge with us with the intention of taking responsibility at fellow Division One club

Birmingham City. Chairman Simon Jordan refused at first to accept Bruce's resignation, insisting that Bruce would be held to his contract even if all he could do was to tend his garden. In the end of course a measure of decorum prevailed, but not before Palace had appointed the former Birmingham manager, ex-England international Trevor Francis to take charge at Selhurst Park, and Trevor received a generous welcome from the Blues' supporters when Palace met Birmingham at St Andrews in mid-December (0-1) in a midweek game.

Trevor had had a brilliantly successful playing career. He had been the game's first £1 million player and gained 52 full international caps. He was by now vastly experienced in management and had led Sheffield Wednesday and Birmingham to the verge of distinction. He was also a popular football pundit, erudite, well-spoken, equable and conscientious. Actually it was in Trevor's second match in charge of the Eagles, when Palace were at home to eventual champions Manchester City, on Saturday 8 December, that our club secured its best result of the entire season. Palace included former City defender, Welsh international Kit Symons, who had joined us from Fulham the day before as Francis' first signing, while City's goalkeeper was the former Eagles favourite Carlo Nash. Palace led a little after the half hour when Dougie Freedman converted a Hayden Mullins free-kick and Jovan Kirovski added a second during a mix-up in the City defence just before half-time. City reduced their deficit midway through the second half to set up an exciting finale in which Alex Kolinko made several good saves to ensure that we retained all three points and therefore rose to within three places of City in the table.

Regrettably, however, the rest of 2001/02 became one of general decline for the Palace, although the goalscoring exploits of Dougie Freedman and Clinton Morrison continued most positively for, when the former netted from the penalty spot against visiting Walsall on 23 March (2-0) it took his season's tally of Division One goals to 20 strikes. Clinton had reached that mark earlier in the same month and the duo were our Club's first pair to achieve such a level since the fabulous days of Bright and Wright in the late 1980s.

Although Palace fell out of the play-off places in February – we eventually finished tenth – the second half of 2001/02 was not without its interest for our fans as Trevor Francis brought in men whom he believed could blend into an effective unit. Defenders Curtis Fleming, a £100,000 buy from Middlesbrough who became club captain but lost out to injury two years later, and Danny Granville (£500,000) from Manchester City, whose career was rescued in 2003/04 and played a major role in our return to the top flight, made their debuts together at Stockport in January. In February powerful striker Ade Akinbiyi arrived for £2.2 million from Leicester City, but the big man scored only two goals for us and, while it would not be fair to blame our failure to reach even the play-offs on him, that disappointing return ensured a bland, uneventful and frustrating run-in to the end of the term for Palace and their fans.

The Easter weekend saw the Eagles' last hopes all but extinguished. On Easter Saturday we were unable to continue our hitherto excellent form at Norwich, where we had been unbeaten in four visits and won twice, going down this time to two strikes late in the first half to which only Clinton Morrison could offer a reply with what proved to be his last goal for the Eagles.

Easter Monday saw the return of Steve Bruce to Selhurst Park with his Birmingham City side. There was a hostile reception awaiting him as the Blues' team coach entered our precincts and he was subjected to a torrent of abuse from Palace fans made angry by his desertion of our club earlier in the season. The game itself finished goal-less. Palace fans gave their team a standing ovation at the end and Steve Bruce sprinted to the dressing room from the dug-out to avoid any further humiliation.

Trevor Francis was Bruce's successor as Palace manager.

While Clinton Morrison was among Eire's World Cup squad in Japan throughout June 2002, it was actually a second round match between the USA and Mexico on 17 June that provided a new Palace 'first' at that level, because our defender Greg Berhalter appeared for the former in their 2-0 win. Indeed, Greg was within inches of scoring for his country a few days later when his quarter-final effort against Germany was prevented from crossing the goal-line by the forearm of a defender, although no penalty was awarded for the offence since the referee deemed it to have been unintentional.

A new but attractive feature of football at Selhurst Park emerged in the spring of 2002 with the staging of two prestigious women's matches for the Football Association. The ladies' 2002 FA Cup final between Doncaster Belles and Fulham (1-2) was held here on Bank Holiday Monday 6 May, then a World Cup qualifier between England and Germany took place on Sunday 19 May (0-1).

SEASON: 2001/02

GROUND: Selhurst Park

MANAGER: Steve Bruce to October 2001, then Trevor Francis from 30 November 2001

LEAGUE/DIVISION: Football League Division One

FINAL POSITION: 10th

BIGGEST VICTORY: 5-0 *v.* Grimsby Town, 18 September 2001

HEAVIEST DEFEAT: 2-5 *v.* Grimsby Town, 2 March 2002

FA CUP – ROUND ELIMINATED: 3rd

LEAGUE CUP – ROUND ELIMINATED: 3rd

FULL MEMBERS CUP – ROUND ELIMINATED: –

LEADING LEAGUE APPEARANCES (MAX: 46): 45 – A. Riihilahti, C. Morrison, 35+8 – J. Gray

LEADING LEAGUE GOALSCORERS: 22 – C. Morrison, 20 – D. Freedman

2002/03

BRILLIANT CUP WIN AT ANFIELD BUT NO LEAGUE PROGRESS

Crystal Palace made a handful of new signings during the summer of 2002, each of whom made a useful contribution to the Club during the forthcoming season, while four of them were quite invaluable in the promotion success that was to follow twelve months later.

Defender Danny Butterfield came from Grimsby Town and produced an awesome record of appearances in our colours. Not only was Danny seldom absent for any reason, but his level of performance barely varied – he was consistency personified in every respect. Striker Andy Johnson joined the Palace from Birmingham as a virtual makeweight in the deal that took Clinton Morrison to St Andrews, but Palace fans soon grew to reckon that we received the better part of that particular transfer.

Shaun Derry, a former Portsmouth captain, added knowledge and experience in this 2002/03 season while his considerable adaptability became priceless when the following term drew towards its climax. Darren Powell had captained Brentford: he was a towering, commanding central defender in the mould of Eric Young and had an excellent first season with us, but he sustained a cruel injury early in 2003/04 and could only return right at the end of the season, but with enormous impact.

Striker Dele Adebola completed the quintet. He played 48 games for Palace in 2002/03 but, for all his experience, netted only 7 goals for us and chose to move on to Coventry City at the end of this season.

The first part of the season enabled Palace fans to witness two superb feats of sustained goalscoring by Eagles men, though curiously, probably neither Andrew Johnson or Tommy Black would have been regarded before the term began as potentially prolific in front of goal. Nevertheless, in October and November Andy netted an astonishing 10 strikes for us in 5 games – the Club's best post-war effort in such matters and surpassing even Cam Burgess' feat almost precisely fifty years earlier – then shortly afterwards Tommy Black scored 9 times in 8 games. Andy's record was glorious: he netted his first League goal of the season during Palace's 2-2 draw with Wimbledon on 19 October, then delivered two hat-tricks in consecutive games, the 5-0 demolition of Steve Coppell's Brighton and a wonderfully entertaining 4-3 win at Walsall in midweek. Perhaps an even better result was the 2-1 Sunday victory at Ipswich on 3 November

Above left: New arrival Danny Butterfield.

Above right: Andy Johnson joined Palace from Birmingham.

when Andy's nineteenth-minute drive from Dele Adebola's pass put Palace on their way. Three days later, in third round Football League Cup action, Andy netted Palace's first two goals, both fiercely hit drives, in the first and last quarters of the contest in a 3-0 victory over Coventry.

This 2002/03 season saw not only the emergence of dynamic, energetic Tommy Black as a dangerous attacking midfielder or striker, but also that of his ex-Highbury colleague Julian Gray, whose skill, pace and sheer dexterity on the ball out on the left wing became increasingly effective, and both men surged in popularity among Palace fans.

As the season progressed, so too did the Eagles in the cup competitions. Favoured with home draws in the early rounds of the League Cup, Palace eased their way to the last eight by beating Plymouth (2-1 after extra time), Cheltenham (7-0 in our first competitive meeting with the Robins), Coventry, as already mentioned and Oldham (2-0), who were managed by our former striker Iain Dowie, who was to arrive at Selhurst Park little more than a year later and to such great effect. But, at Sheffield United in the quarter-final we were beaten after having levelled the scores. The Blades' substitute Paul Peschisolido netted twice late on but the first of these, a darting, glancing header, was patently converted from several yards offside. The decision to allow the goal was regarded by Clive Allen, by now the London ITV football pundit, as 'the worst refereeing decision of the season', but Palace were soon to fall foul of another one that was equally as bad.

Even more commendable was Palace's showing in the FA Cup. Two Tommy Black goals saw us safely past Blackpool at Bloomfield Road, the reward for which was a tie against Liverpool. Sky TV showed the initial match at Selhurst Park, a 0-0 draw in which chances were few, but Liverpool had chosen to deploy England striker Emile Heskey largely in his own half, working on the premise that they would be too strong for us in an Anfield replay. Such arrogance was shortly to be revealed as grossly optimistic!

An unlikely Palace hero in the replay was goalkeeper Cedric Berthelin. With his back to the Kop and having betrayed the inevitable early nervousness, our French custodian saved wonderfully, in particular from Bruno Cheyrou and several times from Michael Owen before the break, and then crucially from Emile Heskey early in the second half, when the England international contrived merely to hit the ball straight at the 'keeper after making a sixty-yard run. Moments later, Palace were ahead. First, right in front of the disbelieving hordes of Liverpool fans on the Kop Julian Gray despatched a volley that rocketed past Dudek on its way into the net, the move that created the opening having been inspired by a wonderful break down the right flank by Danny Butterfield.

Now the Reds were reeling. Andy Johnson was barely denied but then Dougie Freedman was dismissed for reacting to Sami Hyypia's protracted kicking, which was unaccountably missed by the referee, and it seemed that 'Pool might now have the chance to grasp a victory. However, come the seventy-ninth minute Julian Gray crowned a wonderful left-side run with a cross that so bemused Swiss international defender Stephane Henchoz that the ball deflected off that poor fellow's right calf and into the net!

Julian Gray is seen crossing the ball that Liverpool's Stephane Henchoz could not avoid deflecting into his own net for Palace's second goal of the night in an Anfield replay.

Palace rightly received plenty of plaudits for this victory, which was followed by another tie against Premiership opponents. Leeds United brought our former manager Terry Venables back to Selhurst Park. The Eagles fans relished this opportunity to express their feelings towards Terry, who had twice deserted the Club in unsavoury circumstances.

Selhurst Park was cold, despite the pale winter sunshine, when the game kicked off at 1.15 p.m. before the Sky TV cameras. The first half hour was undistinguished: Tommy Black drew a first-minute save from Paul Robinson but Palace were unable to trouble the England 'keeper further, and if Leeds were fluid and mobile they equally found it difficult to penetrate a disciplined rearguard. Then, with little more than half an hour played, Leeds were awarded a free-kick some twenty-five yards out. Gary Kelly took it while Palace were still laboriously organising their defensive wall, and the ball flew into the far top corner of our net in front of the disbelieving Holmesdale Road stand. But Palace were level almost immediately when a Julian Gray volley following a poorly cleared right-side corner ripped into the Leeds goal at the other end of the ground.

As half-time approached, so came the game's crucial moment. Leeds twice cleared off their goal-line but, as TV replays clearly showed, a close-range effort from Tommy Black was both over the line and handled by Michael Duberry – yet the referee and his assistant awarded nothing.

A tense, tight second half ensued that offered few chances to either side, but Leeds' Australian international star Harry Kewell won the tie for the visitors with a fine run from the right flank that took him past two Palace defenders before he shot beyond the reach of Cedric Berthelin. But Palace fans, together with the army of pundits and the Sky audience, all knew that the game had turned on the absence of any decision in the key incident a few minutes before the interval.

Faced now with just the challenge for the play-offs Palace matters became rather banal. Certainly there were items of interest, at both ends of the pitch. During 2002/03 our Club fielded four different goalkeepers in Matthew Clarke, Alex Kolinko, on-loan Nick Michopoulos and Cedric Berthelin. That in itself is not unique at the Palace, for we did so in 1950/51 and during the Second World War – but observant readers will already have discerned that each one of the 2002/03 quartet is of a different nationality!

Further upfield, Palace fans were provided with glimpses of the emerging talent of Wayne Routledge. A sixteen-year-old debutant as a substitute in October 2001 and slight of build to the point of almost being petit, Wayne's shorts covered his knees and almost touched the top of his socks, but his pace, balance and control were already such that he could bemuse even experienced defenders of some quality.

Sad to say though, the second half of Palace's League season was most disappointing. There was little doubt that the glamorous FA Cup run or the manner of our ejection from the competition, or both, had a definite distracting effect upon our team-members. A drab 0-0 draw with relegation-haunted Sheffield Wednesday at Selhurst Park was followed by a 0-4 humiliation at Wolves, which virtually ended our interest in the race for the end-of-season knock-out competition. Palace could not win at home in 2003 until late March, so that it was not altogether surprising when chairman Simon Jordan blasted the team: 'We have flattered to deceive for most of this season,' he announced, perfectly correctly, and Simon then ordered a summer clear out of players who had failed to deliver. 'Big-time Charlies', he called them and his patience finally snapped just before Easter when it was announced on Good Friday, 18 April, that Trevor Francis had left the Club 'by mutual consent'.

Steve Kember steered Palace through our final four games and we finished down in fourteenth place in Division One with some small consolation to be gained by the Reserves winning the Football Combination championship.

SEASON: 2002/03

GROUND: Selhurst Park

MANAGER: Trevor Francis to 18 April 2003, then Steve Kember

LEAGUE/DIVISION: Football League Division One

FINAL POSITION: 14th

BIGGEST VICTORY: 5-0 *v.* Brighton & Hove Albion, 26 October 2002

HEAVIEST DEFEAT: 0-4 *v.* Wolverhampton Wanderers, 1 March 2003

FA CUP – ROUND ELIMINATED: 5th

LEAGUE CUP – ROUND ELIMINATED: 5th

FULL MEMBERS CUP – ROUND ELIMINATED: –

LEADING LEAGUE APPEARANCES (MAX: 46): 46 – D. Butterfield, 43 – H. Mullins

LEADING LEAGUE GOALSCORERS: 11 – A. Johnson, 9 – D. Freedman

2003/04

IAIN DOWIE INSPIRES A MEMORABLE PROMOTION

Hope and expectations at Selhurst Park were high when Crystal Palace embarked upon the new season. Steve Kember had been installed as Palace manager by chairman Simon Jordan on 24 May 2003 and former Palace striker Neil Shipperley returned to us from Wimbledon two months later. The aspirations for 2003/04 appeared to be confirmed at the opening game on 9 August, played in extreme heat at Burnley, where the Eagles won a volatile clash 3-2 against the Clarets and Dougie Freedman netted a brilliant hat-trick – the club's first on the opening day of a new season since 1960 and the first such away from home! Palace had two players sent off in this match and played the last quarter of the game with only nine men – an astonishing feat of endurance and professionalism in the searing heat.

Vastly experienced Northern Ireland midfield international Michael Hughes signed for Palace the following week. He made his Eagles debut in our low-key 1-0 victory over Watford forty-eight hours later, but was sent off for obscure reasons shortly before the end. Wimbledon 'hosted' their last game against the Palace at Selhurst Park on Saturday 23 August but we secured our third successive League victory, winning 3-1 with goals from Danny Butterfield, Dougie Freedman (his 82nd for the club and taking him past Dave Swindlehurst into fourth place in Palace's post-war scoring charts) and Michael Hughes against his former club.

Palace were top of the table after these three victories, but the season began to deteriorate from there on. We won only one more home game before mid-December and one away game in the same period. We also lost our manager. Steve Kember was dismissed on 3 November 2003, two days after an awful 0-5 defeat at Wigan Athletic but following other previous dreadful away performances such as those at Norwich (1-2) and West Ham (0-3). Palace fans were naturally utterly loyal to Steve Kember but recognised that his departure was inevitable as the club slid rapidly down the Division One table. The chairman put the club into the temporary charge of our former Portsmouth, Manchester City and Fulham centre half, Welsh international Kit Symons, but a short-term initial improvement was followed by a not unexpected League Cup reverse at Aston Villa, then by two bad defeats at Preston (1-4, with the player-manager sent off – Palace's first such dismissal since the days of Ronnie Rooke in October 1949) and at home to Crewe (1-3) before achieving a gutsy 1-0 victory over Nottingham Forest at Selhurst Park.

Former Palace striker, Northern Ireland international Iain Dowie was appointed as the club manager on Friday evening 19 December 2003, although Kit Symons took charge of his last game at Steve Coppell's Reading the following day, when Palace gained a most-praiseworthy 3-0 win. Then, despite the disappointment of defeat by Millwall at Selhurst Park on Boxing Day in Iain's first match in control of the team, the new boss made his intentions clear for all to see in dynamic fashion two days later by driving Palace to a brilliant 3-1 victory at promotion hopefuls Ipswich.

By chairman Simon Jordan's own admission, his success rate over previous managerial appointments had been 'mixed' – but no-one would argue that this one was absolutely splendid. Iain Dowie transformed Palace's season from a relegation dogfight into a genuine push for the Premiership via the divisional play-offs. Building upon the victory at Reading, Iain added four more of his own in succession to rewrite the Palace record books with five consecutive League wins on the road and establish us just four points off the play-off places. Then Stoke were beaten in imperious fashion 6-3 at Selhurst Park in our first nine-goal League game at Selhurst Park since before Christmas 1961 and the first in any competition here for over forty years!

Other marvellous victories included the 1-0 but relatively comfortable home win over table-topping eventual champions Norwich in mid-March, a 2-0 success at play-off hopefuls Cardiff on Easter Saturday followed by a tense but deserved home win over West Ham two days later and, most majestic of all, the 3-0 demolition of Sunderland in a rearranged night game at the Palace. Sunderland were the pundits' favourites to win the imminent play-off contest, but by now Palace were the strongest side in the division and quite unstoppable on their own pitch.

Key to this transformation were the return to the Palace of left winger Julian Gray, who had been away unsuccessfully seeking a Premiership contract, the return to favour of experienced left-back Danny Granville and the loan signing of central defender Mark Hudson from Fulham along with those of goalkeepers Thomas Myhre and Nico Vaesen from Sunderland and Birmingham respectively. Striker Andy Johnson had a marvellous run of 14 goals from just 10 Division One games, while Michael Hughes performed outstandingly in midfield and skippered the side in the absence of Neil Shipperley against Reading in early March (2-2) and against West Ham.

Despite a 1-2 defeat at Coventry in the last match of the League programme, Palace took their place in the play-offs where we were pitted in titanic semi-final action against Sunderland. The shadow of Palace's impressive victory over the Wearsiders three weeks earlier loomed large over the first leg proceedings for, on a warm, dry and eventually passionate evening, with the second leg in the North-East to follow, the visitors were simply content to repulse Palace's raids and rely upon their proven strikers, Marcus Stewart and Kevin Kyle, to grab something for them. It could have been a huge mistake, for early in the first half both Neil Shipperley and Finnish international Aki Riihilahti were just inches away from converting a long cross from Julian Gray, then Gray himself fired over from some fifteen yards following an incisive run and pass from Wayne Routledge as the half drew to a close.

After the break Sunderland were much more adventurous, although they might have paid a heavy price in the first minute of the second half when an unintended parry from a retreating defender took the power away from a Routledge shot. They then appeared to have gained the initiative when Marcus Stewart coolly converted a forty-ninth-minute penalty, but barely two minutes later Palace were level with a clever, looping Neil Shipperley back-header into the top right-hand corner of the Holmesdale Road goal from a cross by Danny Granville. Then, a little after the hour Palace were ahead! Michael Hughes played a free-kick square for Danny

Iain Dowie transformed the Eagles.

Butterfield to fire fierce and low at the Sunderland target. The ball deflected off Gary Breen, and Mart Poom was unable to adjust his position sufficiently to prevent it passing him and entering the net just inside the right-hand post.

John Oster shaved a Palace post with some twenty minutes left, though with six minutes remaining Kevin Kyle despatched a loose ball in the Palace penalty area to restore parity, but the Eagles were still not done and with just four minutes to go Andy Johnson proved the match-winner. He broke clear on Palace's left flank, cut inside along the edge of the penalty area then unleashed a right-foot drive that beat Poom at the far post, so that we were able to take a slender advantage into the second leg, which took place at the Stadium of Light just seventy-two hours later.

Palace might have settled the outcome in the opening minutes. Only three minutes had elapsed when Julian Gray's shot was smothered by Mart Poom following a pinpoint cross to the far post from Michael Hughes, and shortly afterwards an Aki Riihilahti header from Danny Granville's cross rebounded off the left-hand post. Palace looked the better side after this but in the forty-third minute Kevin Kyle was able to chest the ball down from a Jason McAteer cross and slam the ball into our net between Nico Vaesen's legs. Then, two minutes into stoppage time Marcus Stewart nodded a McAteer cross past Vaesen to put Sunderland ahead on aggregate.

Julian Gray was dismissed for a second bookable offence as Palace sought a late leveller but then came the moment that turned the contest once again. Remember the name of Darren Powell? The tall centre half's season had appeared to be over seven months earlier, but now here he was, on as a seventy-second-minute substitute for Danny Granville and heading in at Sunderland's back post from a Shaun Derry corner to send the match into extra time! But even this could not separate the sides. With the aggregate now level at 4-4, the contest entered the mandatory penalty shoot-out. Again the teams were locked together at four conversions apiece after six kicks each. Then, Sunderland's Northern Ireland international Jeff Whitley saw his effort saved by Nico Vaesen and Palace's own Provincial star, Michael Hughes, strode up and converted his kick to send the Eagles through to the final at Cardiff's Millennium Stadium.

West Ham were our opponents on Saturday 29 May 2004 and the financial prize for the winners, beyond the prestige of appearing in the Premiership again, was calculated to be between £25 million and £30 million – in this respect certainly the biggest match in which Crystal Palace had ever been engaged. Piquancy was added because not only had Iain Dowie graced the West Ham colours as a player, but also because the Hammers were managed by former Eagles hero Alan Pardew though, as at Selhurst Park the previous month, there was little of the historic Upton Park culture to be seen this afternoon, even if Trevor Brooking was watching from the stands.

Palace brimmed with confidence and brio, simply refusing to yield anything to the opposition, denying territory, possession and even tiredness in their unrelenting quest for supremacy. In the end the 2004 Division One play-off final was settled by a simple tap-in from four yards executed by Palace's skipper Neil Shipperley, to the delight of our fans ranked behind the goal into which he turned the ball, after goalkeeper Stephen Bywater was unable to do more than parry a scorching diagonal drive across the turf from Andy Johnson. Few observers would deny that the Eagles deserved their success as the better team on the day, with our men coming out on top in every one of the crucial duels.

Top of the club's appearances chart for the second season running was Danny Butterfield, who missed just one League game through injury and made 53 starts. However, Player of the Year could go nowhere other than to the Nationwide League's top scorer Andy Johnson, who hit 27 goals in the original programme with one more in the play-offs, a tally that exceeded even that of Ian Wright in 1988/89 and became Palace's highest in the upper reaches of English football.

Darren Powell, our late substitute, whose crashing header at Sunderland took the play-off semi-final second leg into extra time.

The Palace players and management team celebrate our play-off victory at Cardiff's Millennium Stadium.

SEASON: 2003/04

GROUND: Selhurst Park

MANAGER: Steve Kember to 3 November 2003, then Kit Symons to 19 December 2003, then Iain Dowie

LEAGUE/DIVISION: Football League Division One

FINAL POSITION: 6th

BIGGEST VICTORY: 5-1 *v.* Watford, 17 January 2004

HEAVIEST DEFEAT: 0-5 *v.* Wigan Athletic, 1 November 2003

FA CUP – ROUND ELIMINATED: 3rd

LEAGUE CUP – ROUND ELIMINATED: 4th

FULL MEMBERS CUP – ROUND ELIMINATED: –

LEADING LEAGUE APPEARANCES (MAX: 49 including play-offs): 48 – D. Butterfield, 35+12 – W. Routledge

LEADING LEAGUE GOALSCORERS (including play-offs): 28 – A. Johnson, 13 – D. Freedman

2004/05

ANOTHER PREMIER LEAGUE ADVENTURE

Understandably and completely forgivably, Crystal Palace FC and its host of fans preened their way through the warm midsummer weeks of 2004. Our club was back in the top flight of domestic football and that fact was made all the sweeter because such an outcome had appeared – if we are honest and open about it – to be utterly impossible less than six months before it occurred.

But football is a fast-moving sport, even when no games are being played and, although it took place a week or so later than usual, the publication of Palace's Premiership fixture list certainly brought a dose of healthy realism to those fans whose heads were still in the clouds after our victory over West Ham in the Cardiff play-off final.

However, after Iain Dowie's transformation of the club from relegation possibles into the best team in Division One by some distance, and in such a short time too, Palace fans simply placed their confidence in the former Northern Ireland international and backed his judgement as he recruited the players he believed he needed to augment our squad for the stern test that the Premiership would undoubtedly provide and to ensure our survival among its membership. That said, everyone with Palace's good fortunes at heart realised just what a tough task lay ahead. Our own previous experiences at this level had seen us twice before gain the much-coveted Premier League status only for it to be immediately surrendered, while the twelve-year history of the Premiership was littered with the names of clubs that had been promoted, perhaps even as champions or runners-up, and fallen swiftly from grace back into the confines of the lower divisions.

Most of Iain Dowie's signings for Crystal Palace in the summer of 2004 were men who were unknown to Palace fans. Altogether, Iain recruited fourteen new players, of whom few readers would argue that tall, strong central defender or midfielder Fitz Hall, who joined us almost on the eve of the new season in a £1.5 million deal from Southampton, and Hungarian goalkeeper Gabor Kiraly, who was actually Palace's first signing after promotion had been secured and arrived on a free transfer from Hertha Berlin, were the best acquisitions. Initially, Gabor was not our first-choice 'keeper but he took over from Argentinian Julian Speroni in late September and proved an able if occasionally eccentric custodian at Premiership level, composed and confident even when facing proven top-flight and international strikers, while certainly being distinctive in his baggy tracksuit bottoms, which resembled nothing so much as much-loved pyjamas!

Other useful signings were Finnish international left winger Joonas Kolkka, who replaced want-away Julian Gray, and ex-Luton Town defender and Player of the Year Emmerson Boyce who, deputising for Danny Butterfield (who had the misfortune to sustain a torn hamstring in a pre-season friendly at Queens Park Rangers in July), performed effectively at Premiership level and disproved the theory that the stars of the most senior league should be regarded as a class apart.

All the above stated and accepted, it should be understood that Palace's top star throughout the season was once again goal-scorer Andy Johnson who, despite frequently playing in a lone striker's role, was not only Palace's leading target man but also the Premiership's leading English goal-getter. Overall, he was behind only the fabulous Thierry Henry of Arsenal.

Our 2004/05 Premier League campaign opened at Norwich, the Division One champions of the previous season but, with no fewer than five debutants in our starting line-up, the Eagles gained a deserved point from the 1-1 draw secured by Andy Johnson's first strike of the season, touched in from some eight yards following a neat pass from Wayne Routledge. However, though probably not surprisingly, the early weeks of the season saw Palace encounter real difficulties in coming to terms with the sustained demands of the Premiership, and it was partly in response to this that Iain Dowie secured the season-long loan signings of two foreign stars from Inter Milan, the former Italian Under-21 international forward Nicola Ventola and tough, left-footed Uruguayan central defender or right-back Gonzalo Sorondo. Both players'

Palace's Hungarian international goalkeeper Gabor Kiraly.

Eagles' skipper and Northern Ireland international midfielder Michael Hughes.

Palace's club captain and Australian international defender Tony Popovic.

contributions to our cause were hampered by injuries but, certainly before Christmas, Sorondo's presence was invaluable in our rearguard.

A splendid late autumn sequence of results saw the Eagles gain victories over Fulham and West Bromwich Albion at Selhurst Park and at Birmingham, before coming within a whisker of even beating the champions Arsenal on our turf. We thereby rose to fourteenth in the Premiership table, but by the Sunday before Christmas were again ensconced in the relegation places. After the top-flight clubs had all played eighteen games, we were ahead only of West Bromwich Albion and Southampton, but a point behind Norwich and Blackburn. The Sunday Boxing Day clash, with a 1 p.m. (delayed until 1.40 p.m.) kick-off against Portsmouth, under new Croatian manager Velimir Zajec, at Selhurst Park was crucial to our cause. The Eagles attempted to force the issue in the icy chill upon Danny Butterfield's return to our senior side, but Pompey won with a headed set piece with twenty minutes to go so that it became obvious to Palace fans everywhere that the second half of our season was inevitably going to be a decidedly fraught affair.

Fraught it most certainly was – and more and more fraught it became as it progressed! Palace climbed out of the bottom three, above Norwich, after beating a spineless Aston Villa side (with our first goal being Andy Johnson's fiftieth League strike for us) on 3 January 2005. The next game at Selhurst Park saw Tottenham humiliated 3-0 and, at the end of February, the Eagles completed a morale-boosting 'double' over Birmingham by winning the home clash 2-0 with two Andy Johnson penalties. However, when we unsurprisingly lost at champions-elect Chelsea in mid-March, both West Bromwich Albion and Southampton secured away successes to push us back into the relegation places.

Palace gained one more stirring victory in 2004/05 by beating Liverpool at Selhurst Park towards the end of April with an Andy Johnson header after little more than half an hour, but our prospects took a downward turn when Southampton levelled at 2-2 late into added time and before our own fans in our penultimate fixture.

On the morning of Sunday 15 May 2005 the positions at the bottom of the Premiership, where only one of the four clubs involved could survive, now stood as follows and captured massive media attention:

		P	W	D	L	GD	Pts
17th	Norwich City	37	7	12	18	-29	33
18th	Southampton	37	6	14	17	-20	32
19th	CRYSTAL PALACE	37	7	11	19	-21	32
20th	West Bromwich Albion	37	5	16	16	-27	31

Palace were at Charlton for the showdown. It was essential that we gained a point on Norwich, who were at Fulham, and improved upon Southampton's result against Manchester United at St Mary's by a point or two goals, so realistically we had no option but to go for a win at The Valley.

The afternoon was warm and sunny. Palace had the better of the first half yet went in a goal behind at half-time. Suddenly though, and wonderfully, matters changed in our favour: substitute Dougie Freedman calmly lobbed the Valiants' goalkeeper to bring us level just a minute-and-a-half after making his entry, then shortly afterwards we were awarded a penalty, which Andy Johnson converted. For eight or nine minutes we were safely in seventeenth place – only for another late defensive lapse to concede an equaliser. Thus, with West Bromwich

Albion beating an anaemic Portsmouth, the Baggies claimed the one remaining position of safety and the Eagles were down.

However, as this book has shown from beginning to end, Palace are nothing if not resilient, and we'll be back – you can count on that.

SEASON: 2004/05

GROUND: Selhurst Park

MANAGER: Iain Dowie

LEAGUE/DIVISION: FA Premiership

FINAL POSITION: 18th

BIGGEST VICTORY: 3-0 *v.* West Bromwich Albion, 23 October 2004, 3-0 *v.* Tottenham Hotspur, 22 January 2005

HEAVIEST DEFEAT: 1-5 *v.* Arsenal, 14 February 2005

FA CUP – ROUND ELIMINATED: 3rd

LEAGUE CUP – ROUND ELIMINATED: 3rd

FULL MEMBERS CUP – ROUND ELIMINATED: –

LEADING LEAGUE APPEARANCES (MAX: 38): 38 – W. Routledge, 37 – A. Johnson

LEADING LEAGUE GOALSCORERS: 21 – A. Johnson